Anonymous

History and Antiquities of the County of Norfolk

Vol. 3

Anonymous

History and Antiquities of the County of Norfolk
Vol. 3

ISBN/EAN: 9783744774253

Printed in Europe, USA, Canada, Australia, Japan

Cover: Foto ©ninafisch / pixelio.de

More available books at **www.hansebooks.com**

THE
HISTORY AND ANTIQUITIES
OF
ROXBURGHSHIRE
AND
ADJACENT DISTRICTS,

From the most Remote Period to the Present Time.

BY ALEXANDER JEFFREY,

AUTHOR OF THE "GUIDE TO THE ANTIQUITIES OF THE BORDER," &C.

VOL. III.

EDINBURGH: THOMAS C. JACK,
92, PRINCES STREET.

ANDREW JACK, PRINTER CLYDE STREET EDINBURGH.

PREFACE.

WHEN the author closed the second volume, he hoped that the work would be concluded in this one; but notwithstanding all his efforts to do so, he has only been able to complete the district of Kelso—a district so rich and full of interest, that it was with great difficulty the important materials with which it abounds were condensed within the narrow compass of the present volume. He therefore trusts that, under the circumstances, the extension of the work to another volume, with the view of including a great mass of valuable matter—without which the work would be imperfect—will meet with the approval of subscribers and the public.

To the Rev. James Jarvie, Kelso, the author is indebted for valuable information in regard to the modern history of Kelso.

The concluding volume will be published in the course of the next year.

A. J.

JEDBURGH, *September*, 1859.

CONTENTS OF VOL. III.

I. INTRODUCTION.

	PAGE
1. Old names of the country lying along the Forth, and from Tweed to Avon	1
2. Between 635 and 1020, churches in Teviotdale and Lothian belonged to Lindisfarne	2
3. After 1020, the Bishop of St. Andrews assumed jurisdiction	3
4. Boundary of the episcopates of Glasgow and St. Andrews	3
5. The people inhabiting north side of Tweed	4
6. Names of places on north and south of river	5
7. Druidical remains on north of Tweed	5

II. KELSO.

1. Etymology of its name	6
2. Situation of the town and scenery around it	8
3. The town and streets	10
4. The Town-hall and Market-place	11
5. Bridge-street	13
6. Havannah, or Ednam House	16
7. Abbey-close, Butts, and Kirkstyle	17
8. Mill of Kelso	19
9. Roxburgh-street, Cunzie-nook, Horse-shoe, Chalkheugh, and Windy Goul	21
10. Approaches to the town, roads, bridges, and ferries	23
11. Town formed part of regality of Abbey.	29
12. Site of burgh, burgh records and statutes, whipmen	30
13. Markets and trade of the town	35
14. Literature, Chalkheugh library, newspapers and reading-rooms	37
15. The schools of the town	39

CONTENTS.

PAGE

16. The manor of Kelso and Abbey 40

First notice of the manor—the boundaries thereof—governed by a provost—Wester Kelso—Faircross—first settlement of monks at Selkirk, at Kelso—benefits conferred on a district by foundation of abbey—property of the monks in flocks and herds, in lands and fisheries—right of the monks to a tenth of all the bucks and does taken by king's huntsmen—skins of animals—tradition of Northumberland as to monks visiting Delavel's kitchen—monks the early bankers—they enjoyed wardship of heirs—grants made to the abbey for interment in the cemetery—the monks exporters—the property of the monks in lands and churches in the counties of Selkirk, Berwick, Peebles, Lanark, Dumfries, Ayr, and Edinburgh—colonies of monks sent from Kelso—revenues of house.

17. Confirmation Charter of Malcolm IV. 355
18. Annals of the Abbey and Town 67

Of the Abbey.—Abbots—Herbert, Ernold, John, Osbert—interdict by Pope Alexander III., its form—Geoffrey, Richard de Cave, Henry, Richard Maunsel, Hugh de Maunsel, Robert de Smalhame, Patrick, Henry de Lambeden, Richard, Walron, Thomas de Durham, William de Alyncrom, William de Dalgernock, William, Patrick, William, Allan, Andrew Stewart, Thomas Ker, James Stewart, commendator, Duke of Guise, commendator, Sir John Maitland, commendator, Bothwell. *Of the Town.*—Two of Shrewsbury's captains burn Kelso in 1522—next year town and monastery burnt by Dacre—Duke of Norfolk burnt town and abbey—Bowes and Laiton's visit to it, 1544—next year the Earl of Hertford destroyed town and abbey—garrison of Wark ravaged the town—Queen Mary at Kelso, where she slept two days—bond signed at Kelso to put down Border thieves—parties to it—Earls of Angus and Marr, the Master of Glammis at Kelso—joined by Bothwell, Home, Cessford, and Coldingknowes, and barons of Teviotdale—town of Kelso fined 2000 merks—town destroyed by an accidental fire in 1645—Montrose at Kelso same year—in 1715 Scottish rebels at Kelso—persons of the surname of Kelso.

III. FLEURS.

	PAGE
1. The palace of the Duke of Roxburghe, its situation, name, and scenery around it	87
2. Fair-cross, origin of the name	88
3. Woods around Fleurs	89
4. The family of Ker	90
5. Bond between the Scotts and Kers	93
6. Sir Robert Ker, first Earl of Roxburghe	98
7. Competition between Brigadier-General Walter Ker of Littledean and Sir James Norcliffe Innes for the honours and estates of Roxburgh	104
8. The House of Innes	105

IV. EDNAM.

1. Etymology of the name	107
2. Charter by Thorlongus of church of Ednam to the monks of Durham	108
3. Description of Ednam	109
4. Property of the monks of Coldingham, Kelso, and Dryburgh, in Ednam	110
5. Hospital of Ednam	111
6. The family of Edmonstone, origin and end of the race	112
7. Wych elm in brewery garden	113
8. Ednam the birth-place of Captain Cook, notices of family	114
9. James Thomson, the poet, was he born in Ednam?	115
10. William Dawson, the agriculturist	115

V. HENDERSIDE.

1. Situation	116
2. Greater part of estate included in the old barony of Ednam	116
3. Mansion of Henderside Park	116
4. The estate was acquired by one Ormston, and was carried by marriage to John Waldie	117
5. Lineage of the family	118

VI. NEWTON AND NENTHORN.

1. These two manors the property of the Morvilles during 12th century, at whose death in 1196 the manors passed to his only sister, Helena, wife of the lord of Galloway	118

2. When Sir James Douglas became proprietor of these
   manors 119
3. Grants made to the church 120
4. Newton-Don House; its site—the woods around
   house—beautiful weeping birches near garden—
   woolly-leafed poplar nurses an ivy—yew-trees
   —wych elms—remarkable thorn-trees for size and
   beauty—the river Eden—trap dyke across river—
   melancholy incident 121

VII. STITCHEL.

1. Etymology of the name 123
2. Situation and view from the hill 124
3. Barony of Stitchell part of barony of Gordon ... 124
4. Origin of the family of Gordon and its descendants 125
5. Nicolas de Sticcenil 125
6. The church of Stitchel 126
7. Persons who bore the surname of Stitchel ... 127
8. George Redpath minister of Stitchel 127

VIII. HOME.

1. Etymology of name and situation 128
2. The manor of Home formed a part of the territory
   of the Earl of Dunbar 128
3. The manor of Home was given by Patrick, Earl of
   Dunbar, as a marriage gift to his daughter Ada,
   on her marriage with her cousin, William of
   Greenlaw 129
4. Assumed name of the manor as a surname after
   marriage 129
5. Dispute between Home and monastery settled ... 130
6. Castle of Home—notices thereof 131
7. Badge of the Homes 133

IX. SMALHAM.

1. Etymology of name 133
2. The manor of Smalham 133
3. The family of Olifard the first owners—origin of the
   name of Oliver—he was Justiciary of Lothian—
   grants to Dryburgh Abbey and the house of Soltre 134
4. Walter of Moray succeeded Oliver in the barony ... 135
5. William Earl of Douglas acquired the barony in
   1451 360

		PAGE
6. Hospital of Smalham	...	136
7. Edward I. was at Smalham	...	136
8. Persons who bore the surname of Smalham	...	137
9. The mother of Captain Cook resided in Smalham		137
10. Smalham Crags	...	138

X. WRANGHAME.

1. Situation of this place	...	139
2. Residence of the nurse of St. Cuthbert	...	139
3. Legend of St. Cuthbert	...	139

XI. MAKERSTON.

1. Situation and extent of the barony	...	140
2. The mansion of Makerston, and scenery, trees, &c., in park	...	141
3. Etymology of its name	...	141
4. Walter Corbet proprietor about the middle of 12th century	...	142
5. The Macdougals next proprietors of barony, 1370		144
6. Origin and history of the family—Appendix	...	360
7. Notices of the family	...	145
8. Property of Kelso monks in barony	...	150
9. Camp on left bank of the Tweed above Mackerston		150
10. Charterhouse	...	150

XII. MANOR OF ROXBURGH.

1. Extent of manor and possessions thereof in early times	...	151
2. Friars, the seat of the baronial court	...	152
3. Remarkable trysting-tree at Friars	...	153
4. Is any part of the peninsula in Kelso parish?	..	154
5. Inquiry as to the site of the old church of Roxburgh	...	157
6. Church and graveyard—old tombstones—grave of Edie Ochiltree	...	158
7. Village of Roxburgh; Wallace's Tower	...	159

XIII. SUNLAWS.

1. Situation	...	160
2. The estate formerly belonged to the family of Ker of Greenhead	...	161
3. It now belongs to William Scott Ker of Chatto	...	161
4. Lineage of the family	...	161
5. Prince Charles slept a night at the tower of Sunlaws		162

XIV. RINGLEY HALL.

		PAGE
1.	Etymology of the name—its situation—description of fort	162
2.	Traditions regarding it and Rutherford	164
3.	*Tumulus* in front of Mackerston House, its appearance and extent	165
4.	Trows—etymology of name—description of the *Tors*	167
5.	Legend of the Church of Rome as to St. Cuthbert's corpse floating down the river in a stone boat	168
6.	Stockstrother	362

XV. FAIRNINGTON.

1. First appearance of barony in record during 12th century ... 170
2. Notices of the early proprietors—Burnards ... 171
3. The Rutherfurds possessed it about the beginning of the 17th century ... 172
4. Tradition of the Bloody Well ... 173
5. Baron Rutherfurd, notices of ... 174
6. Notice of Major Rutherfurd—Burns visited him in 1787 ... 176
7. Downlaw—ruins of an observatory on its summit—Stanan Stane, near Watling-street, on farm of Heriotsfield—Harlaw—traces of an old ditch referred to in charter of the 13th century ... 176
8. Hospital of Fairnington; its site—belonged to bishop of Glasgow in 1186—grants to chapel, &c. 177

XVI. BARONY OF MAXWELL.

1. First appears in record during the days of David I., by whom the territory was granted to his follower *Maccus*, who conferred on it his name ... 178
2. Situation and extent of the barony ... 179
3. Notices of the family of Maxwell ... 180
4. Bridgend purchased by James Douglas from Ker of Greenhead—the name changed to Springwood Park—notices of the family of Douglas—lineage of the family ... 183
5. Situation of the old mansion of Bridgend ... 185
6. Description of the mansion of Springwood Park, and scenery around—the woods—young trysting-tree—remarkable poplar at Maxwellheugh, 92 feet high and 32 feet 6 inches in girth ... 186
7. Maisondieu, or hospital ... 187

		PAGE
8.	Town of Maxwellheugh—*tumulus* within the grounds of Pinnaclehill—view of, from the ridge to the west of town	188
9.	Softlaw—notices of its early proprietors	189
10.	Church of Maccuswel—existed before 1159—it was dedicated to St. Michael—the graveyard	190
11.	St. Thomas' Chapel, where situated?	191

XVII. SPROUSTON.

1.	Etymology of name—it is first seen in charter of David—the early proprietors—granted by William the Lion to Sir Eustace de Vesci, who married his daughter	193
2.	Robert Bruce conferred the barony on his son Robert—David II. gave it to Thomas Murray—William Earl of Douglas obtained it in 1451—it was afterwards granted to Sir Robert Ker of Cessford	193
3.	Property of monks of Kelso in Sprouston, and by whom granted	197
4.	Village of Sprouston	198
5.	King and Queen of England at Sprouston for several days in 1256	199
6.	Lands of Easter Softlaw	199

XVIII. REDDEN.

1.	Situation of the territory	199
2.	Was the property of the monks of Kelso—notices of the town and grange of Redden—David II. erected it into a royalty in favour of monks	200
3.	Reddenburn	201

XIX. HAUDEN.

1.	Manor granted by William the Lion to Bernard, an Anglo-Norman	201
2.	Notices of the family—assumed Hauden as a surname	202
3.	Estate now property of Sir William Elliot of Stobs	202
4.	Property of monks in Hawden	203
5.	Haddenstank	204

XX. LEMPETLAW.

1.	Barony granted by David I. to Richard Germyn	204
2.	Sir Adam Quinton got Wellflat as a marriage portion with Floria, daughter of Germyn	205

CONTENTS.

	PAGE

3. James III. conferred the barony on Walter Scott of Kirkurd ... 205
4. Geoffrey of Lempetlaw was chamberlain to William the Lion ... 205
5. The barony was originally a separate parish—graveyard still used—the church, which was the property of the house of Soltre, is not in existence ... 205

XXI. LINTON.

1. Etymology of name—Linton mistaken by previous writers for Linton Roderick in Peebleshire ... 206
2. The barony was the property of William Sumerville in 1160—origin of the family of Sumerville—Linton first estate in Scotland—notices of the family ... 207
3. Legend of Linton ... 209
4. Monument over the church-door—remarks thereon 215
5. The skull of a beaver and the remains of an ox, *bos primogenius*, found in Linton loch ... 217
6. Barony now possessed by Robert Elliot of Harwood and Clifton ... 223
7. Graden, Fauside, and Greenlees ... 224
8. Blakelaw—Thomas Pringle, the author of "The Excursion," born here—beautiful view of vale of Tweed and Merse from Blakelaw ridge ... 225
9. Old town of Linton ... 226
10. Church of Linton—tumulus of sand on which it is built—legend thereof ... 227
11. Font of the church used by a blacksmith to hold small coals ... 228

XXII. YETHAM.

1. Etymology of name ... 229
2. Early history of the territory—property of the monks of Kelso in it—Colpinhopes ... 230
3. Chapel of St. Ethelrida, where situated—tradition regarding it ... 232
4. In 1375, Yetham the property of the family of Macdougal of Makerston ... 233
5. James IV. granted to Sir Robert Ker the lordship of Yetham ... 234
6. William Bennet was owner in 1647 ... 234
7. Halterburnhead—origin of name, &c. ... 235
8. The church and graveyard of Yetham ... 235

CONTENTS. xiii

PAGE
9. The town of Yetham—notices thereof 237
10. Shrovetide at Yetham—football, &c. 239
11. Christmas festivities 241
12. Account of the gipsy tribes 241
13. Barony of Town Yetham 258
14. Town Yetholm 261
15. CHERRYTREES and Thirlestane 262
16. King Edward at Yetholm for two days 264
17. Persons who bore the surname of Yetholm ... 265

XXIII. MOW.

1. Etymology of name—boundaries and extent of territory 265
2. Territory originally formed part of Northumbria ... 267
3. First owner named Liulf—Uctred, his son, succeeded, and then the lands passed to *Eschena de Londiniis*, called Lady Molle—she married Walter the first Steward of Scotland—origin of the family—persons who followed Walter to Scotland—charter of Malcolm in favour of Walter ... 269
4. Anselm of Whitton possessed part of Molle ... 273
5. Lands in territory belonging to monks of Kelso—monks had a grant of the forest in Molle ... 273
6. Property of the house of Melrose in territory ... 278
7. The monks of Paisley 279
8. The canons of Jedburgh 280
9. Lands of Robert de Croc in territory—surname of Lindsay 280
10. Cocklaw—powerful castle on sources of Beaumont—besieged by the English in 1401—it belonged to the family of Gledstones 282
11. Town of Molle and church of Molle 285
12. Woods of Molle 289

XXIV. MOREBOTTLE.

1. Etymology—situation and extent of territory—its early history 290
2. The family of Corbet appears to have possessed the lands in 12th century 291
3. Town of Morebottle—church of Morebottle—prophecy in regard to it—dedicated to St. Lawrence—disputes with the monks of Melrose ... 293
4. Dissenting meeting-house—Mrs. Morrison introduced spinning-wheel into Morebottle ... 295

5. WHITTON—etymology, situation, extent, and boundaries—was an ancient possession of the family of Riddel ... 297
6. Fort of Whitton ... 298
7. PRIMSIDE—granted by Earl Henry, son of David I., to Ridel—believed to have been the earliest possession of the family in Scotland ... 299
8. CROOKEDSHAWS—its situation—remarkable bar of sand at Loch ... 300
9. CLIFTON—etymology—its early history—it belonged to St. Cuthbert during the seventh century—notices thereof ... 302
10. GRUBET—etymology doubtful—in 12th century property of Uctred, who took the surname for the territory—De Vescis were over-lords of this territory in the 13th century ... 303
11. WIDEOPEN—its situation—property of the maternal uncle of the poet Thomson ... 305
12. GATESHAW—situation and extent—belonged originally to the monks—fermed by Kers—the family of Ker of Gateshaw ... 306
13. Corbet House—tower of Gateshaw ... 307
14. OTTERBURN, Tofts, Cowbog, Heavyside, Lochside, and Foumerdean ... 308

XXV. HOWNAM.

1. Etymology—property of *Orm* during the beginning of the 12th century—origin of name—Rasawe the property of the monks of Melrose ... 310
2. Church of Hunum—disputes between bishop of Glasgow and monks of Melrose as to titles ... 313
3. Town of Hownam and Hownan Kirk, Capehope, &c. 314
4. Rings—legend thereof ... 315
5. CHATTHOU—etymology—situation—notices thereof 316
6. PHILOGAR, Beirhope, Burvanes, Buchtrig, and Over Whitton ... 317

XXVI. ECKFORD.

1. Etymology—situation and extent of old territory of Eckford ... 320
2. A family of Geoffrey one of the earliest proprietors 321
3. Mowbray acquired it during the reign of William the Lion—lost Cessford in 1316, and Eckford in 1320 ... 322

CONTENTS. xv

PAGE
4. On forfeiture of Mowbray, territory granted by Robert I. to Walter, steward of Scotland ... 322
5. Moss Tower 323
6. Town of Eckford—church thereof—jugs still to be seen at the door of church—notices of church ... 324
7. Moss Tower farm—Church's oats—remarks thereon 324
8. GRAEMSLAW—etymology—situation and extent—hospital on banks of Cayle 325
9. HAUGHEAD—situation—property of Hall, called Hobbie Hall, in 17th century—his son, Henry Hall, commanded at Drumclog and Bothwell Bridge—his banner—he was taken in company with Cargill—died of his wounds—tried after death—remarks on this form of trial, and "Jeddart Justice" 327
10. Richard Cameron licensed here by Welsh—notices as to Cameron 330
11. PRIEST'S CROWN—etymology—situation—remains found there in 1857 331
12. CESSFORD barony, a part of the old territory of Eckford—etymology of name—situation and extent—the early proprietors of the manor—Castle of Cessford: description thereof—besieged by Surrey in 1523—Hall of Haughead imprisoned in it—a large ash-tree which grew there at the end of last century 333
13. MARLEFIELD—lies between the modern baronies of Eckford and Cessford—property of William Bennet in the middle of the 17th century 337
14. Is the scene of the "Gentle Shepherd" laid here? ... 338

XXVII. CAVERTON.

1. Etymology—thought to be the Keveronum in the Inquisitio Davidis 340
2. It belonged originally to the celebrated family of Sulis, of Anglo-Norman race in Northamptonshire—notices of the family—family forfeited the barony in 1320—new grants by Robert I. to Robert, son of Walter Stewart—notices of the barony ... 342
3. Chapel of Caverton 343
4. A tumulus called the Black Dyke 344
5. MAINHOUSE—formerly included in the territory of Caverton—at one time belonged to the family of Chatto—now property of Ralph Nisbet ... 345

XXVIII. ORMESTON.

1. Etymology—situation—description of barony—belonged first to *Orm*, the son of *Eilar*—it became a surname to a family, in the end of the 13th century, of *Ormeston*—it continued in the family of Ormeston till 1573, when James Ormston was executed for his share in Darnley's murder ... 346
2. It was then granted to Ker of Cessford—it afterwards belonged to William Elliot—to William Mein—now to the Marquis of Lothian ... 349
3. Tower and town of Ormeston destroyed by Dacre and Hertford ... 350

XXIX. HETON.

1. Etymology—its situation—the first person who appears as owner was Alan de Perci—notices of family ... 350
2. It belonged to the family of Colville in 1230—it remained with that family till 1509, when it passed to the Kers—it is now property of Sir George Douglas and William Scott Ker of Chatto—notices of the town of Heton ... 353

THE

HISTORY AND ANTIQUITIES

OF

ROXBURGHSHIRE, &c.

OF THE DISTRICT OF KELSO.

THIS DISTRICT comprehends, on the north of the river Tweed, the parishes of Kelso, Makerstoun, Ednam, Smailholm, and Stitchel; on the south of the river, that part of Kelso which formed the old parish of Maccuswel, and the parishes of Roxburgh, Sprouston, Yetholm, Morebattle, Linton, and Eckford.

Before entering upon a particular description of this district, it will be necessary, for the proper understanding of the subject, briefly to sketch its ancient history. As already stated in a previous part of this work, all the country lying along the

Forth, and from the Tweed to the Avon, was known in the age of Bede as Bernicia. In the "Scoto-Irish Chronicle," it is named Saxonia. After 843, the territory acquired from the Saxon settlers, who had come in on the Romanized Ottadeni and Gadeni— the name of Lothian, which it still bore in 1020, when it was ceded by Eadulf-Cudel to Malcolm Ceanmore, the King of Scotland. About 1097, that part of the district lying along the Tweed, as far up as the confluence of the Gala and the *Lamermoors* came to be known as the MERSE. In after times, the three districts, *Merse, Lamermoor,* and *Lauderdale,* were formed into a sheriffwic under the name of Berwickshire. At the death of Edgar, in 1107, his brother Alexander succeeded to the throne, and, by a settlement of the deceased king, his youngest brother, David, had assigned to him as his appanage all the territory lying to the south of the Friths of Forth and Clyde *except Lothian.* While Alexander reigned over Scotland and the country on the north of the Tweed, David enjoyed all Teviotdale and Tweeddale. It was not till the death of Alexander, in 1124, that David, after he became king, was enabled to exercise jurisdiction over the land to the north of the Tweed.

Between the erection of the bishoprick of Lindisfarne in 635 and 1020, all the churches in Lothian and Teviotdale were considered as dependencies of the see of Lindisfarne and Durham. But when Lothian was ceded to the Scottish King, the Bishop of St. Andrews assumed the ecclesiastical jurisdiction of the whole churches in the district. At the dawn of record, many of the churches of Teviotdale belonged to the Bishop of Glasgow.* When the pious David ascended the throne, he renovated the bishoprick of Glasgow, and placed all the churches of Teviotdale under the jurisdiction of the church of Glasgow, and appointed John, his *tutor*, as the first bishop of the restored see. In 1238, the bishoprick of Glasgow was divided into two distinct archdeaconries, of which Teviotdale was one, and from that time enjoyed its own archdeacon.†

The river Tweed formed the boundary between the two episcopates of Glasgow and St. Andrews, from Carham Burn to the mouth of the Gala, and from the Gala it ran along the ridge which separates Lothian from Tweeddale and Clydesdale. It will thus be seen that the parishes of Kelso, Stitchel, Ednam, Smailham, and Makerstoun, were included in the deanery of the Merse, and bishoprick of St. Andrews.‡ No part of any of these parishes lay on the south side of the Tweed.

Before 1020, the river Tweed was the boundary

---

* Inquisitio Davidis, 1116.

† It had its *Dean* during the days of Bishop Jocelin, between 1174 and 1180. The Archdeacon regulated the clergy of Teviotdale, subject to the Bishop of Glasgow.

‡ In 1221 there was a charter granted "*in plena capitulo de Mersa apud Ednham.*" Lib. de Calchou.

between two hostile peoples; and there can be little doubt that many of the strengths which are to be seen on the south margins of the river were to defend the inhabitants of Teviotdale from the Pagan Saxons who dwelt on the north bank of the stream. In after times, when the English seized Teviotdale, and held Roxburgh Castle for more than a hundred years, these forts would be occupied by them as a defence against the lawful owners of the soil resuming possession.* The fact that these strengths are mostly confined to the south bank of the Tweed, leads to the belief that the passages of the river required to be guarded from an enemy advancing from Lothian on the north.

The NAMES of PLACES on the north side of the Tweed evince that the Saxon tribes had gained the complete ascendancy over the Romanized Ottadenian people in this district. The predominance, also, of Saxon names on the south side of the Tweed, to the east of the Teviot river, show the extent of their colonization, and the superinduction of their language on the ancient British. The Saxon "*Hleaw,*" as Law, appears in the names of many little hills and places on the east of the Teviot: *e.g., Sunlaws, Grahamslaw, Blacklaws, Greenlaws, Wormeslaw, Hoselaw, Castlelaw, Todlaw, Lempitlaw, Lurdinlaw, Soft-*

---

* Several writers imagine that a number of these strengths are Danish, forgetting that these robbers had no permanent settlement here.

laws, Spylaw, Pylelaw, in fact, every little hill in that locality bears either a Saxon name or a Saxon termination. On the north side of the Tweed, the "*law*" enters into the names of many places—*Broxlaw, Luntinlaw, Galalaw, Tanlaw, Sharpitlaw*. The Saxon *rig* appears in several names, such as *Musrig, Mainrig, Greatridge*. The word *Kaims*, or *Caims*, for a *ridge*, is found in several names of places between Broxlaw and Combflat, a little to the east of Ednam village; the old Saxon word *thyrn* for thorn in *Nenthorn*. *Holm, Home Castle*, Stitchel, and Ham in Edenham, *Smailham*, etc. The word *hope* is also of frequent occurrence. Proceeding westward, the Saxon names of places become gradually fewer, showing that the colonization was from the eastward; and the rareness of Scoto-Irish names on the east establishes, on the other hand, that these people advanced on the district from the west.

It is worthy of notice, that while Druidical remains abound in Teviotdale, scarcely any are to be found on the north of the Tweed. It is thought that the difference between the two sides of the river in this respect arises from the occupation of the country on the north by the Saxons, who continued all pagans for nearly 200 years after their first entrance on the land, and delighted in the destruction of every vestige of the Druid worship, or the remains of the native people. British remains were the object of their special enmity.

KELSO, the capital of the district, makes its first appearance in 1128, in the charter of David to the Selkirk monks, on their being placed on the well-sheltered banks of the Tweed. In that document it is written in three different ways—*Calchou, Kelchou,* and *Kalchu.** The chronicler of Mailros, while recording the foundation of the abbey at Kelso as having taken place on May 3, 1128, enters the name *Kelchehou,*† and in various other entries in that work—recording events between 1128 and 1255 —it appears as *Kelchou.* In the Register of Glasgow it is written *Chelgho,*‡ *Chelcho, Kelcho, Kalcho, Kelechou;* and in 1176, John the abbot writes the name of the place exactly as it is written at the present day, "*Kelso.*"§ In the Book of Dryburgh it appears as *Calcheo, Kelkou, Kelku;* and in the writ of protection granted by the English king to the abbot and convent, the name is written *Kellesowe.*‖ It is thought that the name is derived from the British *Calch* and the Saxon *hou,* descriptive of a small eminence on the margin of a river, on which part of the town is *now* built, and still bearing the appellation of the *Chalkheugh.* I have conversed with several old people who distinctly remembered the Chalkheugh before it was built upon or protected

---

* Charter of David to the Monastery. Lib. de Calchou.
† Chron. Mail., p. 69, &c.   ‡ Circa, 1150.
§ Reg. of Glas., p. 40.
‖ Rotuli Scotiæ, vol. i. pp. 24, 25.

from the river in 1810, and who stated that the face of the cliff had then the appearance of *chalk*, and which they, in their boyhood had digged for *alabaster*. The cliffs on the east bank of the river are also formed of the same kind of calcareous deposit; and it is probable that the name of *Calchou* was, by the native people, intended to describe these cliffs as well as the eminence on the north side of the river. Several etymologists, however, take a different view, and think that the name is derived from the Celtic *caol, caolas*, a narrow channel.* It is no doubt true, that the Tweed does flow through a strait for some miles above *Roxburgh Castle*, and was separated into several *narrow channels* by the annas, which formerly existed near to Faircross and the present anna, lower down the river, opposite the Chalkheugh. These narrow channels were also in close proximity to Kelso, in the olden time. Indeed it might have been appropriately described as the town on the *Caolas; i.e.*, narrow channels on the Tweed and Teviot. Still I am inclined to think that the true etymology of the name is to be found in the British *Calch* and the Saxon *hou*, the more especially as there are no other cliffs of the same nature in that locality. The *Calchhills*, on the Tweed, would be a good description of the place at an early period, and by which it might

---

* Williamson's Etymology, p. 84.

be easily discovered. It must also be kept in view, however, that the Saxon "*Cealc*" is very like the British *Calch*, and it may be that the whole name is Saxon "*Cealchou.*"*

The TOWN of KELSO is situated on the north side of the river Tweed, exactly opposite to the mouth of the river Teviot, on a piece of haughland, formed by a bend of the river. While passing Roxburgh Castle, the course of the Tweed is to the east, till turned in a northerly direction by the cliffs at Maxwellheugh, which are a continuation of the high land forming the east bank of the river Teviot. On the north side of the haugh is a semicircular ridge, which takes its rise at the river Tweed, in the policy of *Floors*, and continuing eastward, forms, at Sharpitlaw, the left bank of the river, and divides the dale through which Tweed flows from the flat land of Edendale. The right bank of the Teviot and Tweed is also semicircular. The locality is remarkable for scenes of great beauty. From the summit of the river's bank at Maxwellheugh, an extensive view is obtained of the surrounding scenery. The eye roams over the broad expanse of waters beneath, and the termination of the beautiful vale where "the silver tide of Teviot loses itself in Tweed's pellucid stream;" the lovely little islet in the midst of the parent river; the moss-clad

---

* Johnson derives the English *Chalk* from the Saxon *Cealc.*

ruins of Roxburgh, and in the distance the cones of Eildon. On the left bank of the Tweed, the palace of the Duke of Roxburgh stands, environed by dark woods, while lower down are beautiful gardens; houses clustered together; a busy mill, with its waterfall; the Havannah, and several other sweet villas, overlook the beautiful sheet of water that rolls past; while over this scene the august pile, in all the solemnity of ruin, frowns majestically. On the right bank of the Teviot, and between it and the Tweed, in the midst of an extensive and well-wooded park, is Springwood, the seat of Sir George Douglas. Eastward, long reaches of the river are exposed to view, the margins in the highest state of cultivation, studded with mansions, among which Henderside Park occupies a prominent position. The country to the north has the appearance of rising in terraces from the back of Kelso to the woody heights of Stitchel, Mellerston, and of Home. A fine view is obtained from the second arch of the bridge next to Kelso, looking up the river; but the view which is held in the greatest admiration by strangers is from the *Chalkheugh*, the picture including the meeting of the waters, the vale of Teviot, and the ruins of the "*Towering Fortress;*"* but it

---

* It is said in the Kelso Records, p. 113, that Lady Holland, whose taste was so celebrated, had been heard to declare, that the scene here surpassed any she had met with in France and Italy.

is in vain to attempt to pourtray with the pen the scenery around this lovely town; the eye must rest upon the luxuriant picture. Well might Leyden sing*

> "Bosomed in woods, where mighty rivers run,
> Kelso's fair vale expands before the sun;
> Its rising downs in vernal beauty swell,
> And fringed with hazel winds each flowery dell;
> Green spangled plains to dimpling lawns succeed,
> And Tempe rises on the banks of Tweed.
> Blue o'er the river Kelso's shadow lies,
> And copse-clad isles amid the waters rise;
> Where Tweed her silent way majestic holds,
> Float the thin gales in more transparent folds.
> New powers of vision on the eye descend,
> As distant mountains from their bases bend,
> Lean forward from their seats to court the view,
> While melt their softened tints in vivid blue.
> But fairer still at midnight's shadowy reign,
> When liquid silver floods the moonlight plain,
> And lawns and fields, and woods of varying hue,
> Drink the wan lustre and the pearly dew;
> While the still landscape more than noontide bright,
> Glistens with mellow tints of fairy light."

The TOWN of KELSO is large and handsome, containing many well-built houses. In the centre of the town is a spacious market-place of a square form. ROXBURGH-STREET, the approach from the north, enters the square at the north-west angle. BRIDGE-STREET leaves the market-place in a line with Rox-

---

* Leyden's Scenes of Infancy, p. 137.

burgh-street, and leads to the Bridge over the Tweed, and to the country on the south and west. The Town Hall stands on the east side of the square, forming the end of a tongue, with each side a street; on the north, the Horse Market; and on the north-east, the Wood and Coal Market-streets. The Millwynd runs from the south side of the market-place to the mill on the Tweed. Besides these streets there are a number of smaller wynds and lanes, forming the means of communication between various parts of the town to the river and to the country.

The HALL was erected in 1816, chiefly by the munificence of James, Duke of Roxburgh, aided by subscriptions of the inhabitants. It is a building with a pediment in front, supported by four Ionic columns, surmounted by a turret or belfry. In the court-room hangs a whole-length portrait of his Grace, placed there at the expense of the inhabitants, to evince the gratitude felt for the benefits which his Grace conferred on the town. The Hall stands upon the site of an old house, which answered the purposes of a council-room and tolbooth, taken down about the beginning of the century. It was raised upon four pillars of stone, and had a high steeple, with a clock. In August, 1764, the lightning struck the steeple, and carried the weathercock into the churchyard.* With the exception of

---

* Kelso Records, p. 124.

the tenement occupied by Stephen Balmer, the whole of the square seems to have been rebuilt since 1790.* Within the recollection of aged inhabitants, the square which now boasts of so many fine buildings was a quadrangle of straw-covered houses, with their high, pointed gables to the front, which led the celebrated traveller Pennant to remark that Kelso resembled a Flemish town. A huge and unseemly *pantwell*, surmounted by a lamp, stood in one corner. To a saddler's apprentice breaking this pant and its lamp, the inhabitants of Kelso were, in after years, indebted for many improvements, and one of its most handsome buildings. The boy, fearing the wrath of the civic functionaries for demolishing the lamp, fled to London, where he succeeded in making his fortune as a navy agent; and on returning to Kelso, when his youthful exploit was forgotten, purchased part of the estate of Ednam from the old family of Edmonstone, built the Havannah, now called Ednam House, and the present commodious Cross Keys Hotel. The old Cross Keys stood on the site of Lindores' House, lately used as a post-office. Where the Commercial Bank now is, formerly stood an old tavern, with a peculiar sign suspended from its front. Pillars and piazzas stretched from the Millwynd in the direc-

---

* An old painting of the market-place, taken about 1790, for Horsenden, of the Cross Keys Hotel, a copy of which is in the possession of Mr. William Smith, Kelso.

tion of Bridge-street. The shop windows, like deeply-seated eyes, afforded a dry promenade, and a play-ground to the youth of the town. The entrance into Beaumont-street from the square was by a low pend. The crockery market was on the opposite side of the entrance into this street.

BRIDGE-STREET owes its existence to the improved communication by the bridge over the Tweed. The access originally was by the Abbey gardens and glebe, the old highway running straight down Maxwellheugh path, beyond the bridge end, across the site of Mr. Brown's cottage, past the Episcopal Chapel, and up to the great west door of the Abbey. Bridge-street was mostly occupied by tombs. There exists to this day Hardie's crypt, underneath the Spread Eagle; and in excavating, about three years ago, in the cellar of the *Mail Office*, dead men's bones were turned up by the workmen. Many wealthy men gave largely to the Abbey, for leave to lay their bones within its sacred precincts, in the vain imagination that they would lie undisturbed for ever. The handsome gateway into Ednam House was not then in Belmont-place, but between the Weigh-house and Forest's shop. The house now occupied by the National Bank and Messrs. Lugton and Porteous, existed at the beginning of the eighteenth century. It is erected over many very spacious, massy, and arched stone cellars, a peculiarity which gave rise to the mistaken notion, that it occupies the site, and was reared upon the old underground foundations, of the Abbot's House.* These subjects were the property of a family of Ormiston; and in the cess books, at the close of the reign of Queen Anne, it is entered as liable in duty for thirty windows.† Charles Ormiston was then the owner. He was a merchant, and carried on an extensive trade with Holland, through the port of Berwick-on-Tweed. In 1721 he was merchant-treasurer, and, on his own behalf and that of the company of merchants, applied for and obtained a decree, restraining, under a penalty of twenty pounds Scots, one John Ord, a fisherman from Old Cambus, and his father, from retailing brandy in Kelso.‡ In an upper room of that house, with an ornamented roof, the fire-place being lined with pictured Dutch tiles, the ancient religious worship of the abbots of the monastery, was, in Ormiston's day, unobtrusively practised by his wife. Though the son of a Quaker, he had contracted an attachment for a Catholic lady, and, being at first impeded by the rules of the Friends, he threatened

---

* Tradition has it, that the Abbot's Stead occupied a stance above the Pipewell Brae, in a field adjoining that of Mr. Williamson, recently the property of Mr. Jordan, now that of Mr. Waldie of Henderside.

† At that time there seems to have been only seven houses in Kelso liable in window duty.

‡ This was a kind of smuggling more directed against the trade of royal burghs than the revenue of the crown.

to run off to the Plantations. One morning a scrap of paper was found by him lying on his dressing-table, with these laconic but significant words: "Thy sister married without my consent, and I did not disown her." It was his father's hand. The heretic bride was brought home, and while the trade of Hollands was conducted below, the mysteries of the mass were celebrated in the room with the Dutch tiles above, though no doubt sorely against the will, but yet without molestation from the old Quaker, whose sect was beyond others tolerant of religious differences. The sister above referred to, who married out of the pale of her party, but without renouncing her peculiarities, was the fine, liberal old Quakeress, to whom the boy Walter Scott was indebted for the use of her library, afterwards the grandmother of the owner of the best preserved books and paintings in the district.* The *Queen's Head Inn* was one of the houses rated for window duty. It came to be occupied by Waldie of Henderside, who succeeded to it through the Quakeress, who was an Ormiston, and through her certain parts of her lands. The arms of the two families are now quartered as the armorial bearings of the house of Henderside. The large apartment adjoining Lauder's ball-room, and interposing between it and the churchyard, was that in which ducal and

---

* Mr. Waldie of Henderside.

baronial visitors were received, and is a modern addition. The house of Andrew Johnston, Horse Market, from its architecture, seems to be one of the seven houses entered in the cess books of 1721, and the tenement modernized for the shops of Messrs. Rutherfurd, booksellers, and Mr. Moore, draper, which then bounded the HYDE MARKET on the north, was another of these houses. The *Havannah*, or Ednam House, noticed above, is comparatively modern. It was erected after the middle of the last century, by James Dickson, the runaway saddler's apprentice, on his return to his native district.* It is a prominent object in Pennant's sketch of Kelso, taken in 1772.† The mansion is elegant, built of square hewn stone, and stands in the midst of a garden opening on the river. It is ornamented by a Gothic temple; and when the learned Hutchieson visited the locality in 1776, " statues were disposed on the grass plots, which were intersected with gravel walks and flower knots." Dickson was owner of part of the old barony of Ednam, in the neighbourhood of Kelso, and of Broughton in Peebleshire. For some time he represented the Peebles district of burghs in Parliament. In conjunction with Sir Alexander Don, and others,

---

* The house was named the Havannah, from its owner having amassed a considerable sum by purchasing, while a navy agent, the shares due to the captors of the *Havannah*.

† Pennant's Tour, vol. iii. p. 278.

he formed the society of the *Bowmen of the Border*, and re-established Kelso races. John Mason, in his Records of Kelso, is studious to tell that Dickson, "at these races, run over Caverton Edge, in the year 1765, ran his gray horse Cheviot," and won. Mr. Dickson was also the projector of a *canal* between Berwick and Kelso, but which was given up at the time for want of support.

The ABBEY CLOSE joins the present Bridge-street opposite the ruined abbey. During the existence of the old bridge, it was one of the principal approaches to the town. On the east of Bridge-street is the parish church, erected in 1773. It is in the shape of an octagon, with an immense roof, tapering to a point like a *marquee*, and supported by eight inner pillars. In 1823, an attempt was made by the principal heritors to improve the appearance of this inelegant structure, but the proposal was rejected by the smaller heritors, and Kelso continues to be disfigured by one of the ugliest edifices that ever was reared. Between 1649 and 1771, part of the ruins of the Abbey was formed into a parish church, by arching over the transept and head of the cross, with a wing taken from the ruined choir.* The church was deserted at the period mentioned, in consequence of

---

* Engraving of the Abbey and adjoining subjects, in Hutchinson's Northumberland, vol. ii. p. 263, date, 1776; also, view taken by Grose in 1787, vol. i. p. 115.

some fragments of plaster falling from the ceiling during divine worship, the congregation believing that a prophecy of Thomas the Rhymer, to the effect that the kirk was to fall at the fullest, was about to be fulfilled; and although the alarm proved groundless, the congregation could not be induced to assemble again within the walls of the ruin, a result not to be regretted, as it ultimately led to the opening up of the beautiful structure to public view. A tier of arches thrown over those under which the Protestant people assembled to worship formed the prison of the town, and was the original from whence the Author of Waverley sketched the Tolbooth, to which the celebrated Border Bluegown was consigned, on his being carried away from the sports of the adjacent BUTTS.* According to old Bluegown, it "wasna sae dooms bad a place as it was ca'd; ye had aye a gude roof ower your head to fend aff the weather; and if the windows werena glazed, it was the mair airy and pleasant for the summer season, and there were fock enow to crack wi', and he had bread eneuch to eat, and what need he fash himsell about the rest o't?"† The BUTTS is supposed to be the place, where "the young men, availing themselves of the fine evening, were engaged in the sport of long bowls on a *patch of common*, while

---

* The ashes of Andrew Gemmels, the original of Edie Ochiltree, lie in Roxburgh grave-yard.

† Antiquary, vol. ii. p. 213.

the women and elders looked on."* Scott was a frequent inmate of the cottage situated at the south-east corner of the KNOWES, or Butts, occupied by his aunt, who had been his patient preceptress at Sandyknowe; and no doubt he had often enjoyed the sight of the games on the patch of common hard by. The church and grave-yard are enclosed by a high wall; but when Hutchinson (1776) and Grose (1787) visited Kelso, the Knowes and yard were open and intersected with roads in every direction. The entrance at the KIRK-STYLE, between Grey and Balmer's house, was formerly a massive flight of steps, with a solid landing-place in the centre, and the *Style* at the *Butts* as it is now; and the path that winds so crookedly on the east side of the manse to the river, taking off from the old school-house, and the whole extensive space had its only entrance for funerals by an *iron gate* into the abbey north door from the Abbey Close. There was formerly no carriage way between the houses and grave-yard.

The MILL of Kelso is thought to have been erected shortly after the foundation of the Abbey. It is certain that it existed at the end of the 12th century. During the reign of King William, he granted liberty to the monks of Kelso "to grind, free of multure, for three or four days, at his mill of

---

* Antiquary, vol. ii. p. 105.

Edinham, when their mill of Kelso should be stopped by floods or frost."* Next to the abbey, it is the greatest monument of the mechanical skill and enterprise of its monastic proprietors. Tradition has it that the cauld of the mill was run away with every flood, and that the present dam-head was erected by the familiar spirits of the great wizard, Michael Scott. It would seem that, in the early days, the *weirs* were erected something like a stake and rice fence of the present day. During the 13th century, Thomas *de* Gordon, amongst many other favours, conferred on the monks of Kelso, on their agreeing to bury him in the grave-yard of the monastery, granted them "*the free use of his woods, both stock and branches, to build their mill-dam.*"† In this locality is the beautiful islet in the Tweed, appearing, in the language of the minister of Kelso, as "a basket of flowers in the flood."‡ A glimpse of this Anna, as it appeared to the tourist Pennant in 1772, is obtained through one of the arches of the bridge, in his picture of the town, taken from the right bank of the river, between the present bridge and Maxwellheugh. The river seems to have been flooded at the time the drawing was executed; and the *islet* appears as a cluster of foliage resting on the waters.

---

* Lib. de Calchou, pp. 18, 19, 303, 304.
† Ib. "Stock et ramail ad edificandum stagnum suum."
‡ Statistical Account.

In 1755, a dispute occurred between the feuars of Kelso and the Duke of Roxburghe as to this anna; the inhabitants claiming a right to wash and dry their linen on it, as they had been immemorially accustomed to do; and the Duke, as proprietor of the land on both sides of the river, claimed as his own the anna in the middle of the stream. The Court held that, as the inhabitants had been in the constant use of whitening and drying their linen on the island, they were entitled to continue the possession thereof as formerly, but decided that the mill was the property of the superior. Another mill once existed at a place called the CUCKOLD'S LANE, propelled by water from the site of the present *Poors'-house*, and past the Dispensary, into the Tweed.

ROXBURGH-STREET is a modern name imposed by a person of the name of Matheson, about sixty or seventy years ago. This part of the town formerly consisted of four divisions: the *Cunzie-nook*, the *Horse-shoe*, the *Chalkheugh*, and the *Windy Goul*. The *Cunzie-nook* is supposed by some to have obtained its name from being the site of a mint, "*Cunzie*" *coin*, although no coins have been found inscribed with the name of Kelso; yet Kelso may have been at one time a place of coinage, and that the coin bore the name of the King's burgh of Roxburgh; but certainly no coin yet discovered bears the impress "*Kelso*." During the siege of Roxburgh by James II., in 1460, there was a coinage, and the coin bore on the interior circle the inscription, "*villa Roxburgh;*" but how the coinage could have been in the town of Roxburgh at that time, is not clear. From 1346 to the siege in 1460, when James II. lost his life, Roxburgh had remained in the hands of the English king, and could not, during that time, have been a place of coinage. It is probable that, while the siege was proceeding, the coin was executed at Kelso, and impressed with the name of Roxburgh, the King's town. It is not easy to get over the name of the town on the coin, but it is certainly as difficult to reconcile the fact of a coinage existing in a town that remained in possession of the English king during the life of James II. Though not attaching much importance to the name of *Cunzie-nook*, as the same name is to be found in many places of the county, yet it certainly is an element in support of the view, that the name was intended to describe the place where money was coined. The only thing tending to throw a doubt over the etymology is, that the coinage may have been in the town of Roxburgh, as the coin itself testifies, while the English held the Castle. The origin of the name of the HORSE-SHOE is also involved in difficulty. A short way up Roxburgh-street, a *horse-shoe* is firmly fixed in the middle of the street, and when one is worn out, a new one is substituted; but there exists no tradition or document to tell the object of the *shoe* being placed in the street. I have made the most careful inquiries from persons who have lived to an old age without having left the place, and searched every document accessible to me, without getting any light on the subject. It is certain, however, that it has long formed a well-known boundary in the town, and many houses in its locality are described as being bounded by the *Horse-shoe*. Were I to hazard a conjecture, it would be that the horseshoe is descriptive of some noted hostelry that stood in that locality, or that it received its name from being occupied by *stables*, or *smiths'* shops. In almost every town of importance was to be found, in times bygone, a hostelry with the sign of the *horse-shoe*. But the puzzle here is, that the *Horse-shoe* is evidently descriptive of a locality or a division, and not a single tenement.

After the streets, the APPROACHES to the town naturally suggest themselves for consideration. Before the erection of the old Bridge in 1754, which fell a victim to the autumn floods of 1797, the only access from the south and west was by ford or ferry. In the *Theatrum Scotiæ*, published near the beginning of the 18th century, the ferry-boats are seen in full operation. A flat-bottomed boat is engaged conveying the horse-loads, and two small boats transporting the foot-passengers at the ferry at the Millwynd. There was also a cobble at the head of the town opposite St. James' Green, and another plying on Maxwell.* All these ferries were, previous to the dissolution of the monastic establishments, in the hands of the friars of Roxburgh.† In 1754, a bridge of stone was thrown over the Tweed, of which the stone piers are still to be seen at a short distance above the present bridge. In Pennant's engraving of the town and river, this bridge is in the foreground, consisting of six arches, the third and fourth of which appear to be higher than the others. Pennant says it was an "elegant bridge of six arches," and Hutchinson, that he had access to the town "by a fine stone bridge of six arches." At the time this bridge was erected, it is believed that no other bridge existed on the Tweed between Berwick and Peebles.‡ Coldstream Bridge was opened for traffic in the autumn of 1766, and the elegant bridge at the confluence of the Leader with the Tweed, in the beginning of the present century.§ All the old bridges

---

* Retours, No. 282.

† All the passages on the river seem to have been in the hands of the clergy. In 1199, when the Bridge of Berwick was carried away by the flood, a dispute arose between the King and the Bishop of Durham as to rebuilding it, as it abutted on his land. The bridge which they erected only lasted nine years. In 1334, the bishop got a grant of the passage.—Ayloff Cal. 147.

‡ The present bridge at Berwick, of 16 arches, was built of stone in the reign of Elizabeth.—Wallis' Northumberland, vol. ii. p. 41. It is said that it is founded upon wool packs, from the sources whence the expenses of building were drawn.

§ Vol. i. pp. 75-77.

which existed during the days of the Romans, and in the period of Border contention, had fallen into decay or been destroyed. Perhaps no bridge on the river was the scene of greater strife than the Bridge of Roxburgh. It is a pity there is no evidence to mark the exact situation of this well-contested access. In Patten's Narrative of Somerset's expedition, it is stated that between Kelso and Roxburgh there had been a great *stone* bridge with arches, which the Scots had broken down to prevent the English crossing over to them.* In 1370, Edward III. granted the burgesses of Roxburgh forty merks for the repair of this bridge.† In 1398, Sir Philip Stanley, the Captain of Roxburgh Castle, claimed for the King of England £2000, against the Earl of Douglas' son and others, for having broken the bridge, burnt the burgh, and destroyed a great quantity of hay and fuel.‡ In 1410 the bridge was again broken down by the Earl of March and others.§ In the burgh books of Kelso, there is an entry under March, 1718, bearing that Sir William Kerr of Greenhead's house and offices at Bridgend were burned, with all his

---

* Patten says that the Tweed at Kelso was of great depth and swiftness, running thence eastward into the sea at Berwick, and was notable and famous for two commodities, especially salmon and whetstones.

† "Pro reparatione et emendatione pontes ultra aquam de Twede."—Rotuli Scotiæ, vol. i. p. 937.

‡ Border History, p. 365. § Ib. p. 380.

furniture and goods. This place was situated in the policy of Springwood Park, a little way to the south of the old graveyard, and at a place where the river Teviot was forded before the erection of the present bridge. In the map of Timothy Pont, drawn by him in the beginning of the 17th century, published after his death in Blaeu's Atlas Scotiæ in 1655, a *fort* is seen near the mouth of the Teviot; and in Stobie's map of 1772, a considerable number of houses are shown on the right bank of the Teviot, a short way above Maxwellheugh Mill. This place could not have got its name from the old bridge which was carried away by the floods, because it was only erected in 1754, and the name existed long before that date. There must have been a bridge here in early times, either over the Teviot or on the Tweed, which imposed a name upon the place, although the bridge over the Tweed, connecting Roxburgh with Kelso, has always been looked for higher up the river, yet it may have been in this locality. The present bridge was begun in 1800, and finished in 1803, at a cost, including approaches, of about £18,000. It is, in length, 494 feet, breadth of roadway, 25 feet, and its height from the foundation is about 57 feet. There are five elliptical arches, the span of each being 72 feet, and the piers 14 feet. The late Mr. Rennie was the architect; and it is said that Waterloo Bridge over the Thames in London was built after the same plan. The structure is very elegant, and is worthy of the lovely locality in which it is placed. There is a fine painting of Kelso by Macculloch, in which the bridge is a prominent object.* "Few scenes,"

---

* In addition to what is stated in vol. i. p. 73, as to the river Tweed, I may further refer to an earthquake which happened in April 27, 1656, and which followed the course of the Tweed from its source to the ocean. The shock was felt only in the river and places adjacent, but in no other part of the kingdom.—Balfour's Annals, vol. iv. p. 8. In the Newcastle Journal, March 19, 1748, is a letter from a gentleman in Scotland, stating that, on the 25th of January previous, the river *Teviot*, for two miles before it joins the river Tweed, had stopped its current, and its channel became dry, leaving the fishes on dry ground, many of which were taken up by the country people, and sold at *Langton* and other places. It continued in that condition for the space of nine hours; and when it resumed its course, it did so gradually, till it ran as usual, but in no greater quantity. On the 19th February of the same year, the river *Kirtle* was dry for six hours, leaving fishes at the bottom, which alarmed the country so much, that Sir William Maxwell, who lived within 500 yards of it, and many of the country people, rode along the banks of the river, and found it dry for six miles, but could not find out the cause of the water stopping. Four days afterwards, the river *Esk* itself stopped its course, and the channel became quite dry, except some deep holes, for the space of six hours. The strangeness of the facts communicated, and the doubtfulness of the public concerning them, induced the proprietors of the journal to make inquiries on the subject from persons living on the spot, and they received a report from a gentleman of whose veracity they had faith, and who was in part an eye-witness. He stated that

says the writer of the New Statistical Account of the Parish, "are more imposing than that which opens to the tourist, as he descends from the opposite village of Maxwellheugh, with the prospect beneath him of this fine architectural object, the

---

he observed the *Esk* sink several inches perpendicularly that day, and at first attributed it to frost, or the dryness of the times, but he considered that the greatest frosts, nor the greatest drought in summer, never had such effect. The rivers *Sark* and *Liddell* stopped their course, and the shallows became dry, on Saturday the 20th of February; *Sark*, near Philipstown, in the parish of Kirk Andrews; *Esk* and *Tine* were both dry on the 25th; Esk, at a place called the Row, about a mile below Langton; as also above Langholm and Tine near West Linton; Kirtle was dry some days before, near Springhill. There was some little water running among the small stones, but several persons passed through without wetting their feet. The places where Esk and Liddell were dry are seldom under sixteen or eighteen inches deep in the driest times. There was very little frost on the Esk that day. There was no swell of the water as if stopped by frost, but a general sink or lessening of the water. Liddell was dry in the afternoon, and the other rivers in the morning, and continued so till ten o'clock, when they began to flow again gently, and rose to the usual height in a short time. The reporter concludes by saying that "this account is not disputed here any more than that the sun shines in the clearest day." In the same journal, March 5, 1753, it is stated "that some years ago the river Tweed was dried up near Peebles, from six in the morning till six at night, the current being suspended during that time, of which many persons were eye-witnesses." Since the first volume of this work was published, a stoppage of the river Tweed was observed about Innerleithen, and which was attributed to frost.

majestic Tweed, the picturesque town and abbey, and the noble background of the castle, woods, and surrounding heights of Floors.*

The TOWN, while the property of the monks, formed part of the regality of the Abbey. Soon after the Reformation, it was granted to Francis, Earl of Bothwell, but returned to the Crown at his forfeiture in 1594. In 1605, it was bestowed on Sir Robert Ker, of Cessford, the ancestor of the present Duke of Roxburghe. In 1634, Kelso, which was previously included in the barony of Holydean, was separated and erected into a free burgh of barony, with powers to the baron and his male heirs in all time to receive and admit new burgesses, to appoint baillies, clerk, officers, and other members necessary for the government of the burgh, to hold weekly public markets, and two free fairs yearly for the space of eight days, to receive and uplift the customs and duties thereof, and to apply the same to the common good of the burgh, and to establish regulations for the general good of the town, advancement of trade, and encouragement of manufactures. The town was incorporated after the passing of the act, but the sett in existence is dated 1757, and under it the town is governed by a baillie appointed by the Duke of Roxburghe, and fifteen

---

* New Statistical Account, p. 321.

stentmasters. The corporate bodies are seven: viz., the merchant company, skinners, weavers, tailors, shoemakers, hammermen, and fleshers. These bodies admit freemen, and enforce obedience to the regulations of the burgh. Each trade elects its preses and deacons. The baillie judges in all disputes as to admission to the trades, and holds courts for the decision of cases falling under his jurisdiction. The inhabitants having some years ago adopted the Police Act, the town may now be said to be almost entirely under the management of the Commissioners of Police, elected by the ten-pound householders. The Records of the Burgh Court commence in 1647, Andrew Ker of *Maison Dieu*, baillie of the regality. The earliest date in the convenery trade books is in 1658. The Merchant Company's Record, so far as yet discovered, does not go back farther than 1771. The power of the baillie, as well as the customs of the inhabitants of the town, may be illustrated by a few excerpts from the burgh books previous to the passing of the Heritable Jurisdiction Act in 1749. In 1641, certain acts were passed by the baillie of the regality—PATRICK DON—with the view of keeping good neighbourhood among the neighbours of the nether fields at Kelso, with consent of the hail neighbours and persons concerned, viz., "That no person whatsoever presume to lift or take away any march stones betwixt neighbours' lands, under a penalty of fifty shillings to the *Burlaw* men."* No person presume to gather other men's pease, or to *gleane* the same, without leave asked and given by the owners thereof, under pain of five pounds to the baillie, and fifty shillings to the *Burlaw* men for ilk fault. No persons whatsoever offer to lead away stones, or clay, or pick broom off other persons' lands or dykes, without leave asked and given by the owners of said lands, under penalty of forty shillings; that no person gather thistles or weeds from among the corn without leave asked and given. No person in the time of harvest to bring in any shorn corn, either peas, oats, or other corn, into town after eight o'clock at night, though the corn be their own. In 1711, "the whilk day the baillie (*Gilbert Ker*) understanding that there are several prentices, journeymen, and other persons molests and troubles the boys at the Grammar School in the *Churchyard* whyle at their innocent dyvertione, and that to the effusion of their blood, and hazard of their lives; and considering the laudable custom of this place for crushing fresh abuses, does ratify and approve thereof; and farder, whatever damage is done to the

---

* Each barony had its *Burlaw* men, for the settlement of disputes between neighbours, as to any loss or injury sustained by the cattle belonging to each other. They met forthwith on the ground, and administered summary justice. The word itself means *short law*, or speedy justice.

scholars, it is hereby declared, that parents shall be liable for their children, and masters for their servants, prentices, and journeymen, as guilty of blood wyt, and in case of not in a condition to pay the fine, ordains application to be made to the justices of the peace for delivering them over as *knaves* or other *public pests* and *vagabonds*, and ane extract hereof to be given to the next district meeting of the justices of the peace here." In 1716, the same authority endeavoured to prevent football from being played within his jurisdiction: "Forasmuch as there were several unallowable abuses, tumults, and riots committed the last year at the football, and that the same did create feud and enmity amongst several of the neighbours and inhabitants, and also considering, by divers old laws and acts of Parliament, the football is discharged: these do therefore prohibit and discharge the football from being played by any of this jurisdiction, either within the town or the precincts thereof." In 1717, Baillie CHATTO passed the following enactment, which shows the rudeness of a comparatively modern age:—" The baillie, in ane lawful fenced court this day, having considered of ane evil custom and practice of the feuars' servants, and others who possess the land, and labours the same in Kelso, that they compel their neighbour servants at their entry to serve any master in this place, to give money or ale to them under the notion of brothering the said men servants, and, in case of refusal, abuses their masters by taking away their pleugh and other labouring graith, to the great disturbance of the peace in this town and incorporation, which ought to be prevented in .time to come. Therefore, and for remeid thereof, the baillie, by the force of this act, prohibits and discharges all the servants within the burgh, and commonly called *Whipmen*,* frae craving, forcing, or exacting frae

---

* The society or brotherhood against which the law was directed consisted of farmers' servants, ploughmen, and carters, commonly called whipmen. The regulations of the society were secret. Once a-year a public meeting was held, for the purpose of amusement, at which the members were dressed in their best clothes, and heads adorned with bunches of ribbons, hanging over their shoulders. The members assembled in the market-place about eleven o'clock forenoon, mounted on horses, armed with clubs and wooden hammers, in military form, from whence they marched, with drums beating, music playing, and flags waving, to the common, about half-a-mile from the town, the place of rendezvous, to their sports. The first part of the performance, which was called the *cat in barrel*, consisted in putting a cat into a barrel stuffed with soot, and hung up upon a beam fixed upon two high poles, under which the members rode in succession, striking the barrel as they passed with their clubs or hammers. On the barrel being broken, the cat jumped down from the sooty prison, when it soon fell a victim to the whipmen and the crowd of townspeople assembled to witness the sports. A goose was next hung up by the feet on the beam, and the members then rode one after another under it, each trying to catch hold of the head in passing, till some lucky brother plucks off the head, and carries it away in triumph. Horse-races followed, after which the brotherhood

any other servant, new or old, any money or ale, coming under the notion of their right frae tenantry or brotherhood, or molesting or troubling them or their masters' pleugh graith, on the head foresaid, with certification, he or they who shall transgress this act shall ilk ane of them pay a fine to the Procurator-fiscal of the soume of ten groats *toties quoties;* and further, that there has been a base custom among the said whipmen of electing and choosing of ane of their ain number to be their lord or baillie, and ane other to be their officer, whereby they, to the disturbing of the peace, make laws and orders among themselves, contrare to the laws of the kingdom, and their masters' prejudice, such as the discharging any of their number to work, when any of them are convened before the magistrate for misdemeanours and offences, so that they turn to a party, and mob, and threatens, and dares the magistracy and authority itself, which ought to be prevented in time coming. Wherefore, for preventing the like

---

returned to Kelso, and ended the day in feasting and drinking. These cruel sports continued to be practised down to the beginning of the present century, when they ceased, and the sports confined to running races, chiefly in consequence of strictures written by Robert Mason, a native of Kelso, published in 1789 by James Palmer, the founder of the newspaper press in Kelso. It is thought that the strong arm of authority was directed against the whipmen, not only on account of the practices mentioned in the proclamation, but also that the society was secret, and at that period deemed dangerous.

in time coming, the baillie discharges the said servants, called whipmen, from choosing any baillie or lord officer amongst themselves, or to convene themselves as formerly, under any pretence whatsoever, and that with certification, the contravener thereof, by choosing or being choosed, or meeting as above, shall pay a fine, ilk person guilty, of £10 Scots *toties quoties;* and discharges the whole inhabitants of the town from giving the said whipmen shelter for such meetings, or selling ale to them on such occasions, and that under the penalty and certification aforesaid."

THE MARKETS AND TRADE OF THE TOWN.—The markets of Kelso appear at a very early period. By a charter of William the Lion, the monks of Kelso were allowed right of market under certain restrictions. The men of the monks living in the town were allowed to buy in the town fuel, materials for building, and provisions, on any day of the week excepting the day of the king's statute market at Roxburgh; they might expose in their own windows, bread, ale, and flesh; any fish which they had carried to Roxburgh, either on horseback or in wains, and which remained unsold, might also be exposed in their windows for sale; dealers passing through the town with wains should not unload or sell, but pass on to the king's market at Roxburgh. On the day of the statute market at Roxburgh, it was declared unlawful to sell or buy anything in Kelso;

and the inhabitants of that place were enjoined on that day to go to the king's market, and buy what they wanted in common with his burgesses of Roxburgh, according to their customs.*

The weekly market of the town is held on Fridays, and is attended by a great number of people, at which grain of every kind is sold by sample, both in the market-place and in the Corn Exchange—a large, elegant, and commodious building, erected by subscription in 1856. There are also two market days for hiring servants, before each term of Martinmas and Whitsunday. In March, there are good markets for horses; and, during the winter season, monthly markets for sheep and cattle. The butchers used to offer flesh for sale in a public market, but for many years they have followed the regulations laid down in the charter of William the Lion, and exposed it in their shop windows. The foundation of the Abbey was the epoch of trade in Kelso. The monks and their men in early days were skilled as artisans. Between 1165 and 1171, William the *Dyer* lived in Kelso.† The various dealings in this town were greatly promoted by the establishment of a branch

---

* Lib. de Calchou, pp. 15, 305.

† Ib.—Dyers were forbidden to be drapers, and the wools of Scotland were, during the 14th and 15th centuries, draped in Flanders. The nation was supplied with *mercerie* and *haberdasherie* out of the low countries.

of the Bank of Scotland in 1774. At present there are five bank agencies in the town.

LITERATURE.—Under this head the libraries of the town may be first noticed. The Kelso library was founded in 1750, and contains about 6000 volumes. It is kept in a commodious building at the Chalkheugh, the property of the shareholders. In the library is a manuscript copy of Archbishop Spottiswoode's History of the Church of Scotland. The date of the copy is supposed to have been after 1625, as it contains an unsigned "*Epistle Dedicatorie*" to Charles I. The volume bears the word "*Lauderdale*," and it is thought to have been one of two MSS. of the work possessed by the Duke of Lauderdale, and disposed of at a sale by auction of his Grace's books, in "Tom's Coffee-house, Ludgate-hill," in 1692, by a friend of Evelyn's to whom they had been pawned. The catalogue of the sale contains two MSS. of Spottiswoode's work, Nos. 11 and 12. The Duke of Lauderdale died in 1682. This MS. is said, by Bishop Russell, to be an exact copy, with the exception of a few verbal alterations, of a manuscript marked "*Ex bibliotheca apud Spottiswoode*," which was put into his hands by the present representative of the *Primate's* family.* The *New*

---

* Preface, by Bishop Russell, to a new edition of Spottiswoode's History of the Church of Scotland, p. 3.

Library, founded in 1778, and the Modern Library in 1800, were united in 1858, and consist of about 4000 volumes. There are also libraries in connection with the churches of the town. The *"Physical and Antiquarian Society"* was founded in 1834. A suitable building has been erected in Roxburgh-street, adjoining the Chalkheugh Library, and in which is an extensive collection of rare and valuable specimens of natural history and antiquities. Sir T. M. Brisbane is President. The Society was fortunate in securing the services, as Secretary, for many years, of the accomplished Dr. Charles Wilson, late of Kelso, while the skill exhibited by Mr. Heckford in the preservation of the animals is not surpassed by the best artists in London. The first newspaper started in Kelso was the *British Chronicle*, or *Union Gazette*, in 1783, by a person of the name of James Palmer. It was published every Friday morning in Bridge-street, and adjoined the Bank of Scotland. The *Chronicle* advocated liberal principles, which gave offence to those who held different opinions, and the result was the establishment of the *Kelso Mail*, under the superintendence of James Ballantyne, which still continues to be the organ of conservatism. At this press the first edition of the Border Minstrelsy was printed. In March, 1823, the *Border Courier* was brought out by the late John Mason, in opposition to the *Mail*, but failed to gain sufficient support, and the last number was published in the October following. In 1832, the *Kelso Chronicle* was set on foot by the Whigs of the district, for the purpose of advocating the principles of the party, and is still in existence. About three years ago, a *reading-room* was erected by shareholders, and is well supplied with newspapers.

The SCHOOLS of Kelso have long been famed for eminent masters. In the Grammar School the Latin and Greek classics are taught, with French, geography, and mathematics. The rector has the maximum salary and the statutory accommodation. The fees charged are, for classics, 10s. per quarter, and for mathematics, 10s. 6d. The late Dr. Dymock, one of the rectors of the Grammar School of Glasgow, was master of this school from 1791 till 1808, and during that period attracted to the seminary sons of the most eminent scholars of the day. It was at this school that the great novelist Scott received part of his education. The master of the English School has a salary of £5, 11s. 1d., paid equally by the heritors of the landward part of the parish and the burgh, and the interest of £240 of money mortified for teaching poor scholars recommended by the kirk-session. The fees charged are, for reading, 3s. 6d., for writing, 4s. 6d., arithmetic, 6s. 6d. There are also a number of excellent private schools in the town, and boarding-schools for young ladies. Besides the week-day schools, there are Sabbath schools connected with the Established Church and dissenting congregations in the town.

The town of Kelso has long been famed for its *Races*. The original course was on Caverton Edge, and afterwards, for a few years, on Blakelaw Edge. In 1822, James, late Duke of Roxburghe, converted the *Berry Moss* into one of the finest race-courses in the kingdom. It is a mile and a quarter round, sixty feet broad, and from there being no rising ground, the horses are seen distinctly from the starting till the termination of the race. On the west of the course is an elegant stand, with suitable accommodation. There is a spring and an autumn meeting, the latter often enhanced by the presence of the Caledonian Hunt. The first race run on the new course was in September, 1822.

THE MANOR OF KELSO AND ABBEY.—Although the first intimation of Kelso is to be found in the charter of David I., there can be little doubt that a town and church existed there at an earlier period. At the date of the charter, a church, dedicated to St. Mary, was planted in that situation; but the state of the country may be inferred from Edenham being described as a *waste* in the days of King Edgar, who reigned between 1097 and 1107. At that period the manor of Kelso was the property of the King, and remained so till 1128, when it was granted by David to the monks of the order of St. Benedict, whom he had settled in the *desert* at Selkirk, in 1113.* There is no information existing to point out the exact boundaries of the manor of Kelso, but it is thought to have comprehended the whole parish of Kelso lying on the north of the river Tweed, if not all the land lying between Brocsmouth and the influx of the Eden. When Malcolm IV. confirmed the grant of his grandfather David, he described it as " the town of *Kelcho*, with its due bounds in land and water, discharged quit and free from every burden; also the lands which Gerold gave me near the confines of the said town, which lands came down to the road which goes to *Naythanthyrn*." At the date of this charter there was only one town of Kelso; but in the reign of Robert I., two towns appear in the records. The wester town seems to have been incorporated at an early period, and governed by a *provost*, between 1165 and 1214. During the reign of William, Arnold the son of Peter of Kelso granted a messuage and some land, with a toft and croft in Kelso, and three shillings of annual rent paid by Ralph, the *provost* of the burgh. In 1323, the burgesses of wester Kelso appeared in the court of the abbot, and acknowledged that they had done wrong in making a new burgess without his consent. In an old rent-roll of the abbey, supposed to have been made up about

---

* Foundation Charter of Kelso. Chron. Mail. p. 64.

the beginning of the 14th century, *easter Kalchou* is entered as being in their own hands, and the mill of the *easter* town is said to be rented at £22. It is impossible to say, with any degree of certainty, the distinct boundaries of these two towns, but I think it may be fairly inferred, that the principal or wester town of Kelso lay along the river's bank, beyond the Duke of Roxburghe's old garden. The garden wall runs across what was of old the market-place of Kelso. The feuars of the third generation by-gone could point out to their children their former steadings in the burgh. The market cross of this town stood, it is said, north of the Coblehole, from whence it was removed to the King's Tree. During the night the cross was abstracted from this place, and all trace of it has as yet been lost. A little to the west, and nearly opposite to St. James Fairstead is the FAIR-CROSS, which appears to have been in former times a village; and after the erection of Broxfield into a barony, it was one of the seats of the baronial court. In the valuation-book of the county of Roxburgh, made up in 1791, and corrected to 1811, is entered as belonging to Isabella Trotter, "a small piece of ground surrounded by the pleasure-grounds of Floors;" and "*lands in Fair-cross*" are stated as having formerly belonged to Richard Learmonth.* The abbot's seat or stead was

---

* Valuation Book, p. 43.

at the Pipewell-brae, or ground which now forms a part of the estate of Henderside. In the valuation-book already referred to, there are a number of fields entered as being situated in this locality. Baillie John Jerdone was possessed of "one enclosure in Abbotseat." Charles Williamson has two enclosures there, and the heirs of Robert Happer three enclosures in Abbotseat.* In the Retour of the service of John Duke of Roxburghe, in 1696, the manor of Kelso is described as comprehending the lands called Almirielands and bakehouses of Kelso, the mills thereof, the fishings on the Tweed, and four ferry boats on the river, "the lands called Westercrofts; the lands of Broombalks and Hoitt; Broomlands; lands of Angreflat; the lands of Broomcroft; the lands of Towncrofts; lands of Blackbalks and west meadows; the lands of Eshieheugh, and all other moors and mosses lying near to the town of Kelso, and which were of old possessed by the abbots of Kelso and their tenants."† There can be no doubt, however, that nearly all the present town of Kelso, built on the haugh, including the market-place, is erected upon what was formerly the gardens and domestic buildings of the abbey. In the rent-roll given up by the Earl of Roxburghe, in 1630, there were twenty-seven feuars of the lands in the town and territory of

---

* Valuation Book, pp.41-43.   † Retours, No. 318.

Kelso; twenty-one feuars of Willands and crofts in Kelso.

The colony was settled in Selkirk by David, to be near his castle and hunting-seat in the forest, where he often lived while Earl of Cumberland. While the abbey was erected near to the earl's castle and village, the men of the monks soon reared a town, which became known in after times as the Abbot's Selkirk, to distinguish it from the town of the king. RADULPHUS was the first abbot of this fraternity, and who became abbot of Tyrone on the death of Bernardus in 1115.* The second abbot, WILLIAM, remained at Selkirk till the death of Radulphus, whom he succeeded as abbot of Tyrone in 1118.† The third abbot of Selkirk, and the first of Kelso, was HERBERT, who afterwards rose to be Bishop of Glasgow at the death of John in 1147.‡ But on Roxburgh being chosen as a royal residence, Selkirk became inconvenient for both king and monks. It is probable that between 1124—when David ascended the throne—and 1128, preparations had been made at Kelso for the reception of the monks, and the charter only granted when the accommodation was sufficient for the fraternity. While these works were proceeding, there can be little doubt that the monks

---

* Chron. Mail. p. 65.   † Ib. p. 66.

‡ Ib. p. 66, "Et illi successit Herbertus Monachus postea primus abbas de Kelchou." Ib. 73, "Obiit Johannes Glasguensis Episcopus et Herbertus abbas de Calchou successit ei."

were lodged at Roxburgh by their pious founder. Sir James Balfour positively states that, "in May, 1125, David translated the Abbey of Selkirk to Roxburgh;" but it is more likely that the complete removal of the fraternity did not take place till 1128, the date of the charter, although the great body of the monks and their men might be engaged in the erection of the house from the time David became king. Considering the character of David, a proper location for his favourite monks would be one of his earliest cares on being raised to the throne. It is hardly possible at this day to appreciate the great benefits conferred on a district by the foundation of an abbey or religious house within its bounds. The inmates of these houses carried not only the gospel into the wilds and waste places of the land, but peace and civilization followed in their footsteps; they stood between the oppressed poor, the serf, and slave, and the feudal tyrant and military spoilers of those benighted times. The abbeys were the sole depositaries of learning and the arts through many centuries of ignorance. The monks collected manuscripts, and made copies of valuable works. In the *Scriptorum* silent monks were constantly employed making copies of the Bible, which were sometimes sold, but were oftener "bestowed as precious gifts, which brought a blessing equally

---

* Balfour's Annals, vol. i. p. 10.

to those who gave and those who received." To these Benedictines are we indebted for nearly the whole of the works of Pliny, Sallust, and Cicero. They were the earliest painters, and the fathers of Gothic architecture, the inventors of the gamut, and the first who instituted a school of music was Guido d'Arizzo, a monk. They were the greatest farmers of the early times, and the first agriculturists who brought intellect and science to bear on the cultivation of the soil. Wherever they carried the cross, the plough also appeared. In the number of their flocks they rivalled kings and nobles. "The extraordinary benefit which they conferred on society by colonizing waste places—places chosen because they were waste and solitary, and such as could be reclaimed only by the incessant labour of those who were willing to work hard and live hard—lands often given because they were not worth keeping—lands which, for a long time, left their cultivators half-starved and dependent on the charity of those who admired what we must too often call fanatical zeal—even the extraordinary benefit, I say, which they conferred upon mankind by thus clearing and cultivating, was small in comparison with the advantages derived from them by society, after they had become large proprietors, landlords, with more benevolence, and farmers with more intelligence and capital than any others."* Take the

---

* Maitland's Dark Ages.

House of Kelso as an illustration. When David placed the community at Selkirk, the district was overgrown with woods, nearly uninhabited, except by the beasts of the forest. But in a short time a town was built and peopled; churches were raised; the waste was converted into fruitful fields; the rose was seen to blossom where the bramble formerly grew. On the sources of the Beaumont and the Cayle, numerous herds of cattle and flocks of sheep covered the sides of the mountains, and corn waved on the summits of many of the hills. Mills were erected in the granges to grind the corn belonging to the monks, as well as the produce of their neighbours' lands. The deserts of Liddesdale were colonized by them at a time when it was dangerous for a Christian to be found in that wild region. For many years a monk of Kelso lived in the waste near to Hermitage Castle, preaching to the rude men of the district. So early as the days of William the Lion, the monks had converted the morasses on the upper parts of the Ale into arable lands. Wherever they had a grange, they built cottages for the persons employed in labouring on the land, or tending the flocks of sheep, or herds of cattle and swine. They built bridges and made roads throughout the whole country. In the Abbey the sons of the nobility were boarded and educated.* To qualify the

---

* In 1260, Matilda of Moll granted her thirds in the lands Moll to the abbots and monks of Kelso, on condition that of

monks for being instructors of youth, one or more of them were generally in England studying the liberal faculties and sciences.*

While an examination of the Chartulary tells of the wealth of the Monastery in its lands and houses, studs, flocks, and herds, it also exhibits an interesting picture of the social condition of the people during the 12th and 13th centuries. At first the lands were cultivated by the bondsmen and villeyns belonging to the Abbey,† but in the progress of time the hamlets to which a district of land was attached gradually came to be occupied by the free tenants, who rented each a husbandland, and the cattle and swine of all the husbandmen or tenants pastured on

---

they should board and educate her son with the best boys who were entrusted to their care.—Lib. de Calchou.

* In the Book of Kelso there is the form of a license to enable a monk to go to England to study.

† These men might all be bought and sold with the land. In 1144, David granted to the abbot of Kelso the church of Lesmahago, and all Lesmahago, with the men—*cum hominibus*. In 1116, Waldeve, the Earl, gave to the same monks *Halden* and *William*, his brother, and all their children and their posterity. Andrew, the son of Gilbert Fraser, gave the monks some lands in the lordship of Gordon, with Ada, the son of Henry del Hoga my *vileyn* and all his issue: "*Nativo meo cum tota sequla sua.*" All the prisoners not ransomed remained in bondage, and on the Borders they got the name of *Cumerlach*, from their constant wailing while working in the field. In the charters they are styled "*Fugitivos.*"

the common of the hamlet.* There were also a number of cottages in the hamlet in which labourers lived, who possessed with each house a croft of about an acre of land, and the right of pasturing their cows and swine on the common, which consisted of pasture-land and woodland. When the hamlet increased to the size of a village, a mill, malt-kiln, and brewhouse appeared. Each of these husbandlands† used to rent in Roxburghshire on an average of 6s. 8d. yearly, and services, such as the husbandman shearing for four days with his wife and whole family; carrying a wainload of peats to the stableyard, and one cart-load of peats to the abbey in summer; travelling to Berwick with one horse-cart once in the year; finding a man to wash the sheep, and another man to shear them, and assisting to carry the wool of the Grange to the abbey. While performing these services, the husbandmen generally got their victuals at the abbey; but those who

---

* In 1160, John, the abbot of Kelso, granted to Osbern, his man, half-a-carrucate of land in Midlem, he becoming a freeman, and paying yearly a rent of 8s. A carrucate of land was as much land as could be tilled by a plough with eight oxen. The same abbot granted to his man Walden the eighth part of Currokis for half-a-merk yearly, and the third part of Auchenlee, paying for it 2s. 3d. yearly.

† A husbandland was generally equal in extent to a bovate or oxgate, consisting of six, thirteen, and occasionally nineteen acres. The extent depended on the number of oxgates granted to the husbandmen.

washed and sheared the sheep often did so without victuals. To supply the want of capital, every husbandman was in use to lease with his land two oxen, one horse, three chalders of oats, six bolls of barley, and three bolls of meal; a practice which is thought to be the origin of *Steelbow*.* The cottages rented at about eighteen pence yearly; six days' labour in autumn; to assist at the washing and shearing the sheep of the Grange; and weeding the corn of the abbot.† The abbot was entitled to take from every house in every hamlet before Christmas a cock for a penny. A brewhouse usually rented for about 6s. 8d. yearly, with this condition, that the brewer was bound to sell the abbot a *lagen* and a half of ale—equal to about seven quarts—for a penny. A

---

* Steelbow is supposed to be derived from the Anglo-Saxon *steel*, signifying the state of the thing, its condition; and *bod* in the British, *bo* in the Irish, and *bye* in the Saxon, mean *habitation*; *steelbow*, the condition of the habitation. On the tenant entering into the subject, an inventory was taken of the goods belonging to the lord, and declared in the language of the lease of the 14th century, "*Alle this to leve and to delivere to the said William Skrene or to his heyres at the termes ende.*"—Madox, p. 144. The leases were for fifty years, or for life, and the widow of the tenant enjoyed the subjects during life. The monks were liberal landlords and indulgent masters. *Stellnet* seems to have the same meaning as *steelbow*, a *fixed* net at a particular place for fishing.

† The cottages were formed of wood and turf, and of the value of about 20s. Houses were deemed of little importance, the value was attached to the land.

great quantity of malt was used during the 12th century, and it is supposed that the mill of Ednam alone ground not less than 1000 quarters of malt yearly.* All these services were, about 1297, commuted into a payment in money. The monastery acquired from the kings general grants of the use of their forests for pasturage, panage, and for cutting wood for building and burning, and for all other purposes. Earl David granted such a right to the abbot and convent of Selkirk, and on his ascending the throne, he renewed the grant in favour of the house of Kelso. David II. conferred on them a special grant of wood out of Jed forest to repair the abbey. Besides these royal grants, they enjoyed special grants from barons of the same privileges in particular forests, which extended not only to the monks, but to their men, all who were engaged in the cultivation of their lands, and to their shepherds. In these forests vast herds of

---

* Oat malt was generally used; malt of barley appears seldom. Oat malt sold at 3s. 6d. per quarter, and barley at 4s. 4d., during the 12th and 13th centuries. An acre of oats was valued at 6s. Oats and wheat were the grain chiefly cultivated at that period. Wheat sold at from 7s. to 8s. per quarter; flour, 6s. per quarter; oats, 3s. 6d.; barley, 4s. 4d.; pease, 2s. 9d.; beans, 5s.; salt, 5s.; the carcase of an ox, from 5s. to 6s. 8d.; fat hogs, 2s. 2d. to 3s. 9d.—*Wardrobe account.* The multure paid for grinding at the mills was fixed by King William at the sixteenth vessel for a freeman, and a firlot out of 20 bolls as *Knaveship.*

cattle and swine were reared, and in them their breeding mares ran in a wild state. From many barons they had grants of a tenth of the young stock bred in the forests. Gilbert de Umfraville granted to the monks the tenth of the foals of his breeding mares in the forest of *Cottenshope,* and the foals were allowed to follow their dam till they were two years old.* A grant of lands often contained a right of *Scalengas,* in the mountains to which the cattle and flocks were taken to pasture during summer, and returned to the low-lying grounds at the approach of winter. Gospatric, the Earl of Dunbar, bestowed such a privilege of pasturage on the abbey in the lands of *Bothkel.*† During the reign of William the Lion, Patrick, another Earl of Dunbar, granted the monks the same rights. William de Veterepont granted to them the *scalengas* in Lambermore, which belonged to *Hornerdene.*‡ The same practice is described by Cambden as existing in the wastes of Cumberland and Northumberland so late as 1594. He says, "The herdsmen were a sort of *nomades,* who lived in huts dispersed from each other, which were called *Scheales* or *Schaelings.*"§ In all the mountain districts of Roxburghshire the

---

* Lib. de Calchou.

† Ib. "Scalingas de Bothkel per rectas suas divisas."

‡ Lib. de Calchou.

§ *Scalingas* signifies a mountain pasture, the herdsmen's huts, and secondarily, a hamlet.

word *shiel* or *shieling* is to be found in the names of places.

In addition to the grants of WOOD for burning, which seems to have been the earliest fuel, the monks obtained grants of *turves* and *peits*. The principal PEATRIES of the monastery appear to have been in the territory of Gordon. Thomas de Gordon granted to the monks a right to take *peats* from that part of his *peatry* called *Brun Moss*, in the territory of Gordon, with land, for the conveniency of working the moss; and also the liberty of pulling heath wherever they could in the territories of Thornditch and Gordon, and timber from his woods, on their agreeing to allow his bones to repose in the cemetery of Kelso. In carting the peats from this peatry, the men of the monks required to cross the rivulet of Blackburn on the lands of Melochstane, which being at times attended with danger, William de Hetely, the owner of the lands during the 13th century, granted leave to them to build a bridge over the stream, and to carry their peats and goods through his grounds beyond the bridge.*

The monks were also the owners of a number of FISHERIES. Earl David granted to the monks of Selkirk and their men the right to fish in the waters around Selkirk, in the same manner and as fully as his own men. As king, he conferred the same right

---

* Lib. de Calchou.

on the monks of Kelso, and added the fishings in the Tweed from Broxmouth to the confluence of the Eden. Malcolm IV. issued a precept to his sheriffs and other officers in Lothian, and in his whole land, to allow the monks the half of the fat of the royal fishes which might be stranded on either shore of the Forth.* In the reign of David I., Bernard de Baliol granted to the monks at Kelso a fishing in the Tweed at Berwick, called *Wudehorn Stell*, and which was confirmed to them by the king. They had another fishing at the same place called North-Yare, and a fishing at Upsettlington.† In the 12th century John de Huntingdon, rector of Durisdeer, conferred on them a fishing on the Tweed called the *Folestream*. They had also a fishing in Renfrew. The monks were also possessed of *Saltworks*. David I. bestowed upon them a *saltwork* in the carse on the upper shore of the Forth. They had another saltwork at *Lochkendeloch* on the Solway, granted by Roland the constable, with sufficient easements from his woods to sustain the pans.

The monks had a right from David I. to the tenth of all the bucks and does which his huntsmen and hounds should take. They had also a right to a certain portion of the cows, swine, and skins of beasts, which he received from Nithsdale; the skins and fat of beasts from Carric; the half of the skins

---

* Lib. de Calchou. † Ib.

and fat of the beasts slaughtered for his use on the north side of the Forth, with all the skins of the sheep and lambs; the tenth of the deer skins; and the tenth of the cheeses he was in use to receive from his estates in Tweeddale. The exercise of this right became in after times so inconvenient, that Alexander II., with the view of freeing *his kitchen* from the intrusion of the monks, granted to the monastery, in commutation thereof, one hundred shillings yearly out of the firms of Roxburgh.*

---

* The monks were not always safe visitants of a kitchen. In the neighbouring county of Northumberland, there exists a tradition of a monk, who, strolling abroad, arrived at the ancient house of Delavel, while the chief was absent on a hunting expedition, but expected back to dinner. Among the dishes preparing in the kitchen, was a pig, ordered expressly for Delavel's own eating, which suiting the palate of the monk, he cut off its head, reckoned by epicures the most delicious part of the animal, and, putting it into a bag, made the best of his way to the monastery. Delavel being informed at his return of the doings of the monk, which he looked upon as a personal affront, and being young and fiery, remounted his horse and set out in search of the stealer of his pig's head, whom overtaking, he so belaboured with his hunting gad that he was hardly able to crawl to his cell. The monk dying within a year and a day, although not from the beating, his brethren made it a handle to charge Delavel with his murder, who, before he got absolved, was obliged to make over to the monastery, in expiation of the deed, the manor of *Elsig* in the neighbourhood of Newcastle, with several other valuable estates; and by way of an *amende honorable*, to set up an obelisk on the spot where he corrected the monk. Elsig afterwards became the summer

While princes and barons borrowed money from the monks "*in their great need,*" and gave land in security, it was customary for many men to resign their lands into the hands of the monks, on obtaining an obligation for a decent provision in the abbey, where they were sure of amusement, instruction, and pardon. In 1311, Adam de Dowan, the elder, resigned his lands in Greenrig to the abbots and monks, and they obliged themselves to support him in victuals in their monastery, and to give him yearly a robe, or one merk sterling.* The abbot, in consideration of Reginald de Curroch's resigning his lands of Fincurrochs, granted to him the lands of Little Kype, with decent maintenance in victuals for him and a boy within the monastery. The abbot granted to William Forman, during life, a *corody* of meat and drink, such as a monk received, with a chamber, bed, and clothes, and grass for a cow. Andrew, the son of the foresaid Reginald, got a pension of four merks a-year from the abbot, on his resigning to the monastery his tenement of Little Kype. The great of the land were anxious that their ashes should rest in the burial-ground of the abbey. Adam de Gordon granted important

---

retreat of the monks. The obelisk is said to have been ten feet high, and on the pedestal, the inscription, "*O horror, to kill a man for a piggis head.*" The obelisk bears the name of the Monk's Stone.

* Lib. de Calchou.

privileges for interment in the cemetery; and Margaret, the natural daughter of William the Lion, who married Eustace de Vesci, gave lands in Moll to the monks, to be received with her husband and their heirs into the fraternity of the monks.* In 1203, William de Vetrepont relinquished every claim he had against the monks, in consideration of their services in bringing his father's bones out of England, and burying them in the cemetery. Earl Henry, David's son, lies in this graveyard.† The abbots enjoyed the wardship of the heirs of their vassals, which was the source of great patronage and profit. Hugh, the abbot of Kelso, from 1236 to 1248, granted to Emma, the widow of Thomas de Bosco, the custody of her son and heir till he should come of age, "*cum maritagu*" of her son, she paying L.20.‡

The monks exported their skins, wool,§ and corn at Berwick, with the horse and carts of their husbandmen and cottagers, who brought in return coals, salt, and wine, &c. for the use of the monastery. When Berwick was in the hands of the English king in 1369, David II. erected Dunbar into a port, and declared it to be co-extensive with the Earldom

---

* Lib. de Calchou.

† Noticed in charter of William de Vetrepont to the abbey.

‡ Lib. de Calchou.

§ The usual mode of packing wool in Teviotdale during the period alluded to, was by the sack, which contained twenty-six stones. By a statute of David II. each sack of wool paid a duty of one penny.

of March, and to be the port for Teviotdale so long as Berwick remained in the power of the English. Edward I. was anxious that the men of Teviotdale should use the port of Berwick, and granted protection to them, and all the rights and privileges which they had previously enjoyed.

Besides the granges, farms, and other possessions in Roxburghshire, which will be found under the localities in which they were situated, they had property spread over the shires of Selkirk, Berwick, Peebles, Lanark, Dumfries, Ayr, and Edinburgh. In SELKIRKSHIRE, David granted to the monks whom he had placed at Selkirk the church of his castle, on the condition that the abbot and his successors should be chaplains to him and his successors. The king also granted to the abbey many parcels of land in the forest, but, being inconveniently situated, Malcolm IV. conjoined the whole, and excambed them with lands lying near the town. All the lands of the abbot were let in husbandlands of a bovate each, with right of common pasturage for a certain number of beasts. He had also many cottages with crofts, containing each nearly an acre of land. About the end of the 13th century, the monks had at Selkirk, in *demesne*, a carrucate and a-half of land, which rented for ten merks, fifteen husbandlands, each containing an oxgate, which rented for 4s., and the usual services—sixteen cottages, with ten acres of land, one of which rented for 2s.,

and the other fifteen for 1s. and services. The abbot had three brewhouses, which rented at 6s. 8d. each, and a corn mill, which rented at *five merks* yearly. Out of their *demesne*, they had thirty acres separately rented at 5s., and four acres at 6s. yearly. Alexander II. granted to the abbot of Kelso sixteen acres of land on both sides of the Ettrick, for the perpetual repair of the bridge of Ettrick. These lands are known by the name of the *Briglands* at the present day. The abbot held his court at the bridge over the Ettrick. In BERWICKSHIRE, in the territory of *Waderley*, the monks had, during the 12th century, five acres of tofts and crofts and five acres of arable land, with common of pasture for 100 sheep and forty cattle, with their lambs and calves, till three years old, granted to them by Gilbert, the son of Adam of Home. During the 13th century, Andrew, the son of the late Gilbert, granted to the monks a carrucate of land, which he had bought in the territory of Wester Gordon, and three acres of meadow in the lordship of Gordon, with common of pasture for five score of young cattle and 400 wedders, wheresoever the cattle or sheep of the lord of the manor pastured without the corn and meadowland.*
During the days of David I., Richard de Gordon granted to the monks of Kelso and to the church of

---

* The carrucate of land and privileges rented for two merks.

St. Michael at Gordon, in free alms, a piece of land adjacent to the churchyard at Gordon; an acre of land in Todlaw; an acre of meadow in Hundley-strother; and whatever chaplain the monks placed in the church should have the pleasure of pasturage within his territory of Gordon, as his own men enjoyed the same. In the state furnished by the abbey to Robert I., they valued the church at L.20, and added that they had at that place half-a-carrucate of land pertaining to the church, with pasture for 100 young cattle and 400 sheep, and a toft whereon to build a mansion-house for the chaplain. In *Greenlaw*, Earl Gospatrick granted in 1147, to the monks of Kelso, the church of Greenlaw, with the chapel of Lambdene. Patrick, brother of Earl Waldave, while he confirmed the munificence of his father, gave them the right of pasture within the manor of Greenlaw for 100 sheep and oxen, 4 cows, and 1 work-horse. William, his son, added two tofts and crofts in the town, with other lands; and in consideration of these grants, leave was given for the erection of a private chapel in Greenlaw, on assurance being given that the mother church should not suffer thereby. At *Mellerstones*, they had a carrucate of land, with common of pasture, and other easements, within the territory. In *Halyburton*, David, the son of Truck, gave them, in 1176, within his vill, the church with two bovates of land, and some tofts and crofts, which was confirmed by his son Walter, and, in the reign of Alexander III., by his great-grandson Philip. This Philip was the first who was called *de Halyburton*. At *Fogo*, the monks got the church of that place from Gospatrick, in 1147, with a carrucate of land, confirmed by Malcolm IV., William the Lion, and approved of by Roger, the Bishop of St. Andrews. William, his grandson, added the mansion possessed by John the Dean within the adjacent croft and contiguous land, reaching southward to Greenrig, besides the lands which John the Dean enjoyed with the church. During the days of David I., the church of *Langton* was bestowed on the monks by Roger *de Ow*, a follower of Earl Henry, which was confirmed by his successor, William de Vetrepont, who added the lands of Coleman's-flat, in the same parish. Allan the constable gave them five ploughgates of land in *Oxton*, with easements, as a composition for revenues which they had out of Galway. In *Horndean*, Vetrepont gave them two acres of meadow, called *Hollenmedu*. In the time of Robert I., their property had increased to half-a-ploughgate, with pasture for 100 ewes, 6 oxen, 2 cows, and 2 horses, along with the lord's cattle. In *Symprine*, they got from *Hye* of that place the church with a toft and croft, and eighteen acres of land, under reservation of *Thor* the archdeacon's liferent. At *Spertildon*, they had a grange which they laboured with two ploughs; they had pasture for fifty score of ewes, twenty score of wedders, forty plough cattle, and great herds of swine. On this grange they had sixteen cottages for their herdsmen, labourers, and their families. They had here a brewhouse to supply the wants of the villagers, which rented at 6s. At *Bondington*, they had two carrucates of land, with two tofts and common rights, all which rented at six merks. In 1370, Nicholas Moyses gave them his right in his cottages, with a garden, which Tyoch, the wife of Andrew, held of him. In *Tweedmou*, they had three acres of land, and a house with a *spring*, for which they got 20s. yearly. In HADDINGTONSHIRE, Allan, the son of Walter the steward, confirmed by a charter a lease by his men of *Innerwick* to the monks of Kelso for 33 years, from Martinmas, 1290, of certain woods and pastures in that place for 20s., free of all services, "*inward or de outward.*" In *Humbie*, Sir Robert de Keith, the Marshal of Scotland, granted to the monks leave to build a mill on the lands, with a right for their work oxen, ploughs, and *carts, to pass and repass over his lands*. During the reign of William the Lion, the monks obtained the advowson of the church of *Pencaithland* from Everard de *Pencaithland*. In the time of Malcolm IV., Simon Fraser granted to the monks the church of Keith, with the whole wood from the southern side of the rivulet which runs near the church, with pertinents and other privileges. A dispute arose between the monks and the marshal as to the tribute he was bound to pay for the church of *Keith Hervie*, and so serious did it become, that the Pope delegated Joceline, Bishop of Glasgow, and the Abbot of Paisley, to settle the controversy, which they did by fixing the tribute at 20s. yearly out of the living, the marshal obliging himself to part with the church only to the monks. In the reign of William the Lion, they had a toft and other lands in Haddington, at a rent of 10d. yearly. In EDINBURGHSHIRE, the monks acquired the church and lands of Dodinston during the reign of William the Lion; but the charter does not mention the name of the person whose bounty added so largely to the possessions of the abbey. The lands were erected into a barony, and the abbots appointed their baron baillie, who administered justice within the boundaries. Owing to the distance of the lands from Kelso, they were usually let on lease. About the beginning of the 13th century, the lands of Easter Duddingston, with the half of the peatry of *Camberun*, were let to Reginald de Bosco for 10 merks yearly. Thomas, the son of Reginald, held the lands for the same rent. In the reign of Robert I., the abbot let the half of the manor of Wester Duddingston to Sir William de Tushelaw for 12 merks of yearly rent. In 1466, Cuthbert Knightson held part of the lands of Duddingston in fee for the yearly rent of 4 merks. This barony remained with the monks till the Reformation, and, after successive changes, it was purchased by James, Earl of Abercorn, in 1745, from the Duke of Argyle. In the city of Edinburgh, the monks held a toft, situated between the West Port and the Castle, on the left of the entrance to the city. They had a tenement in the town, which rented at 16d. per annum, but as to its situation, the rent-roll is silent. They had also a piece of ground, which lay beside the Abbey of Holyrood, let to John Clerk* in 1492. In PEEBLESHIRE, King William confirmed to them the church of the Castle of Peebles,—"capellum Castelle de Peebles" —with a *carrucate* of land adjacent to it, and ten shillings yearly granted by his grandfather out of the firms of the burgh, to found a chapel in which to say mass for the soul of his son, Earl Henry. The church of *Innerleithen* was given to them by David I., to which Malcolm IV. added a toft, and because the body of his son rested there the first night after his decease, he commanded that the church should have the same power of sanctuary as was enjoyed by *Wedale* and *Tyningham*. In 1232, William, the Bishop of Glasgow, confirmed the grant of the church to the monks. They had also a carrucate of burgage lands near the church, which rented for 12s. per acre. At Hopecailzie, they had three acres of land, which rented at 1s. per acre. Ralph de Clerc gave the monks the church of St.

---

* Acta. Dom. Con. p. 264.

Cuthbert of *Caledoure:* Caldour, with the tithes of the mill, on payment of ten merks annually to the vicar. King William confirmed to them the church of Cambusnethan in Clydesdale, together with the tithes of the profits of his mills. Dunsyre church was granted by Helias, the brother of Josceline, Bishop of Glasgow. Wicius gave the monks the church of Wiston, of which the church of Symington was a dependency. *Thankerton* was conferred by Anneis de Brus. Robert de Londonius, brother of King Alexander, granted to the monks a part of his land of *Kadihu,* with pasture for ten cows and ten oxen. The convent had also an annual pension of 40s. from the church of Lynton, and they had the church of Craufurd John. Robert I. granted to them the church of Eglismalescho, in Clydesdale, in 1321, as a compensation for their sufferings and losses during the wars of the succession.* They had an annual pension of 10 merks out of the living of Campsie. William the Lion confirmed to the monks the church of *Culter.* Brice Douglas gave the convent the church of Birnie in the beginning of the 13th century. In DUMFRIES they got the church thereof, and the church of St. Thomas, with lands, tofts, and tithes, from King William, and four acres of land. They had the church of *Morton, Close-*

---

* Robertson's Index, iii. 3.

burn, *Staplegorton*, and the church of *Wilbaldington*, and the patronage of the church of *Lesingibi*, Cumberland, confirmed by Pope Innocent III.

In 1144, David I. granted to the abbey the church and whole territory of Lesmahago, for founding a cell for monks from Kelso, and Bishop John of Glasgow freed it and its monks from Episcopal dues and subjection. It was dedicated to the Virgin and St. Machutus. The festival of the saint was on the 15th November. The cell had a right of sanctuary to every one who came within its four crosses to escape peril to life and limb.* In 1296, Alexander II. granted to the prior and convent to hold their lands in free forest. The prior had a seat in Parliament. In 1335, John, the brother of Edward III., burned the abbey while on his way to Perth by the western marches.

Colonies were sent from Kelso to the foundations of Kilwinning, Aberbrothick, and Lindores.

The revenues of the abbey of Kelso were, at the Reformation, in money, £3716, 1s. 2d.; 9 chalders of wheat; 106 chalders, 12 bolls, of bear; 112 chalders, 12 bolls, and 3 firlots of meal; 4 chalders and 11 bolls of oats. From these revenues it will be seen that the abbot of Kelso was more opulent than most bishops in Scotland.

The property of the abbot and convent was not liable to be poinded or distrained.

---

* Lib. de Calchou, p. 9.

THE ANNALS OF THE ABBEY AND TOWN.—In 1147, HERBERT,* the first abbot of Kelso, was raised to the see of Glasgow, and was succeeded in his office by ERNOLD, who, in 1160, was appointed bishop of St. Andrews.† JOHN, the precentor of the abbey— a man of a very ambitious character—was the next abbot.‡ In 1165, he obtained a *mitre* from the Pope. He also got himself named first in the rolls of the Scottish Parliament. The Archbishop of York having claimed the supremacy of the Scottish Church, was opposed with spirit by the abbot, who refused to obey a summons to meet him at the Castle of Norham. In the end the question was referred to the Pope, who decided against Roger of York, and declared the Scottish Church independent of any other, save Rome. Flattered by the many favours conferred on him, the abbot claimed precedence of the other religious houses in Scotland, which was not finally settled till 1420, when a decision was given in favour of St. Andrews. About the same time a dispute arose between him and the monastery of Tyrone, the abbot of Kelso claiming superiority over the abbot of that house, from which the convent of Kelso had its origin. John died in 1180, when OSBERT, the prior of Lesmahago, was elected to the office.§ While he was abbot, Scotland was

---

* Chron. Mail., pp. 66, 73–76, 77–79.   † Ib. pp. 73, 78.
‡ Ib. pp. 77, 90.   § Ib. pp. 99–92, 105.

interdicted by Pope Alexander III., which was afterwards removed by his successor, Lucius III., who also conferred upon the abbey of Kelso the privilege of exemption from excommunication proceeding from any other quarter than the apostolic see; and though the whole kingdom should be interdicted, they might worship in the church with closed doors, and in a low voice, without ringing of bells.* During Osbert's time, a controversy arose between the monks of Kelso and Melrose as to the boundary be-

---

* It required no ordinary resolution to withstand an interdict. The announcement of the interdict was usually made at midnight, by the funereal toll of the church bells; whereupon the entire clergy might presently be seen issuing forth in silent procession, by torch-light, to put up a last prayer of deprecation before the altars, for the guilty community. Then the consecrated bread that remained over was burnt; the crucifixes, and other sacred images, were veiled up; the relics of the saints carried down into the crypts; every memento of holy cheerfulness and peace was withdrawn from view. Lastly, a papal legate ascended the steps of the altar, arrayed in penitential vestments, and formally proclaimed the interdict. From that moment divine service ceased in all the churches; their doors were locked up, and only in the bare porch might the priest, dressed in mourning, exhort his flock to repentance. Rites, in their nature joyful, which could not be dispensed with, were invested in sorrowful attributes; so that baptism could only be administered in secret, and marriage celebrated before a tomb instead of an altar. The administration of confession and communion was forbidden. To the dying man alone might the viaticum, which the priest had first consecrated in the gloom and solitude of the morning dawn, be given; but extreme unction and burial in

tween the lands of the barony of Bolden and the property of Melrose. The matter was remitted by Pope Celestine to King William, who heard the parties at Melrose in 1202, and thereupon directed an inquisition to be made by the honest and ancient men of the district.* In 1204, the parties appeared again before the king, in his court at Selkirk, when judgment was given in favour of the monks of Kelso, and a charter granted by him, in which the whole proceedings were recited. Osbert died in 1203.

---

holy ground were denied him. Moreover, the interdict, as may naturally be supposed, seriously affected the worldly, as well as religious, cares of society.—(Life of Aidan, vol. iv. p. 36.) Such was the nature of the interdict under which Scotand lay for above three years, in consequence of King William resisting the pope's interference in the appointment of a successor to Richard, Bishop of St. Andrews. The chaplain elected the learned John Scott, and the king nominated Hugh, his own chaplain. Roger, the Archbishop of York, legatine of the pope, excommunicated William, and interdicted the kingdom. The pope supported the archbishop, but William remained firm, and swore, "by the arm of St. James, that, while he lived, John Scott should not be Bishop of St. Andrews." The legate then excommunicated Morville the constable, and Prebenda the secretary. The king banished every person who obeyed the pope and legate. During the contest, both pope and archbishop died. A compromise was effected between Pope Lucius and William; both the prelates resigned their claims, and the pope, with the consent of the king, appointed *Hugh* to St. Andrews, and John to Dunkeld. England lay under an interdict from 1207 to 1213.—(Hoveden, 599; Fordun, i. vi. c. 35, 36; Chron. Mail. 89-92.)

* "Per probos et antiquos homines patria."

GEOFFREY, the prior, was raised to the dignity of abbot, and filled the office for three years.* RICHARD DE CAVE was elected abbot, but died in two years.† HENRY, the prior, was elected by the monks in June, 1208.‡ Next year, the Bishop of Rochester, frightened from England by the fulminations of the Pope, found an asylum in Kelso Abbey; and, though he lived at his own expense, the King of Scotland sent him 80 chalders of wheat, 60 of malt, and 80 of oats—a proof that, in that age, corn was of more value than money.§ Henry was at the general council at Rome in 1215, for the purpose of concocting measures against the Waldenses, who preserved, in their remote habitations, the pure truths of Christianity, and but for the cruel measures adopted to suppress it, would soon have overthrown the papal tyranny. At this assembly there were 1283 prelates, 673 of whom were bishops, including the bishops of St. Andrews, Glasgow, and Moray. The council sat fifteen days, at the end of which the abbot of Kelso returned to his abbacy. The abbot died on October 5, 1218. RICHARD, the prior, was called to fill the chair; he died in 1221.∥ HERBERT MAUNSEL, the secretary, succeeded; and, after filling the office for

---

* Chron. Mail. p. 105. † Ib. pp. 106, 107.
‡ Ib. pp. 107–121, 134.
§ Ib. p. 109. Gilbert Glenville was at this time Bishop of Rochester.
∥ Ib. pp. 134, 138.

fifteen years, he resigned on September 2, on the day of the nativity of St. Mary, when HUGH DE MAUNSEL was installed;* but OTHO, the Pope's legate, in 1239, compelled Herbert to resume the mitre, and Hugh—being a mild, peaceable man—quietly resigned his pastoral charge.† The Chronicler of Melrose has the death of Hugh recorded as taking place in 1248.‡ About this time the abbot and convent, and their successors, received authority from the Pope to excommunicate known thieves and invaders of their estates, and those guilty of doing evil to the Church. The sentence was to be pronounced with lighted candles and ringing of bells, on a Sunday or holiday, and they had power to repeat the sentence every year, the Thursday before Easter, the Feast of the Assumption of the Blessed Virgin, and other solemn occasions.§ ROBERT DE SMALHAME, one of the monks, was appointed abbot,

---

* Chron. Mail. pp. 147, 148: "Item dompnus Herbertus abbas calcovensis in die Nativitates beata Maria baculum cum metri super magus altere possut et taliter pastorali cure valedixit."

† Ib. p. 150.   ‡ Ib. p. 177.

§ The form of excommunication was by the priest using the following words: "By authority of Almighty God, the Father, Son, and Holy Ghost, and the blessed Mary, the mother of God, and all the saints, I excommunicate, anathematize, and put out of the confines of the Holy Mother Church, A. B., that evil-doer, with his abettors and accomplices; and unless they repent and make satisfaction, thus may their light be put out before Him that liveth for ever and ever;" and at

in 1248.* In 1256, Alexander, and Margaret, his queen, made a grand procession from Roxburgh Castle to the abbey of Kelso, where the King of England was royally entertained.† The abbot died in 1258, and was succeeded by PATRICK,‡ one of the fraternity, who retained the mitre for two years, when he was forced to resign in favour of the intriguing HENRY DE LAMBEDEN, the chamberlain, whose conduct was such, that his death, in 1275, of apoplexy, as he sat at table, was looked upon by the inmates of the convent, and others connected with the monastery, as a punishment for his wicked ambition. They refused to watch his corpse, and interred him on the same day on which he died.§ RICHARD was the next abbot. In 1285, he presided at a court at Reddon, when Hugh de Revedon resigned all the lands held by him in the baronies of Revedon and Home, which had been purchased by the convent.‖ The abbot seems to have kept the writs and titles of the nobility. In 1288, William de Duglas gave an acknowledgment to the abbot, that he had

---

the same time taking lighted torches, and trampling them out on the ground while the bells were ringing. Excommunication does not seem to have produced the least effect on the Border mosstroopers. They entertained greater fear for the doings of the Justiciaires at Jedburgh than any monkish ceremony.

* Chron. Mail. p. 177. † Ib. p. 181.
‡ Ib. pp. 184, 185–189. § Ib. p. 189.
‖ Lib. de Calchou.

received from him all his charters which were in the abbot's custody.* When Bruce and Baliol disputed the succession to the crown at the death of King Alexander, Richard was chosen by Baliol to support his pretensions. In 1296, the abbot was received into the peace of Edward I., and the lands and property belonging to the convent were restored.† About this time WALRON was abbot. In July 22, 1301, Edward I. was at Kelso on his way north.‡ The mitre was next worn by an Englishman of the name of THOMAS DE DURHAM, it is said, by usurpation during these perilous times, till Robert Bruce was finally established on his throne by the fortunate result of the battle of Bannockburn, when WILLIAM DE ALYNCROM was made abbot.§ In 1316, an exchange was made of the church of Cranston for Nenthorn and chapel of Little Newton, with the Bishop of St. Andrews. WILLIAM DE DALGERNOCK was next abbot. He was preceptor of David II., the young king, and when the King of England invaded Scotland in 1333, on the pretence of supporting Baliol, David and the abbot retired into France, where they remained nine years, and the monastery was in charge of a warden. In 1333, Edward granted letters of protection to the abbey,|| and when Baliol made over the counties of Roxburgh,

---

* Lib. de Calchou. † Rotuli Scotiæ, vol. i. p. 8.
‡ Ib. vol. i. p. 53. § Lib. de Calchou.
|| Rotuli Scotiæ, vol. i. p. 268.

Berwick, and Dumfries, the abbot of Kelso was one of those who witnessed the degradation. In 1344, David II. granted leave to the monks to cut wood in the forests of Jedburgh and Selkirk, to repair the convent. He also granted to the monks that they should possess the town of Kelso, with its pertinents, the barony of Bolden and the lands of Redden, with their pertinents, with exclusive jurisdiction of justiciars, sheriffs, with other privileges.* WILLIAM was abbot about 1354. In 1366, protection was granted to the abbey and convent by the English king.† In 1368, Edward III. granted liberty to the abbot and convent of Kelso to buy victuals in England for themselves and families, in consequence of the miserable state to which they were reduced by the war.‡ In 1373, the same king granted protection to the abbot, the monks, and the lands and possessions of the convent. In 1378, Richard I. granted protection to the monks of Kelso, and their convent, and lands, wherever situated.§ PATRICK is seen acting as abbot from the year 1398 to 1406. About 1428, WILLIAM was abbot. Another WILLIAM was abbot in 1435, and continued so till 1444. In 1460, Roxburgh Castle and town were wrested from the English, after having continued for more than 100 years in their possession; but it was purchased by the death of the king, who was killed by

---

* Reg. Mag. Sig. p. 190, No. 26.
† Rotuli Scotiæ, vol. i. p. 902.   ‡ Ib. vol. i. p. 924.
§ Ib. vol. ii. p. 8.

the bursting of a cannon. Immediately after the castle was taken, Prince James was solemnly crowned in the abbey church of Kelso, in the seventh year of his age. ALLAN appears as abbot between 1464 and 1466. ROBERT was next abbot, and GEORGE filled the office in 1476. After James III. was slain at Bannockburn-mill, his son James was crowned in the abbey of Kelso in 1488. In 1490, Henry VI. granted special letters of protection and license from the abbot and convent of Kelso, including the town of Kelso, the town of Redden, Sprouston, Wester Softlaw, and the barony of Bolden, and all their lands and tenements, servants, corn, and cattle, and all their goods, moveable and immoveable. License was also granted to one or two monks to go with their servants into England, and buy lead, wax, wine, and other merchandise, for the use of the convent, and also to go to the wardens or lieutenants of the borders, and demand restitution of their goods.* In 1493, ROBERT, the abbot of this house, was appointed by the Three Estates one of the auditors of causes and complaints. Henry, the prior, was famed for his great learning. In 1511, ANDREW STEWART, bishop, had the abbey granted to him in trust.† Four years after, the famous Dand Ker of Fernieherst marched to Kelso, assaulted the abbey, took it, and turned the superior, one of the Cessford family, out of doors.

---

* Rotuli Scotiæ, vol. ii. p. 494.

† About this time the kings were beginning to encroach on the privileges of the Church.

It is said that this assault took place the night after the battle of Flodden. THOMAS KER, the brother of Dand Ker, was the next abbot. In 1520, commission was given to the abbot to meet with Dacre, warden of the marches, at Heppethgate-head, on the Colledge-water, and a truce was concluded till January following; at that time the abbot and KER of Cessford met the English warden at Redden, when they agreed to prorogate the truce till the last day of June. The Governor of Scotland was then anxious to conclude a truce, but Henry rejected all offers of peace, and prepared to march into Scotland. He also ordered all the French and Scots to be imprisoned, their goods seized, themselves marked with a cross and sent home to Scotland. In the end of July, 1522, two of Shrewsbury's captains, the Lords Ross and Dacre, pillaged and burnt the town. The men of Teviotdale flew to arms, and amply revenged the loss they had sustained. Next year, Dacre, one of Surrey's captains, paid a visit to Kelso, and reduced the monastery and town to ashes. The monks were forced to leave Kelso and take shelter in the neighbouring villages. In 1526, the abbot assisted in concluding a truce for three years. At the death of Thomas Ker, JAMES STEWART, an illegitimate son of James V. by Elizabeth Schaw, was, while in minority, made commendator of the abbey. The abbot was a pupil of George Buchanan. In 1542, the Duke of Norfolk entered Scotland by the river Tweed, burning and destroying everything that fell in his way. No place was held sacred. The town of Kelso and the abbey, which had been partially repaired since Dacre's inroad, were again reduced to ashes. Two years later, an inroad was made by Bowes and Laiton, and in 1545, the Earl of Hertford attacked the abbey. Three hundred men retired into it, and made an obstinate resistance, but were forced to yield, and were nearly all slain or taken prisoners. Next year, the abbey was defended by thirty footmen against Eurie, but taken. In the report of Eurie to the English king, two "bastille houses" are referred to as being in the town. In June following, when the garrison of Wark made an incursion into the town, the church was defended by sixteen men, who had builded them a strength in the old walls of the steeple. The abbey afforded a shelter to a few monks till 1560, when they were expelled by the fanatical mob, the images broken, and all its internal furniture and decorations destroyed. In 1558, Mary of Lorraine gave the commendatorship of Kelso and Melrose to her brother the Duke of Guise, on the abbot being slain by his own relation, one of the Kers of Cessford. Sir JOHN MAITLAND was temporarily commendator. BOTHWELL next got the abbey in trust, by exchanging Coldingham for Kelso with Maitland. On the 9th of November, Queen Mary arrived at Kelso from Jedburgh. Next day she held a council, and on the 11th left with the design of viewing Berwick, attended by her court and about 1000 horsemen, belonging to the border shires. She travelled by Langton and Wedderburn, and on the 15th looked upon Berwick from Halidon-hill.* On the 6th of April, 1569, a remarkable bond was agreed to and subscribed at Kelso by the inhabitants of the sheriffdoms of Berwick, Roxburgh, Selkirk, and Peebles, and provosts and baillies of burghs and towns within the bounds, whereby the parties bound and obliged themselves to the king's majesty and his dear cousin James, Earl of Murray, Lord Abernethie, regent, to concur together to resist the rebellious people of the country of Liddesdale, and other thieves inhabiting Ewisdale, Anandale, and especially persons of the surnames of "Armestrong, Ellot, Niksoun, Croser, Littell, Batesoun, Thomsoun, Irwing, Bell, Johnnestoun, Glendonyng, Routlaige, Hendersoun, and Scottis, of Ewisdaill," and other notorious thieves, wherever they dwell, and their wives, bairns, tenants, and servants, that none of them would at any time thereafter reset, supply, or intercommune with any of the said thieves, their wives, bairns, or servants, or give them meat, drink, house, or harbour, or suffer any meat, drink, or victuals, to be brought, had, or carried to them, forth or through the lands, baillieries, towns, and bounds, where they could

---

* Life of the Scottish Queen, vol. i. p. 193.

hinder; nor should they tryst or have intelligence with them in private or apart, without knowledge or leave of the warden obtained to that effect: or suffer them to resort to markets or trysts through the bounds : nor permit them, their wives, bairns, tenants, or servants, to dwell, remain, or abide, or to pasture their flocks of sheep or cattle upon any lands outwith Liddesdale, except such as within eight days of the date of the bond found responsible sureties to the wardens of the marches and their clerks, that they would reform all enormities committed by them in time bypast, and keep good rule in time coming, and be obedient to the laws when called upon : All others not finding the said security within the said space were to be pursued to the death with fire and sword, and all other kind of hostility, and exposed in prey and all things in their possession to the men of war, as open and known enemies to God, the king, and the common good, without favour, assurance, or friendship : all kindness, bonds, promises, assurances, and conditions that had been entered into with any of them in time bygone, before the date of the bond, were to be renounced, as the subscribers should answer to God, and on their duty and allegiance to the king and regent. In case any of the parties to the bond failed in any part of the premises, or revealed not the contraveners thereof, if known, they were to be punished in terms of the general bond and pains contained therein. As also, in case—in the resistance or pursuit of any of the said thieves—it should happen that any of them be slain and burnt, they should ever esteem the quarrel and deadly feud equal to all, and should never agree with the said thieves, but with one consent and advice. In the meantime, the subscribers bound themselves to take a sincere and true part ilk ane with the other, and specially should assist the laird of Buccleuch and other lairds nearest to the said thieves. There are three columns of signatures to the bond. The first contains the names of "Sir Nicholas Rutherfurd of Hundoley, knyt.; Jhone Rutherfurd of Hunthill; John Mow of yt Ilk; Richard Rutherford, provost of Jedbur[t]; James Scott, baillie of Selkirk; James Gledstanes of Coklaw; Wat Scot, in Bellhauch; Wat Scot of Tuschelaw; Hector Turnbull, tutor of Mynto; Cuthbert Cranstoun of Thirlestan Manis; Robert Scot, baillie of Hawyke." The second column—"Andrew Ker; Gilbert Ker of Prinsydeloch; John Edmonstoune of yat Ilk, Knyt; William Douglas of Cavers; Jhone Haldane; Thomas Turnbull of Bederowll; Richard Rutherford of Edgerstone; Alexander Cokburn; Robert Scot of Edilstane; Thomas Makdowell." The signatures on the two first columns are autographs, but the third column is all written in the same hand—"Alex[r] L. Home; Walter Ker of Cessford; Bukclewch, Knyt; Thomas Ker of Fernhirst; William Ker; Patrick Murray of Faulahill; Walter

Ker of Dolphinstone; Andro × × ×; Andro Ker of Fa × × ×; T. Cranstoune of yt Ilk; Thomas Ker of Nether Howdane.*

This bond certainly discloses a sad state of Roxburghshire in the beginning of the reign of James VI. Without the aid of the powerful barons, the king and his lieutenants could do little to maintain rule on the Borders, as the clans, by means of their signal-fires, could gather the country in an incredibly short space, rendering success on the part of the royal troops impossible. The king had often to resort to stratagem to secure the persons of some of the leading clans before entering on an expedition to the Border land, to enforce the law among his unruly subjects. By means of such bonds, the clans were kept in some degree of control, although the numerous entries in the criminal records show that the obligations in the bonds were seldom faithfully implemented. In 1569, the Regent Murray obtained from the boy Francis Steuart, his nephew, and William Lumisden, the rector of Cleish, his administrator, a grant to him and his heirs, in fee-firm, of the whole estates of the abbey of Kelso, comprehending the town of Kelso, and many lands, mills, fishings, and other property in the four shires of

---

* The original of this document is deposited in the General Register House, but a copy of it is given in Pitcairn's Trials, vol. iii. pp. 394-396.

Roxburgh, Berwick, Dumfries and Peebles, which was confirmed by a charter under the Great Seal, on the 10th December following.* In October, 1585, the Earls of Angus and Marr, the Master of Glammis, and others their associates, banished to England, came to Kelso, and were received at Floors, the laird of Cessford's house. † Here they were joined by Bothwell and Home, the lairds of Cessford and Coldingknowes, and many of the barons of Teviotdale and Merse. The inhabitants of Kelso seem to have assisted Bothwell, for in May, 1593, they, with the exception of William Lauder, came in his Majesty's will for the treasonable reset of the Earl, and found security that they would satisfy his Majesty in "*siluer*," provided the sum did not exceed 2000 merks. The king's will was, that he freely pardoned the "*haill* inhabitants" and their posterity, but ordained the town to make payment to the treasurer of 1700 merks money, and to find caution, acted in the books of Secret Council, that they should not intercommune with Bothwell, or his accomplices, in time coming, under a penalty of two thousand pounds.‡ On Bothwell being attainted in 1592, the abbey of Kelso and the priory of Coldingham were annexed to the Crown. The whole property of the abbey was then conferred on Sir

---

* Privy Seal, Reg. xxxviii. 106.
† Memoires of Scotland, p. 101.
‡ Pitcairn's Criminal Trials, vol. i. pp. 291-2.

Robert Ker of Cessford, a great favourite at court, and who had, in 1590, been created a peer, with the title of Lord Roxburghe. Twenty of the churches and advowsons thereof were surrendered to the king in 1639. These estates are now enjoyed by the Duke of Roxburghe. In the spring of 1645, Kelso was almost wholly consumed by an accidental fire, by which the inhabitants were reduced to such a state of distress as to render it necessary for the neighbourhood to furnish supplies of victuals for their support, which was done with a liberal hand. In the months of April and May, 227 bolls of corn were sent, "*to relieve the honest and poor distressed householders in Kelso.*" Of this supply, Teviotdale sent 184 bolls, the Merse 45 bolls; to the supplies of corn were added 34 horse-loads of bread, 43 hogsheads of ale, six loads of salt-herrings, eight stones butter, money £414 Scots. No apology, it is thought, is needed for giving the names of the chief contributors. The first name on the list is that of Robert Pringle of Stitchel, who gave 11 bolls of oatmeal; Lady Linton, 1 boll 2 firlots; next follow the names but not the donations of Sir William Scott of Mertoun; John Ker of Hadden; Sir William Douglas of Cavers; the laird of Hunthill; the laird of Gateshaw; the laird of Fairnington; Mr James Mather; Sir James Ker of Gateside; Sir Walter Riddell; Earl of Lothian; town of Jedburgh; George Pringle of Craigs, Carchester;

Sir William Ker of Cavers; the laird of Greenhead; Sir Andrew Ker of Primside; the four Bells of Plenderleath; Sir William Elliot of Stobs; town of Dunse; John Hume of Ninewells; the laird of Tofts; John Hume of Crumstains; laird of Wedderburn.* This fire seems to have dwelt long in the memories of the inhabitants, as occasional entries in the court-books show. In November, 1723, the baillie issued the following prohibition :—" These are to advertise all the inhabitants who are concerned in making malt, or carrying on their affairs in malt-kilns, that they no way presume to kindle fires after gloamin, or under night at any time, nor in the day-time, when the wind blows high, under pain of being summarily imprisoned."

In September, 1645, Montrose was at Kelso, on the invitations of the Earls Roxburghe and Home, but when he had arrived within about twelve miles of them, they surrendered their houses and themselves to General Leslie, who, on hearing of the battle of Kilsythe, left the Scottish army before Hereford, and, at the head of 5000 men, marched northward by Berwick and Tranent, with the view of intercepting Montrose at the passages of the Forth; but on arriving at Tranent, he got information that the Royalist troops were in the forest of Selkirk, on

---

* From a paper deposited in the museum of Kelso, extracted by Mr John Steuart, surgeon, from the original in the charter-chest of the Duke of Roxburghe.

which he turned southward, and marched to Melrose by the river Gala. In the meantime, Montrose, although obliged to dismiss his Highlanders, and, deserted by those who had promised him assistance, resolved to pursue Leslie, and prevent him from gathering additional forces. On the 12th, the Royalist general left Kelso, and marched to Selkirk forest, in which he encamped his infantry, between the Ettrick and Yarrow, close to the junction of these rivers, the cavalry and himself taking up their quarters in Selkirk. Next morning the camp was surprised by the Covenanting general, and after a desperate struggle, the Royalist troops were routed with great slaughter.

In 1715, the Scottish rebels met those from Northumberland and Nithsdale at Kelso. The Highlanders were met by the Scots' horse at Ednam Bridge, and conducted into the town, in compliment to the bravery displayed by them in passing the Firth. Next day Mr Paton preached in the abbey church to the soldiers, from Deut. xxi. 17, "*The right of the first-born is his.*" A great number attended. In the afternoon a sermon was preached by a Mr William Irving, full of exhortations to his hearers to be zealous and steady in the course in which they were engaged. On the Monday the troops were drawn up in the market-place, while the proclamation was read, and a manifesto of the Earl of Marr, on which all the people assembled and shouted "*No union; no malt-tax; no salt-tax.*" The Highland army remained in Kelso till the Thursday following, during which time they drew the public revenues, excise customs, and taxes. While at Kelso, word was brought that General Carpenter had arrived at Wooler, intending to give them battle at Kelso next day. A council of war was held, at which the Earl of Winton urged the council to march to the west of Scotland, but the English leaders prevailed, and the army set out for England by way of Roxburgh. In 1718, the commissioners of Oyer and Terminer sat at Kelso, to inquire into the treasons committed in 1715. Lawyers were sent from London to assist on an occasion so new in Scotland as trials for high treason, but all the artifices of the judges and lawyers could not overcome the firmness of the grand-jurors, and the presentments were negatived. On 4th November, 1745, Prince Charles arrived at Kelso, with a division of his army, consisting of 4000 foot and 1000 horse, and on the 6th he left the town and marched for Jedburgh.

Several persons have borne the surname of Kelso. *Richard* of Kelso is mentioned in a charter of Robert I. to Fergus of Ardrossan.* *Thomas* of Kelso was, in 1365, admitted to the peace of Edward III., and license granted to him to dwell in any part of

---

* Reg. Mag. Sig. p. 10, No. 51.

England.* *Allan* of Kelso, and several other merchants, got a safe-conduct in 1367 to go to England and trade.†

FLOWRIS.‡ FLOORS.§ FLEURS.|| The palace of the Duke of Roxburghe occupies a lovely situation on the left bank of the river Tweed. The view, though limited, is beautiful, taking in the ruins of Roxburgh Castle, part of Teviot's fair vale, and all the lovely scenery where Tweed and Teviot meet. Sir Walter Scott, in writing of this locality, says that "the modern mansion of Fleurs, with its terrace, its woods, and its extensive lawn, forms altogether a kingdom for Oberon or Titania to dwell in, or any spirit who, before their time, might love scenery, of which the majesty, and even the beauty, impress the mind with a sense of awe, mingled with pleasure."¶ The palace was built in 1718, upon the site of an older house, greatly enlarged and beautified by the present possessor of the rich domain. The earliest notice of the house under the name of "*Flowris*" that I have met with is in 1545, but it must have existed long before that time, and occupied by the monks of Kelso or some of their *kindly tenants*. A plan of the locality in 1739 shows three islets, com-

---

* Rotuli Scotiæ, vol. i. p. 894. † Ib. p. 919.
‡ Circa, 1545.   § Ib. 1585. || Ib. 1772.
¶ Demonology, p. 119.

prehending a considerable space, formed by the Tweed, in front of the palace. In Stobie's map of the county, executed in 1772, only one of these appear, about half-a-mile in length. Near the lower end of that anna is the site of a cross called the *Fair-cross*, and which gave a name to these islets. This *Fair-cross* is near the spot where, according to tradition, King James was killed while besieging Roxburgh Castle in 1460. The writer of the old statistical account of the parish of Kelso, while treating of this locality, remarks,* " A holly-tree is said to stand on the spot where this happened, a little below Fleurs House. Near this tree stood a large village, which, from a cross that remained within these few years, was generally called the *Fair-cross*. But the probable origin of the name, as it has been handed down, though not generally known, is this:—James II.'s Queen having very soon reached the spot where the lifeless body of her husband lay, is reported to have exclaimed, *"There lies the fair corse;"* whereupon it received the name of the *fair corpse* or *corse*, and in process of time the change from *corse* to *cross* was easily effected." I doubt this derivation of the name of *Fair-cross*, and am inclined to think that the cross owes its origin to the erection of Broxfield into a barony, with right of market cross, in 1642. The name may receive further illus-

---

* Vol. x. p. 582. Article written by the late Dr Douglas.

tration from the fact, that about this time the people of Kelso were anxious to have James' Fair held on the north side of the water, and many attempts were made to hold the fair at this place. The records of Jedburgh contain many acts ordering the burgesses to attend the fair of St. James in force, to support the authority of the magistrates, and to bring the bestial from the north to the south side of the river. Occasionally the flooded state of the river prevented persons and cattle passing to the south side, and the fair or market was held at *Fair-cross*, opposite to St. James' Fair-stead. In 1713, the fair, owing to the flood, was held for two days—Saturday and Monday —on the north side of the river, at this cross.* It may safely be inferred that *Fair-cross* derived its name from being the place where the market or fair was held, in the same way as the haugh on the south side of the river gets the name of *Fair-green* at the present day.

The woods around Fleurs are extensive and valuable. A considerable portion of the wood, however, is not older than the end of the seventeenth century. In 1717, the baillie of the regality passed an act forbidding "the plucking of the haws from the thorns that defended the *young* plantations at Fleurs." On the forfeiture of Bothwell, his estates were divided among Buccleuch, Home, and Sir

---

* Burgh Court-Books.

Robert Ker of Cessford. Buccleuch got Crichton and Liddesdale; Home, Coldingham; and Cessford, the abbey of Kelso, with its lands and possessions. Sir Robert was distinguished for talent and courage, and while warden of the marches, did good service to his country.

The peerage writers say that *John* Ker, of the forest of Selkirk, who lived about 1358, was the founder of the house of Cessford and Roxburgh; that *Henry*, his son, was living about three years after; and *Robert*, supposed to be the son of Henry, got a charter of the lands of Auldtonburn, from Archibald, the fourth Earl of Douglas. Chalmers is of opinion that Andrew Ker of Altonburn, who married a daughter of Sir W. Douglas, the heritable sheriff of Teviotdale, was the founder, and died before 1450. It seems to me that these views are not well founded. Before 1385, *John* Ker was the owner of Altonburn and Nisbet in Teviotdale; at that date these lands were granted by Richard II. of England to John Boraille.* It is probable that the *Andrew* Ker alluded to by Chalmers was the grandson of John Ker of Altonburn and Nisbet, and son of the first owner of Cessford; but he is wrong in supposing that the Andrew Ker who married the sheriff's daughter died before 1450. It was his father who obtained a confirmatory charter from the

---

* Rotuli Scotiæ, vol. ii. p. 75.

Earl of Douglas of the lands of Cessford, which formerly belonged to the families of Oliphant and Cockburn. In 1451, James II. granted Andrew Ker of Altonburn "all and each his lands of the barony of Auldroxburgh, with pertinents," for payment of one silver penny at Whitsunday, in name of blench farme, if demanded.* It was this Andrew who accompanied Douglas to Rome in 1451. In 1474, during the minority of James III., Andrew Ker of Cessford resigned to him the baronies of Auld Roxburgh and Cessford, on which a charter was granted by Lord James Hamilton of the same to Walter Ker, his son and heir, under reservation of the terce for life of Margaret Tweedy, his wife. In 1478, Walter Ker appears as proprietor of Caverton.† On the king attaining his majority, the same lands were again resigned to him by the same Walter Ker, in 1481, to whom he again granted them, with the remainder, in succession, to his brothers Thomas, William, and Ralphe, and the true and lawful heirs whomsoever of the said Andrew Ker. In 1488, James IV. granted to Walter Ker the place and messuage of Roxburgh, with pertinents, castle, and the patronage of the *Maisondieu*, for payment of a red rose at the castle, at the Feast of John the Baptist.‡ In 1500, the grant was confirmed.

---

*Reg. Mag. Sig., Lib. iv. No. 3. † Acta Dom. Con. p. 69.
‡ Reg. Mag. Sig., Lib. xii. No. 16.

In 1509 the *demesne* lands of Auld Roxburgh, with mill, mount, and Castlestead, and the town and lands of Auld Roxburgh, were resigned by Andrew Ker, the son of Walter Ker, into the hands of James IV., who granted them anew to him and his wife, Agnes Crichton, for the usual services. Andrew Ker was one of the border barons who bound themselves to assist the Earl of Angus against the Liddesdale men, and others dwelling within the bounds of Teviotdale and Ettrick forest, in putting them out of the same.* In 1526, while James V. was returning from Jedburgh, accompanied by Angus, with a body of his kindred, they were attacked by Buccleuch with 1000 men, but the result was in favour of Angus. Cessford pursuing too eagerly, was slain by a domestic of Buccleuch, which produced a deadly feud between the families of Ker and Scott, which raged for many years upon the Borders. To reconcile this quarrel, an agreement was entered into at Ancrum, in March, 1529, between the clans of Scot and Ker, whereby each clan was to forgive the other, but it was stipulated that Sir Walter Scott of Branxholm should go to the four head pilgrimages of Scotland, and say a mass for the souls of the deceased Andrew of Cessford, and those who were slain in his company, and cause a chaplain to say a mass daily, wherever Sir Walter Ker and his friends

---

* Pitcairn, vol. i. pp. 126-7-9.

pleased, for the space of five years; Ker of Dolphinston, and Ker of Gradon should also go to the four head pilgrimages, and make a mass to be said for the souls of the Scots and their friends who were slain on the same field, and get a chaplain to say a mass daily for three years, at any place Sir Walter Scott might fix upon; that the son and heir of Branxholm was to marry one of the sisters of Ker of Cessford, and the marriage portion to be paid by Sir Walter Scott at the sight of friends; any difference that might arise in future between the clans was to be settled by six arbiters. But this agreement, which both parties bound and obliged "ilk ane to others be the faith and troth of their bodies, but fraud or guile, under the pain of perjury, manswearing, defalcation, and breaking of the bond of deadly," seems to have been of brief endurance. In 1535, Buccleuch was imprisoned for levying war against the Kers, but in 1542 his estates were restored by Parliament. In 1552, Sir Walter Scott was slain by Ker of Cessford in the streets of Edinburgh. With the view of stanching this feud, a contract was entered into in 1564 between Sir Walter Scott of Branxholm, with the consent of his curators, and Sir Walter Ker of Cessford. In that curious document, Sir Walter Ker takes burden upon him for his children, and for his brother Mark of Newbattle, and his children; Hume of Cowdenknowes, and his children; Andrew Ker of Faldonside, and his children and brother; Ker of Messington, his father's brother and their children; Ker of Linton, and his children and grand-children, and brother's bairns; Richard Ker of Gateshaw, his children and brother; Andrew, William, and John Ker, brothers, of Fernieherst; Ker of Kippeshaw, and his son Robert Ker of Bothtown; Robert Ker, burgess of Edinburgh, and all their children; brother kyn, friends, men, tenants, and servants.* And Sir Walter Scott of Branxholm and Buccleuch, with consent of his curators, took burden upon him for his *haill surname,* and the relict and bairns of the deceased Sir Walter Scott, his grandfather, and also for Cranstoun of that Ilk;† the laird of Chisholme, Gladstones of that Ilk; Langlands of that Ilk; Veitch of Sinton, and Ormstone of that Ilk. On the one

---

* Sir Thomas Ker of Fernieherst; Sir Andrew Ker of Hirsel; Robert Ker of Woodhead; John Haldane of that Ilk; Gilbert Ker of Primisideloch; James Ker of Tarbet; Robert Ker of Gradene and Andrew Ker, and their children, servants, and all others, were *excluded* from this bond, in consequence of their having refused to join in the contract when asked by the laird of Cessford, brother-in-law of Fernieherst.

† Celebrated in the "Lay of the Last Minstrel" as "Margaret of Branksome's Choice," and the substitute of William of Delorain in the duel with dark Musgrave. The minstrel celebrates the marriage at Branksome Castle in presence of the wardens on each side of the Border; but Wood and Crauford give "Teviot's Flower" to Sir John Johnstone of that Ilk.

part, the laird of Buccleuch bound himself and all his clan not to pursue the laird of Cessford, or any other person for whom he was bound criminally or civilly, for any slaughter or blood committed in time past, nor bear hatred, grudge, or displeasure therefore, but bury and put the same under perpetual silence and oblivion, and to live in perfect amity and Christian neighbourhood in time coming. And on the other part, the laird of Cessford became bound that neither he nor any one for whom he took burden should in any way pursue the laird of Buccleuch, or any of his surname, or others for whom he was bound criminally or civilly. And for the better removing of all feud and enmity between the parties through the unhappy slaughter of Sir Walter Scott, it was agreed that Sir Walter Ker should, upon the 23rd day of March instant, go to the parish kirk of Edinburgh, and there, before noon in the sight of the people, reverently and upon his knees ask God's mercy for the slaughter, and forgiveness of the same from the laird of Buccleuch and his friends, promising, in the name and fear of God, that he and his friends would truly keep their part of the contract, which being done, Buccleuch should reverently accept, and receive, and promise, in the fear of God, to remit his grudge, and never remember the same. It was farther agreed that Thomas Ker, the second son of Cessford, was to marry a sister of the laird of Buccleuch, between the date of the contract and the last day of May next, without any tocher to be paid by her brother and her friends, the laird of Cessford being bound to provide them an honest and reasonable living, effeiring to their condition; and also to infeft her in her virginity, in conjunct fee and liferent with her future spouse, and their heirs, in lands or annual-rent of the amount of one hundred merks yearly;* that George Ker, the eldest son of Ker of Faldonside, should marry Janet Scott, the aunt of the laird of Buccleuch, as soon as he became of perfect age, without tocher; and in the event of George dying, the next son was to marry her, and so long as there were sons of Ker to marry; in the event of Janet Scott dying before the marriage, George Ker was to marry the next sister, so on as long as Ker had a son, and Janet a sister, to marry. The bond next provided for the settlement of any dispute that might arise between the parties by arbitration, and failing their agreeing upon a proper person, the Queen and Council were to appoint an oversman. The contract was subscribed by "*Janet Betoune*," relict of the deceased Sir Walter Scott, with her own hand, "in signe of hir consent to the premisses," and in manner following: " Walter Ker of Cessford, Walter

---

* It seems that this arrangement did not take place, as *Janet* the eldest sister married Sir Thomas Ker of Fernieherst five years afterwards; she was the mother of the too celebrated Viscount Rochester.

Scott of Bukleuch, Janet Betoune, Lady of Bukcleuch;* James; Thomas Scott of Hanyng; Mr Johne Spens, curator, above written; Johne Maxwell; J. Bellendine, as curator; Robert Scot of Thirlestane, with my hand at the pen led by *David* Laute, notaric publict."†

At the same time, the king granted a remission under seal to Sir Walter Ker, for his share in the slaughter of the Knight of Branxholm. In 1574, James VI., with consent of Regent Morton, granted the lands and barony of Auld Roxburghe, with their pertinents, to Robert Ker, the son and apparent heir of William Ker, younger of Cessford, with remainder in succession to his heirs; to the heirs male of William Ker; to the heirs of Sir Walter Ker of Cessford; to Mark Ker, the commendator of Newbattle, brother of Sir Walter Ker, and his heirs; to Andrew Ker of Faldonside and his heirs; to Thomas Ker of Mersington and his heirs; to George Ker of Linton and his heirs; to Ker of Gateshaw and his heirs; to the heirs male whomsoever of the said William Ker, younger of Cessford, bearing the name

---

* This lady was a daughter of Beatoun of Creich, and possessed so much ability that the country people attributed her knowledge to magic. She has been rendered immortal by Sir Walter Scott in the "Lay of the Last Minstrel." She rode at the head of the clan after the murder of her husband.

† This gentleman was the ancestor of Lord Napier. Few even among the great men were at that period good clerks.

of Ker and the Cessford arms, reserving the freehold and liferent to Sir Walter Ker, and the terce to Isabel his wife, and after their death, the same to William Ker and his wife Janet Douglas.* On the death of Sir Walter Ker, WILLIAM, his son, succeeded. For many years he was warden of the middle marches. His son ROBERT, afterwards the first Earl of Roxburghe, was one of the most noted spirits on the Border. He acted as depute-warden of the middle marches during the life of his father. While differences existed between the two houses of Cessford and Fernieherst, Sir Robert was guilty of the slaughter of William Ker of Ancrum, one of the clan of the latter family. It is said by Spottiswoode,† that the young chief was instigated to the murder by his mother, for which he obtained a remission the following year. Having met Bothwell near Humbie in Haddingtonshire, the two engaged in single combat for two hours, and parted from pure fatigue, without either having sustained any serious injury. One of the Rutherfurds accompanied Cessford, and was wounded in the cheek by Bothwell's attendant. Of Ker, Sir Robert Carey, who was deputy warden of the east marches, says,

---

* Reg. Mag. Sig. lib. xxxiv. No. 67. Sir Walter was married to Isabel, daughter of Ker of Fernieherst, and William, his son, to Janet Douglas, daughter of Sir William Douglas of Drumlanrig, and widow of Tweedie of Drumelzier.

† Page 383.

that he was opposite warden, and a brave, active officer. By the laws of the Border, it was provided that the wardens of each kingdom should deliver up offenders till satisfaction was made, and the warden failing to do so, was bound to deliver himself up to the opposite warden, and be detained till the judgment of the commissioners of the Border was obeyed. The Lord of Buccleuch and Sir Robert Ker having failed to deliver offenders on the day fixed, were complained of, on which Buccleuch entered himself prisoner to Sir William Selby, master of the ordnance in Berwick, and the Lord Home, by the king's command, delivered up Cessford a prisoner at Berwick, who was at his own request placed under the charge of Sir Robert Carey, who says, in his Memoirs, "I lodged him as well as I could, and tooke order for his diet and men to attend on him, and sent him word that (although by his harsh carriage toward me ever since I had that charge, he could not expect any favour yet) hearing so much goodness of him that he never broke his worde, if he should give me his hand and credit to be a true prisoner, he would have no guard sett upon him, but have free liberty for his friends in Scotland to have ingresse and regresse to him as oft as he pleased. He took this very kindly at my hands, accepted of my offer, and sent me thankes. Some four days passed: all which time his friends came in to him and hee kept his chamber. Then he sent to mee and desired mee I would come and speak with him, which I did, and after long discourse, charging and recharging one another with wrongs and injuries, at last, before our parting, wee became good friends, and great protestation on his side never to give mee occasion of unkindness again. After our reconciliation, he kept his chamber no longer, but dined and supped with me. I took him abroad with mee at least thrice a-week a-hunting, and every day we got better friends. Buccleuch in a few days after had his pledges delivered, and was sett at liberty. But Sir Robert Ker could not get his, so that I was commanded to carry him to York, and there to deliver him to the Archbishop, which I accordingly did. At our parting, he professed great love unto me for the kind usage I had shown him, and that I would find the effects of it upon his delivery, which he hoped would be shortly. After his return home, I found him as good as his word. We met oft at days of truce, and I had as good justice as I could desire, and so we continued very kind and good friends all the time I staid in that march." The Archbishop of York says he "found him wise and valiant, but somewhat haughty and resolute." On the 29th December, 1599, six days after the baptism of the infant Prince Charles, the king created Sir Robert Earl of Roxburghe.* In 1601 he was appointed a commis-

---

* Balfour's Annals, vol. i. p. 409.

sioner of Justiciary "for the torture, trial, and execution of Mr Peter Nairne," charged with having conspired the murder of several Englishmen whom he had induced to enter Scotland on the pretence that he would obtain them employment from the king, and when he got them to Kelso, attempted to murder them.* In 1606 he was made Baron Ker of Cessford and Caverton, and Earl of Roxburghe. He was privy seal in the reign of Charles I. He married, first, Mary, daughter of Sir William Maitland, by whom he had a son, William, who died in infancy, and three daughters. He next married Jane, daughter of Lord Drummond, by whom he had an only son, Harry, Lord Ker, who predeceased himself, leaving four daughters. The earl, seeing that by the death of his son his honours would die with himself, obtained a power to institute a new series of heirs to his titles and estates. On the 17th July, 1643, he resigned his dignities and estates into the hands of the king, for the purpose of obtaining a new grant thereof, to himself and the heirs male of his body, and whom failing, to his heirs and assignees, to be nominated and constituted by him during his lifetime by any writing under his hand. Next year he executed a deed of nomination, by which he called to the succession several near relations, on the condition that they should marry one of his grand-daughters, the children of Harry, Lord

---

* Pitcairn, vol. ii. p. 351-2.

Ker; but this nomination being considered ineffectual, he obtained a new charter from the crown, under which he was infeft, and in 1648 executed a new destination of his dignities and estates. Failing heirs male of his own body, he nominated Sir William Drummond, fourth son of his daughter Jean, Countess of Perth, and the second son of his grand-daughter Jean, Countess of Wigton, in their order, all of whom, and the heirs male lawfully begotten of their bodies, with their spouses, he constituted heirs of tailzie and successors to his titles and estates, under certain restrictions. One of these was the appointment of his heir to marry one of the grand-daughters, offering himself first to the eldest, and so on, and to bear the arms and name of Ker. In the event of the above appointment failing by death, or the not observing the said restrictions and conditions, the right of the said estate was to pertain and belong to the eldest daughter of the said deceased Harry, Lord Ker, without division, and the heirs male—she always marrying or being married to a gentleman of honour, who would obey the conditions of the deed: which all failing, to their heirs male, and the nearest heir male of the Earl of Roxburghe. This entail was ratified by Parliament.

At the death of Earl Robert in 1650, Sir William Drummond succeeded under the entail, and married Lady Jean, the eldest daughter of Harry, Lord Ker. The earl was distinguished for military genius in

Holland; but joining the Royalists, was fined £6000 by Cromwell. His son Robert was the third earl; and was lost in the *Gloucester* frigate, in the Yarmouth Roads, in 1682. His son Robert dying unmarried, his younger brother, John, succeeded to the earldom, and for his services in bringing about the union between Scotland and England, was created Duke of Roxburghe in 1707. He was privy seal in Scotland in 1714, and secretary of state in 1716, but lost office in 1725, in consequence of opposing Sir Robert Walpole. He died at Fleurs in 1741. Robert, his son and successor, died in 1755, and was succeeded by John, his son and heir, who was a great book-collector. He rose high in the favour of George III. He died, unmarried, in March, 1804. It is said that his not marrying was caused by an attachment that "had been formed between his Grace, when on his travels, and Christina Sophia Albertina, eldest daughter of the Duke of Mecklenburgh Strelitz, and that their nuptials would have taken place, had not her sister, the Princess Charlotte, just at that time been espoused to King George III. Etiquette then interfered, it being deemed not proper that the elder should be a subject of the younger sister; but both parties evinced the strength of their attachment by devoting their after-lives to celibacy."* He was succeeded by

---

* Sharpe's Peerage, vol. iii., and papers of the day.

Lord Bellendean, descended from William, second son of William Ker of Cessford, and brother of Robert, first Earl of Roxburghe. On the 18th of June, 1804, Duke William executed a trust disposition in favour of Henry Gawler and John Seton Kerr, of the estate of Roxburghe, for the purpose of paying certain legacies. He also executed a deed of entail in favour of himself and the heirs of his body: whom failing, to John Gawler and certain other heirs. In the same year he conveyed the lands of Byrecleuch and others to the same trustees, and granted sixteen feu dispositions, whereby the whole estate, with the exception of the mansion-house of Floors, and a few acres of ground around it, was disponed to John Gawler and his heirs and disponees, for payment of certain feu duties. He died in October, 1805, without issue, and in him failed all the descendants of Sir William Drummond.

Brigadier-General Walter Ker, of Littledean, claimed to succeed as heir male general of Lady Jean Ker, the eldest daughter of Harry, Lord Ker, the son of the first Earl Robert, and also to Henry Lord Ker.

Sir James Norcliffe Innes claimed, under the same clause of the deed, as heir male of the body of Lady Margaret, the third daughter of Harry, Lord Ker, who married his great-grandfather, Sir James Innes, in 1666, to the exclusion of General Ker, the trustees, and Mr. Gawler. After a long litigation, it was ultimately decided in May 11, 1812, that, as Lady Margaret was the eldest daughter at the time the succession opened, Sir James was entitled to be preferred to the honours and estates.

The house of INNES owes its foundation to a Fleming who settled in Scotland during the 12th century. During the reigns of William Rufus and Henry I., the Flemings migrated in great numbers to England, and were settled in the waste lands of Northumberland and Cumberland, where their language may still be traced in the names of places. In the civil wars of Stephen, the Flemings aided as stipendiaries in his armies; but on Henry II. ascending the throne, he banished them out of England. The Flemings then repaired to Scotland, where they easily obtained settlements; and in the course of a few years they were to be found in every town and hamlet in the kingdom, carrying on trade in the country, cultivating the wastes, and raising villages on their farms; on the sea coast they settled as fishers. In the 13th century, the trade of the country was nearly all in their hands. Berwick was then governed by Adam Flandrensis, and a body of that people defended the Redhall of that place against the English in 1296, till every man perished in the flames. Under David I., a Fleming was Provost of St. Andrews, and in Perth they appear as goldsmiths and saddlers. Jordan, a Fleming, got a grant from David I. of lands on the Tweed; and in 1144 witnessed a charter by the king to the monks of Kelso. It was this Jordan who granted lands in the territory of Orde to the same monks. This eminent man was taken prisoner with William the Lion at the siege of Alnwick. Amongst the earliest immigrants were many Flemings, who had distinguished themselves in the armies of England, and who were received by the King of Scotland into his army, getting payment for their services in land. In every district, from the Tweed and Solway to the Clyde and Moray Frith, the Flemings obtained settlements; and so powerful did they become, that they obtained right to be governed by their own laws.* When the Flemings settled among the Celts of the district of Moray, and introduced new customs and laws, the men of Moray raised the standard of revolt in support of their ancient principles and laws. But Malcolm IV., with the aid of his Flemish stipendiaries, put down the revolt, after a violent struggle. At the suppression of this revolt, a Flandrekin obtained from the king, as a reward for his services, a grant of the lands of INNES, which he afterwards adopted as his surname, and transmitted to the successful claimant of the dignities and estates of Roxburghe, and many other respectable families descended from the same stock. A number of remarkable men sprung from

---

* David II. granted a charter to John Marr, canon of Aberdeen, for the lands of Cruterstoun, in the Gariach. "Una cum lege Fleminga dicitur *Fleming-Lauche.*"

Berowald, and filled high offices in both church and state. In the end of the 14th century, George Innes was a Cardinal and Primate of England. In 1406, John was Bishop of Moray, and John, sprung from the marriage of Sir Walter Innes with Lady Fraser of Lovat, was Bishop of Caithness. Duncan Forbes, the compiler of the pedigree in Douglas' Peerage, says that "there are three things wherein the family are either notable or happy: first, that their inheritance never went to a woman; second, that none of them ever married an ill wife; and, thirdly, that no friend ever suffered for their debt." Sir James Innes, who succeeded as fifth Duke of Roxburghe, assumed the name of Ker, and married, in 1807, Harriet, daughter of Benjamin Charleswood, of Windlesham, and died in July, 1823, aged eighty-seven, leaving issue, the present duke, who was born in July, 1816, being the thirtieth in descent from Berowaldus.

EDNAHAM; EDENHAM; EDNAM.—This part of the district is entitled to be mentioned next, on account of its being one of the earliest settlements to be found on record. It derives its name from the British *Eden*, the *gliding stream*, and the Saxon *ham*, a dwelling—*Edenham*, the dwelling on the Eden. In one of the first of the genuine charters, there exists a grant from King Edgar to *Thorlongus*,* *i.e., Thor*

---

* Thorlongus was a Saxon or Danish colonist from the north of England. There was a *Thor* in Jed forest, and it is the *Long*—to distinguish him from other Thors—of Ednaham, described in the grant as a desert which, with the help of the king, he peopled, and built a church in honour of Cuthbert, the Tweedside saint. In the grant by Thorlongus, transferring this church to the monks of Durham, Ednam is called a *waste*. This curious document is still preserved in the treasury of Durham, and is as follows: "To the sons of Holy Mother Church, *Thor* the *Long* greeting in the Lord: Know that Edgar, my lord King of the Scots, gave me Ednaham, a waste; that with his help and my own means I peopled it, and have built a church in honour of St. Cuthbert and his monks, to be possessed by them evermore. This gift I have made for the soul of my lord King Edgar, and for the souls of his father and mother, and for the weal of his brothers and sisters, and for the redemption of my dearest brother Lefwin, and for the weal of myself, both my body and my soul. And if any one by force or fraud presume to take away this my gift from the Saint aforesaid, and the monks his servants, may God Almighty take away

---

probable that he obtained a grant of the lands from Earl Henry. Swan, his son, obtained the manor of *Ruthven* and other lands in Perthshire. It was his grandson Walter who took the surname of *Ruthven*, and who married a daughter of the Earl of Strathern in the reign of Alexander II. Their descendants became Earls of Gowrie in 1581. In 1297, Sir William Ruthven was governor of Jedburgh.

from him the life of the heavenly kingdom, and may he suffer everlasting pains with the devil and his angels. Amen.* Although the locality is at the present time a fruitful field, it does not require a stretch of imagination to realize the picture drawn of it by Thor the Long. It would not only be a desert in his time, but a *watery waste.* extending from the Eden westward, to Broxlaw near the Tweed, as the names of places as well as the nature of the ground evince. A number of high gravel ridges are to be seen here, and are called *comb-knowes*, and the flat land between them *comb-flat.* These ridges have all been formed by water, and there can be little doubt that the flat lands between these combs were covered with water, and it is probable that the name of "*combs*" was imposed by the Saxon followers of Thorlongus. David I. granted to the monks of Coldingham a toft with houses in Edenham.† The king had a large mill here, from which he granted to the monks of Kelso, in 1128, twelve chalders of malt, with right to dig turf for fuel in the moor of Edenham. King William gave the monks the mill itself, and three carrucates of land in the town, as Erkenbald the abbot of Dunfermline had laid them out in terms of the king's writ, in exchange for the grant of 20 chalders of meal and

---

* Smith's Bede, 763-4. North Durham Appendix, p. 38, N. cxi.

† Chart of Coldingham, 3.

wheat which they had from the mills of Roxburgh, and 40s. from the customs of the same, with power to prevent the erection of any other mill in the parish, and a right to the same services from the inhabitants, which the latter were bound to yield to the proprietors of the mill. Two-and-a-half of these carrucates are described as lying on the north side of the peatry of Ednam, reaching thence along the boundary of the parishes to the southern bounds of Newton, and thence to the river Eden, and along the Eden to the bridge on the west side of Ednam, thence to the road leading to the hospital at the forking of the road which comes from the north side of the peatry, and along the road to the place first mentioned, with pasturage of a piece of ground lying between the peatry and the bounds of Kelso; the other half-carrucate lay on the east side of the quarry belonging to the abbey, and on the side of the road leading to Sprouston Ford.* The same king granted the monks of Dryburgh two-and-a-half merks yearly out of a carrucate of land in Ednam.† During the 12th century, the church of Edenham had two dependent chapels, one at Newton, and the other at Nathansthorn. Before 1158, Robert, Bishop of St. Andrews, confirmed the connection between the mother church and the chapel at Newton.‡ Before 1162, Bishop Arnold confirmed

---

* Lib. de Calchou. † Lib. of Dryburgh.
Chart, Coldingham, p. 41.

both chapels to the church of Ednam. In 1221, there was a charter granted in a full chapter of the Merse at Ednam : "*in pleno capitulo de Mersce apud Edenham.*" There was also an *hospital* at Edenham, dedicated to St. Leonard. In 1349, Edward III. issued a writ for restoring the hospital of St. Mary at Berwick and of Edenham to Robert de Buston, who is said to have been a busy agent of the English king on the Border.* The lands of Edenham seem to have been the property of the crown at the end of the war of independence. At that time Robert I. granted, *inter alia*, the barony of Edenham, which appears to have been co-extensive with the parish, in marriage, with his daughter Marjery. Robert the Stewart confirmed these lands, with the churches and hospital, to Robert Erskine and Christian his spouse, but on becoming king, he granted to Sir Robert Erskine and his wife £100 sterling out of his firms in Aberdeen, in exchange for the lands of Ednam and Nisbet. In 1333, letters of protection were granted by Edward III. to William of Edenham and others. In 1335, the same king gave the property in Berwick which formerly belonged to Robert of Edenham, to Henry of Bamborough. In 1358, a safe-conduct was granted to Fergus of Edenham, a merchant, to travel in England.† The old family of Edmonstone possessed

---

* Rotuli Scotiæ, vol. i.   † Ib. pp. 255, 384, 822.

this property for a long period. The first settlement of the family was in Mid-Lothian, during the reign of David I. *Edmund* is a witness to several charters by that king. The estate of Edmunston in Mid-Lothian went off at an early period with an heiress, but the heirs male retained the barony of Edenham. In 1593, Andrew Edmonstone of that Ilk obtained from James VI. all and hail the lands of Barningtoun, Barleis, and Berryloch, with their pertinents, which formerly pertained in feu farm to Francis, Earl Bothwell, and his sons, John and Francis Stewart, held immediately from the abbey of Kelso, and then in his Majesty's hands, by reason of Bothwell's forfeiture.* The barony was in the progress of time gradually diminished by partial sales; amongst others, Henderside and Newton-don were slices from it. Still, a good estate remained behind, but so burdened, that James Edmonstone, the last laird, was obliged to dispose of it to James Ramsay Cuthbert, about 65 years ago. It is now the property of Lord Ward. With the reversion, Edmonstone purchased the property of Corehouse, on the Clyde, which he left to his sisters, the last of whom was involved in many law-suits. George Cranstoun was her counsel, to whom she ultimately, left her property, and when made a judge, he took the title of Lord Corehouse. She died at the age of

---

* Acta Parl. vol. iv. p. 37.

105, and on her death-bed, she charged Cranstoun to see that she was laid in the graveyard of Ednam by her own relations, of whom she gave him a list. The ashes of the last of the race were laid in the cemetery of Ednam, in accordance with her desire. One of the lairds of Ednam married a princess of Scotland, in memory of which they added the tressure to their arms. When James Dickson became proprietor of part of Edenham, he enclosed the lands, built a neat village, and attempted to establish woollen manufactures for cloth, particularly English blankets.* He built an extensive brewery, which is still successfully carried on. In the garden of the brewery is a wych elm, which measures in girth 23 feet; at the height of 10 feet, where the first large branch springs, 10 feet; and at the height of 25 feet, where the second large branch leaves the trunk, 9 feet. It is about 60 feet high, and the branches cover a space of 23 yards in circumference. The trunk is sculptured with deep ridges like a cork-tree.†

Edenham is said to be the birthplace of the father of the famous Captain Cook. The tradition of the family is, that the father of the captain was born here, from which he went to Ayton, in Berwickshire,

---

* Old Statistical Account, vol. ii. p. 305.
† Johnstone's Natural History of the Eastern Borders, vol. i. p. 177.

and from that place to Martin Cleveland, in England, where the great captain was born. In confirmation of this tradition, the parish record bears: "Dec. 24, 1692, John Cooke, in this parish, and Jean Duncane, in the parish of Smailhume, gave up their names for proclamation in order to marriage. A certificate produced of her good behaviour. John Cooke and Jean Duncane were married, Jan. 19, 1693."—"1694, John Cook had a son baptized, called James, March the 4th day." The same register also bears that John Cuke, the grandfather of the captain, was an elder of the parish in 1692, during the incumbency of Thomas Thomson, father of the poet of the Seasons.

It has generally been believed that James Thomson[1] the poet, was born in the manse of Edenham, on the 11th of September, 1700, about a month before his father's translation to Southdean; and although satisfied myself, that the poet was born at Edenham, I think it right to notice, that there has always existed a tradition on the Cayle water, that the poet was born at a place called Wideopen, which stood on the hill to the south of Lintonloch, the property of his mother, Beatrix Trotter. It is said that Mrs Thomson gave birth rather unexpectedly to the poet, while on a visit to her mountain home; but if there be any truth in the tradition that Wideopen was the place of the poet's birth, it is probable that his mother had gone to that place for the purpose of having the child on her own land, as was customary in the time in which she lived, the more especially as the family was about to leave Edenham. The writer of the "Old Statistical Account" of the parish, published in the end of the last century, states, that "a proposal was made, some years before that time, to erect a monument to the poet, but it had not been accomplished." Several noblemen and gentlemen, with a laudable zeal for the literary fame of their country, were in the habit of meeting annually at Edenham, to celebrate the poet's birthday, as well as with the view of forwarding the execution of that design. The design was not carried out till 1820, when an obelisk, fifty-two feet high, was raised to his memory, on a rising ground on the estate of Henderside. The expense of the erection was defrayed by the members of the club, who held their last meeting in September, 1819.

William Dawson, the distinguished agriculturist, was born at Harpertoun on this manor, and is said to have introduced, in 1753, a regular system of turnip husbandry in this part of Scotland, although Dr. John Rutherford, Melrose, had begun the sowing of turnips in the field in 1747. In Haddingtonshire, turnips had been sown in the fields in 1736. Like every other place lying near the border, Edenham had its full share of the miseries of war. In July, 1544, the captain of Norham Castle, the Wark garrison, and Henry Eure, burnt the village, made many prisoners, took a bastille house, strongly built, and got a booty of forty nolt and thirty horses, besides those on which the prisoners were mounted, each on a horse. In 1558, Edenham, with other villages, was destroyed by the Earl of Northumberland.

HENDERSIDE.—This estate lies between Ednam, on the north, and the Tweed, on the south, a little to the east of Kelso. The greater portion of it was comprehended in the barony of Edenham. The mansion-house called Henderside Park, stands on a considerable eminence, and commands a beautiful view of the valley of the Tweed, the rich country on the opposite bank of the river, with the ruined towers of the abbey rising above Kelso. The house was erected in 1803, in front of a wood planted in 1775, by William Ormiston, then proprietor of the estate, with the view of building a mansion at the place. It has been greatly enlarged and improved by the present proprietor, John Waldie, in 1829 and 1840. The policy is laid out with taste and skill, and the approaches are judiciously formed. The house contains a library of 18,000 volumes, classified and arranged according to the subjects. In this library is incorporated a smaller library, formerly in the house of Mr. Waldie's grandmother, Jane Waldie or Ormston, which was used constantly by Sir Walte·

Scott, when quite a youth, at Kelso school, and where he spent much time with Mrs. Waldie, who was an intimate friend of his parents. Besides the library, which is peculiarly rich in valuable works relative to the fine arts, is a large and very valuable collection of paintings, chiefly of the old masters, and a fine collection of antique marble columns supporting busts, for the most part modern copies. The busts of the Four Seasons, lately brought from Rome, are the *chefs-d'œuvres* of Benzoni, the Italian sculptor. They are said to have been much admired during the winter of 1856-7, at Rome, by the Empress and Grand Duchess Olga, the Dowager Queen of Spain, the King of Bavaria, and Pope Pius IX., who often visited the studio of Benzoni.

The estate was acquired by one of the Ormstones of Kelso about 1600, and was greatly added to by that family till it went with Jane Ormstone, in marriage to John Waldie of Berryhill, which was at one time the property of the Earl of Bothwell. By the death of her father, and other members of her family, Jane Ormstone became vested in all the property which belonged to them, and which she conveyed to her eldest and only surviving son, George Waldie, father of the present proprietor of the Ormstone and Waldie estates, both in Roxburghshire and Northumberland. The first of the name of "*Waldo*" is said to have been a follower of William of Normandy, and who settled in Sussex.

One of the descendants of this Waldo was secretary to an abbot of Kelso, and his offspring acquired lands in and around Kelso. John Waldie of Kelso married Elizabeth, niece of Sir Alexander Don of Newton. The heir-apparent of the present John Waldie is the only son of Sir Richard Griffith.

NEWTON; LITTLE NEWTON; NEWTON DON, and NENTHORN; NAYTHANSTHORN.—The two manors of Newton and Nenthorn were, during the 12th century, the property of the Morvilles, the hereditary constables of Scotland, who were also proprietors of Bemersyde, Dryburgh, and Merton, on the same bank of the Tweed. At the death of William Morville in 1196, without lawful issue, his estates and offices passed to his only sister, Elena, and her husband, the lord of Galloway. They were succeeded by their only child, Allan, who was one of the most opulent barons in Britain. He died in 1234, leaving, by his wife Margaret, a daughter of David, Earl of Huntingdon, three daughters, Elena, Christian, and Dervorgil. Elena married Roger de Quincey, Earl of Winchester, and her daughter Margaret became Countess of Derby; Christian, William de Fortibus, son of the Earl of Albemarle; and the youngest, John Baliol, the lord of Bernard Castle, father of the Baliol who competed for the crown of Scotland. On the accession of the Bruce, he conferred the property on his favourite warrior,

Sir James Douglas. The territory was held by vassals under the Morvilles, their descendants, and the Douglas. It was served by two chapels named after the manors, both dependant on the mother-church at Edenham. Hugh, the first Morville, gave the monks of Dryburgh the tenth of the multure of his mills of Naythansthyrn and Newton, with half-a-carrucate of land in Newton, with pasture for nine oxen and one work-horse.* About 1162, Roger Bertram gave the tenth of the mills of Naythansthorn to the monks of Dryburgh, for the salvation of the soul of Hugh Morville, for his own soul, and the soul of his wife Ada.† Between 1212 and 1281, these grants were confirmed by William, Bishop of St. Andrews.‡ About 1388, Richard de Hanganside, a vassal of the Douglas, gave to the monks of Kelso all his land in the territory of Little Newton, *in the constabulary of Lauder*. These subjects are called *Comflat*, with portions of land and meadows, and described as " bounded by the parish of Kelso on the south, and on the north by the morass of *Kanmuir*, through which the causeway and highway runs." In the end of the 12th century, Arnold, the diocesan of St. Andrews, confirmed to the monks of Coldingham, the church of Edenham, and both chapels of Newton and Naythansthorn. In 1204, these monks compounded

---

* Lib. of Dryburgh, p. 145.   † Ib. p. 106.   ‡ Ib. p. 107.

with William, the Bishop of St. Andrews, for their rights, and conceded to him both chapels. Before the year 1316, the parishes of Naythansthirn and Newton were erected into a parish, when the former was made a parochial church, and Newton a dependent chapel.* On the 17th of March, 1316, William de Lamburton, the Bishop of St. Andrews, gave to William de Alyncrombe, the abbot of Kelso, the parish church of Naythanthirn, and the chapel of Little Newton, in exchange for the church of Cranstoun, and the land of Preston, in Midlothian, which lay contiguous to the bishop's property, as the former did to the lands of Kelso. The bishop, at the same time, agreed to pay for ten years, from and after the Feast of Pentecost, 1317, the sum of 25 merks a-year, under deduction of the salary of the chaplain of said church, unless the revenues of Nenthorn and Neuton should in any year amount to 25 merks. The proceeds of the fruits and tithes beyond the chaplain's salary were to be placed to the account of the bishop and his successors, as payment of part of that sum which the bishop bound himself to pay. The reason of making this yearly payment, was in consideration of the two chapels being reduced in value by the war.† In June, 1317, a precept was

---

* The conjoined parish is only about two and a-half miles long, by one and a-half broad.

† "Et quod dicta ecclesia nostra de Naythanthirn et ca-

issued by the diocesan to his stewart in Lothian, to give the monks of Kelso seisin of the church of Naythanthirn, and two days after, the stewart issued his precept to Henry Stulp, the baillie of Wedale, ordering him to give the seisin as commanded.* In the end of the 16th century, the master of Roxburgh possessed parts of the lands of Little Newton, and was succeeded by Lady Mary Ker, and Lady Carnegie, his sister, in 1634.† In 1669, Mark Pringle was proprietor of the lands of Nenthorn as heir of his father, Andrew Pringle.‡ Nenthorn became the property of General Ker of Littledean, the claimant of the Roxburgh honours and estates, and sold by him to meet the costs of the litigation. The lands are now owned by a family of the name of Roy. Newton passed from the Edmonstones to the family of Don, and is now possessed by a son of the late Balfour of Wittingham. The mansion of NEWTON-DON was built by Sir Alexander Don. It stands on the site of the old chapel, and commands an extensive view in every direction. The park is well wooded, and contains a number of fine trees. On the north of the garden is a beautiful weeping birch, fourteen feet in girth; at four feet from the ground it divides itself into two

---

pella de Newton sunt exiles et per communem guerram destructe et devastate."

* Stow, on the Gala, was the baillie's residence, and one of the palaces of the bishops of St. Andrews.

† Retours, No. 199. ‡ Ib. No. 355.

branches, one of which is eight feet seven inches in girth, the other seven feet; and the height is about seventy-four feet. Near to it is another tree of the same kind, and of about the same size. In the same locality stands a fern-leaved beech-tree of great beauty. Nearer the bank of the Eden is a woolly-leafed poplar, having a trunk of about eight feet in circumference, of considerable height, and its limbs entwined with ivy. The ivy is three feet thick, and for eight feet from the ground is distinct from the tree; at that height a part of it enters the trunk of the poplar, from which it seems to have derived nourishment, and the effect of the poplar's nursing has been to convert the trunk of the ivy into poplar wood. About two feet higher up, the ivy assumes its natural appearance. Several yew-trees are fully four feet in girth. and shade an area of nearly forty feet diameter. A chestnut-tree, near the east end of the house, is fourteen and a-half feet in circumference, and rises to the height of nearly eighty feet. At a short distance from the chestnut are several magnificent wych elms, fifteen feet in girth, and fully eighty feet high. The policy is studded with remarkable hawthorn-trees. About 150 yards east from the house, a thorn-tree measures nine feet at its base; at twelve feet from the ground its trunk is five feet and a-half, and the branches cover an area of forty-three feet diameter. Within a few hundred yards of this place may be seen six other thorns, of nearly equal dimensions with the one described. The Eden forms the northern boundary of the park, and at a place nearly opposite to the mansion, the river throws itself over a trap dyke about thirty-five feet of perpendicular height. The spot is called Stitchel Linn. Forty years ago the Linn was the scene of a very melancholy incident. Two sisters of the late Sir Alexander Don, and a lady guest, were drowned in the pool. They left the mansion to walk in the woods, and had strayed to this romantic scene. Not returning to dinner, a search was made, and their bodies were found in the Linn. No one could tell how the accident happened; but it was conjectured that one of the ladies had slipped from the rock, and the other two were drowned in endeavouring to save their companion.

STITCHELL; STICHEL; STYCHILL; STICCANEL.—The name is thought to be derived from the Anglo-Saxon, and means a steep hill; but it may be that the name is rather intended to describe the situation of the town at two peculiar hills, stuck, as it were, on the top of the ridge on which the town stands. The village cannot be said to be placed on the top of a steep hill. On the west and east, the approach is nearly level, and on the south only there is a considerable rise from the Eden, but not to such an extent as to impose a name upon the village. The situation commands an extensive view of the country to the south and west, comprehending the valley of the Tweed and Teviot, and the whole range of the Cheviot mountains from the west to their eastern extremity, as well as the Eildon hills, Ruberslaw, the Dunion, Penielheugh, and Downlaw. The hills on the north of the town limit the vision in that direction. The view from the top of the hill at the base of which the mansion-house is situated, is well worth the trouble of ascending from the valley of the Eden. Perhaps this prospect is surpassed by the view from Blacklawedge on the road above Easterstead. It is a lovely scene, rich and beautiful; the whole of the Merse spread out as a map before the eye, with the palaces and mansions of the nobility and gentry, environed with wood.

The *barony of Sitchel*, or the whole parish of that name, was of old part of the territory of Gordon, granted by David I. to an Anglo-Norman settler, who assumed from it the name of *Gordon*. During the reign of Malcolm IV., the lands were possessed by the sons of the first Gordon, Richard and Adam; Richard enjoyed the greater part of the lands of Gordon, and Adam, the remainder, with Fanys. The lands were all united by the marriage of Alicia de Gordon with her cousin, Sir Adam Gordon. This Sir Adam de Gordon supported Wallace, and fell doing battle for the independence of his country, about the end of the 13th century. His widow, Marjory, swore fealty to Edward on the 3rd of

September, 1296, and received restitution of her estates. But their son Adam followed in the footsteps of his father, and mainly contributed to the first success of Bruce. He was warden of the marches in 1300, and, as such, warned the Douglas of the approach of the Earl of Arundel, with a numerous army, against his stronghold in the forest. In 1305, he was fined three years' rent of his estates by Edward I. In the same year, he was one of the commissioners for settling the government of Scotland. In the same year, he was appointed one of the Justiciars of Lothian. In consequence of Robert I. granting to Sir Adam the estates of the faithless Earl of Athol, in the shires of Aberdeen and Banff, he and his vassals went north. He fell at the battle of Halydonhill, in 1333, leaving to his eldest son Alexander, the estates of Gordon, and the lordship of Strathbogie in Aberdeenshire; to his other son, William, Stitchel, and Glenkins in Galloway.

The descendants of Alexander rose to be Dukes of Gordon. About the end of the 13th century, *Nicolas de Sticcanel* is seen granting to the hospital of Soltre two *sceppas* of oatmeal, to be yearly received from his granary at Lyda.* This grant was confirmed by Eustacius of *Sticcenil*. In April, 1358, Robert, the Stewart of Scotland, and Earl of Strath-

---

* The *skep* measure is said to have been borrowed from the English practice. It contained twelve bushels.

earn, granted to William Gordon of Stitchel, the heritable office of keeper of the new forest of Glenkins in Galloway, as fully as the Earl himself had got it from his uncle, David II. The family of Gordon possessed the estates of Stitchel till the 17th century. In 1604, Lord Robert Gordon of Lochinvar was served heir to his father in the lands of Stitchel.* In 1598, Robert Hopper seems to have been owner of part of Nether Stitchel. In that year, Robert Hopper was served heir male of his father, Robert Hopper, in two husbandlands, with pasture, in the town and territory of the lordship of Stitchel.† In the course of the 17th century, the lands of Stitchel passed to Robert Pringle, whose grandson was created a baronet of Nova Scotia in 1683. His eldest son, Sir John, succeeded, and married Margaret, a daughter of Sir Gilbert Elliot of Stobs and Wells, by whom he had four sons, one of whom was John, a celebrated physician. His grandson, Sir John, was the last Pringle of Stitchel. A family of Baird now possess the lands.

The church of Stitchel appears at a very early period as held by the priory of Coldingham to their proper use. Thomas, the son of *Ranulph*, settled a chantry in the chapel of Stitchel. Several disputes occurred between the monks of Coldingham and Thomas, in regard to this chapel and its lands, which

---

* Retours, No. 24.   † Ib. No. 24.

required the presence of the delegates of the Pope to adjust. An exchange was afterwards effected between Sir Thomas and the same monks, of lands in the manor of Stitchel.* There seems to have been other disputes in this parish; as the register in 1457 contains notices of several appeals, one of which is at the instance of the vicar of Stitchel. In the reign of Alexander II., the church was rated at thirty-four marks. Although the church belonged to the monks of Coldingham, the Bishop of St. Andrews, and his subordinate, the Dean of the Merse, exercised jurisdiction over it, and the other churches situated in that district.

There is now a church belonging to the United Presbyterian body, having a congregation of about three hundred individuals.

The salary of the parochial teacher is £25, and the school-fees amount to about as much more.

The Melrose *Chronicle* records the death of Philip of Stitchel in 1221.† Robert of Stitchel succeeded Walter de Kirkham as Bishop of Durham, on the 9th of August, 1260.‡

George Redpath, who died minister of Stitchel in 1772, collected materials for a history of Berwickshire, and left in MS. a history of the Borders, which was published in 1776 by his brother Philip, minister of Hutton.

---

* Chart of Coldingham, No. 72.
† Chron. Mail. p. 138. ‡ Ib. p. 185.

HOLM; HOWM; HOME; HUME.—The name of this place is said by Mr Chalmers to be derived from the Saxon *Holm,* signifying a hill, and not from the same word, meaning a river island; but had this learned and laborious writer seen the locality, it is probable that he would have held the name as descriptive of a rocky height surrounded by marsh and moist meadows. It was described by Paton, who accompanied the Protector Somerset in 1547, as standing "upon a rocky crag, with a proud heith over all the country about it, on every syde well nie *fenced by marrysh,* allmost round in forme with thick walles, and, in which is a rare thing upon so hie and stonie a ground, a fair well within yt." The name would more correctly describe the situation in the 12th and 13th centuries, as surrounded with marshes, meadows, and lochs. The view from the castle is extensive and varied, taking in, on the north, the Lammermuir range of hills, and on the south, the Cheviot mountains, with all the fine country lying between these mountain ranges. The MANOR of HOME formed a part of the territory of the powerful family of Dunbar before the end of the 11th century. Before 1166, the fourth Gospatrick, Earl of Dunbar, granted to his younger son, Patrick, the lands of Greenlaw, where he fixed his abode. Patrick *of Greenlaw* was succeeded by his son William, who married his cousin Ada, who was a daughter of the first Patrick, Earl of Dunbar, by *Ada,* a natural daughter of William the Lion. Ada had been previously married to a Courteney, and obtained from her father, Earl Patrick, as a marriage gift—*in liberum maretagium*—the manor of Home. After the marriage with Ada, William assumed Home as a surname, and from this pair sprung the border clan of the Homes. The church of Home was dedicated to St. Nicholas, and was the property of Earl Gospatrick, who granted to it a carrucate of land, with parochial rights over that village and the half of Gordon. He afterwards confirmed the same church, with two carrucates of land, and a meadow called Hawstrother, to the monks of Kelso. Before 1159 this monastery obtained a confirmation of the grant from Robert, the Bishop of St. Andrews. Ada, the wife of William of Home, gave a portion of her land and buildings in Home, called *Pulles*,* on the margin of the Eden, " where that rivulet formed the march between Home and Nenthorn." Afterwards disputes arose between William de Home and the monastery, as to their rights in the territory of Home; but in 1268 he granted an acknowledgment to the monks that he had unjustly treated them, and, according to a custom common at that time, swore upon the holy Evangelists to do so no more, but protect their rights in future, pay 100s. as damages and expenses, and gave security for the payment thereof. The monks do not seem to have put great faith in the promises

---

* Stables and other farm buildings.

of Home, as, in addition to his own seal attached to the deed, the official seal of the Archdeacon of Lothian and the Dean of the Merse were also appended.* He died shortly after the execution of this deed, and his son William bound himself to confirm it as soon as he had assumed military arms and changed his seal. The lands, toft, and messuages in Home, which formerly belonged to Adam Long, were gifted to the monks of Kelso by Lord Walter de Laynale. On the monks obtaining the patronage of the church of Gordon, the territory of Gordon and part of Weststruther was erected into a separate parish by Richard, the Bishop of St. Andrews, who, on that occasion, gave liberty to the men of Adam Gordon to take the sacrament and bury their dead, either at the new cemetery or at the graveyard of the mother church of Home, so long as it pleased the monks of Kelso. The parish of Home is now joined to Stitchel, and is nearly of the same extent as it was on Weststruther being erected into a separate parish.

After Home became the residence of William of Greenlaw, the castle rose to be a place of importance, and was gradually increased in strength as its lords grew in power in the land. It was held by the Homes under the Earl of March till January, 1435, when their chief was forfeited, and they obtained in-

---

* It was the practice in that age for the parties in whose favour a grant was made, to request that the seals of well-known and respectable persons should also be appended to it.

dependence by becoming tenants of the crown. In 1515, the castle was taken by the Regent Albany. In the year following, Lord Home and his brother were executed. In 1517, the castle was retaken by the Homes, and maintained against the authority of King and Regent. In 1522, George Home was restored to the title and estates of his brother, which had become vested in the crown. In 1529, Lord Home was imprisoned. When Bowes, in 1542, entered Scotland, he was met by the Earl of Huntly and Lord Home at Haddonrig, and defeated. Lord Home fell in a skirmish before the battle of Pinkie, and his son and heir taken prisoner. The castle was taken by the Protector Somerset, on returning from his expedition. He pitched his camp at Harecrags, about a mile west from the castle, on the 20th September, 1547, where he was visited by Lady Home, entreating him to take the castle into his protection, which he refused to do; and on his demanding the castle to be delivered up, she begged a respite till next day at noon, to enable her ladyship to consult with her son, who was in the camp, and other friends, keepers of the castle. A second respite was granted till eight at night, and safe-conduct for John Home of Cowdenknowes to meet with Somerset. After considerable debating, it was at last arranged that the castle was to be delivered up, and the inmates to leave by ten next morning, with as much bag and baggage as they could carry, excepting ammunition and victuals. In case the keepers of the castle should alter their mind during the night, the English General caused eight pieces of ordnance, fenced with baskets of earth, to be placed on the south side of the crag next the castle. Next morning, Lord Grey was deputed by Lord Somerset to receive the castle from the hands of the Homes, and Lord Dudley to be keeper thereof. The castle was accordingly delivered up by Andrew Home and four others of the principal persons therein. Within the castle the English found store of victuals and wine and 16 pieces of ordnance. In 1549, the Scots retook the castle by stratagem, and put the garrison to the sword. Lord Grey, the English lieutenant on the Borders, attempted to retake it, but failed. In 1565, Tamworth, the English messenger, was seized at Dunbar by Lord Home, and carried to the castle of Home, where he was detained for some days. In November, 1566, Queen Mary was two nights at Home Castle, on her way north from Jedburgh. After the battle of Dunbar, Colonel Fenwick, on 3rd February, 1650, appeared before the castle of Home, and summoned the governor to surrender it to Cromwell. The governor answered, 'I know not Cromwell; and as for my castle, it is built on a rock;' whereupon Colonel Fenwick played upon him with the great guns; but the governor still would not yield; Nay sent a letter couched in these singular terms:

'I, William of the Wastle,
Am now in my castle,
And a' the dogs in the town
Shanna gar me gang down.'

So that there remained nothing but opening the mortars upon this William of the Wastle, which did gar him gang down."

The badge of the Homes was *Kendalgreen*. Their *slogan*, or war-cry, was, "*A Home! a Home!*"

SMALHAM;* SMALHAME;† SMAILHOLM. — The name of this place signifies a small dwelling, hamlet, or village. The town is situated on the summit of a ridge, rising gradually from the margin of the river Tweed, consisting of a church, school-house, several shops, and a number of other houses. It is six miles north from Kelso. The manor of *Smailholm* appears in record as early as the beginning of the twelfth century. It was granted by David I. to David de Olifard, his godson, who concealed the king after the battle of Winchester, and accompanied him to Scotland. The family of Olifard, or Oliver, is said to have sprung from a Danish chieftain, who gained the surname of Barnakel, or the Preserver of Children, from his dislike to the favourite amusement of his soldiers, that of tossing

---

* Circa, 1160.
† Ib. 1248; Chron. Mail. pp. 177, 179; Lib. de Dryburgh, pp. 109, &c.

infants on their spears.* During the reign of Malcolm IV., he appears acting as Justiciary of Lothian, which extended to the Tweed. He held the same office under William the Lion. David Olifard witnessed many charters of David I., Malcolm IV., and William the Lion. After the death of his godfather, David de Olifard granted, in 1160, to the monks of Dryburgh, a carrucate of land in Smailham, with pasturage for 300 sheep, for the remission of his own sins, and for the souls of "my lord, who gave unto me the lands, and for the souls of my ancestors and successors."† This grant was confirmed by Malcolm IV. during the same year.‡ Olifard also gave to the house of Soltre a thrave of corn from one of his manors of Smalham and Crailing.§ He left five sons, the eldest of whom, David, succeeded to the estates and offices of his father. He died at the end of the 12th century, leaving two sons, Walter and David. The eldest acted as Justiciary for above twenty years under Alexander II., by whom he was greatly trusted. He granted the church of Smailholm and

---

* Vol. ii. p. 319. † Lib. de Dryburgh, p. 109.
‡ Ib. p. 120.
§ Chart. Soltre, Nos. 16, 17. The *thrave* was the common measure of corn at that period. The word is derived from the British *drev*, signifying a tye. The Saxons used the word "*threaf*" for bundle. It is probable that the word *threaf* is from the British. The term comprehended two stooks of 24 sheaves each. It is still in use in various parts of the country.

its pertinents to the monks of Coldingham.* Olifard died in 1242, and was buried in the abbey of Melrose.† After his death, Walter of Moray is seen in possession of the estates of Bothwell in Clydesdale and Smailholm; and it is thought that he obtained them by marriage with the heiress of David Olifard. He seems to have resided at his manor of Bothwell, as a charter by him in favour of the monks of Dryburgh, exempting them from paying multure to *his mill at Smalholm*, is dated at Bothwell in the year 1278.‡ Walter died soon after, and was succeeded by his son William, who swore fealty to Edward in 1291. Not having any issue, his brother Andrew succeeded to the territory of Smalhom, and became celebrated as the companion in arms of the illustrious patriot Wallace. He fell at the battle of Stirling in 1297. His son Andrew, by a daughter of John Cumyn of Badenoch, also joined the ranks of Wallace, followed Bruce, and was the protector of David II., his infant son. About 1465, Halyburton of Merton, and Janet, his spouse, were tenants of the monks of a plow of land of the Bouchicoittis, within the lordship of Smailholm. In the end of the 15th century, the lands of Smailholm seem to have been

---

* The present church is supposed to have been built in 1632. When the church was undergoing repair, a stone was found above one of the doors, bearing the inscription, "SOLI DEO GLORIA, 1632."

† Chron. Mail. p. 155. ‡ Lib. of Dryburgh, p. 110.

possessed by David Purves, who, in 1483, was found guilty of treasonable assistance given to Albany, and in-bringing of Englishmen, and his life and goods forfeited.* Before 1515, the manor passed to Sir William Cranston, grandfather of the first Lord Cranston. About the same time, the Rutherfurds appear as owners of certain parts of the lands of Smailholm. The family of Hoppringell are seen in connection with Smailholm about 1493. In 1602, James Hume of Coldenknowes was proprietor of eighteen husbandlands in the territory of Smailholm; in 1605, George Hoppringell, of Wranghame, two husbandlands and three cottages, with the hills and tower of Smailholm Crags towards the west, within the territory of Smailholm. It is now the property of the Earl of Haddington. There was an hospital within the manor of Smailholm, the property of the abbey and convent of Dryburgh.†

In 1536, James Stewart, the abbot, feued to John Hume of Cowdenknowes all and haill the lands of Smailholm, Spittal, and pertinents, lying within the sheriffdom of Roxburgh, for thirty merks yearly. In 1630, those lands were occupied by Cairncross of Colmslie.

In May, 1303, Edward I. was at Smailholm, on his journey north. He travelled from Roxburgh to Lauder on the same day.‡

---

* Acta Parl. vol. ii. p. 160. † Lib. de Dryburgh, p. 340.
‡ Rotuli Scotiæ, vol. i. p. 53.

Several persons have borne the surname of Smailham. About 1207, Alexander de Smalham, clerk, is witness to a charter of William, abbot of Paisley. Robert of Smailham was abbot of Kelso from 1248 to 1258.* Adam of Smalham was abbot of Dere in 1267.† Robert de Smalham got letters of safe-conduct from Edward III. in October, 1365.‡

Jean Duncan, the mother of Captain Cook, resided in the barony of Smailholm, at the time of her marriage with John Cook of Ednam. It is probable the pair were married at Smailholm.

At a short distance to the west of the village of Smalham, and within the manor thereof, stands the ruins of a strong tower called Smailholm Crags, better known as Sandyknowe Tower, amidst scenery thus described by Sir Walter Scott:§—

> "It was a barren scene and wild,
> Where naked cliffs were rudely piled;
> But ever and anon between,
> Lay velvet tufts of loveliest green.
> And well the lovely infant knew
> Recesses where the wallflower grew,
> And honeysuckles loved to crawl
> Up the low crag and ruined wall."

The tower is a square building about 60 feet high, surrounded with a stone wall, now in ruins, enclosing a courtyard, defended on two sides by a morass, and

---

* Chron. Mail. p. 177.   † Ib. p. 197.
‡ Rotuli Scotiæ, vol. i. p. 53.
§ Introduction to third Canto of "Marmion."

on the third by a precipice of steep rocks, accessible only by the west end, and that so steep and rocky that the approach is exceedingly difficult. The apartments have been placed above each other; the lower apartment arched with stone, and the others with wood; a narrow stair winding up one side. The walls are nine feet thick. On the outside of the wall of the court was the chapel. From the top of the tower is a magnificent view of the surrounding scenery,—

> ———" o'er hill and dale,
> O'er Tweed's fair flood and Merton's wood,
> And all down Teviotdale."

This tower belonged to the family of Hoppringell, and, by various transmissions, came at last into the family of Lord Polwarth. Sir Walter Scott's paternal grandfather was farmer of Smailholm Crags, including the barnikin and the surrounding varied scenery. Here Sir Walter Scott resided for some time while a boy, and it is believed that at the blazing ingle of Sandyknowe the minstrel obtained information which laid the foundation of his Border lore. One of the crags near the tower is called the Watchfold, and is said to have been the station of a balefire during the Border wars. Cromwell besieged this fort, and so obstinate was the defence of the last John Pringle, that the English were forced to batter down the chapel before the keepers of the fort would surrender. This ancient fortress and its vicinity is celebrated by Sir Walter Scott in the "Eve of St. John."*

WRANGHAME.—This place is now a part of the Merton estate, but in early times was the property of the monks of Dryburgh, and, during the 16th century, occupied by the Hoppringells. The town stood in the eastmost field of the farm of Brotherstones, which lies on the north side of the Smailholm road. It is now entirely removed, a few ash-trees only marking the site of the hamlet. This village is thought to be the place where *Kenspid*, the nurse of St. Cuthbert, resided, with whom he lived from the age of eight years till the time he entered into the service of God. Bede relates, that one day, when the saint was invited to Wranghame by his nurse, " a house at the east end of the town took fire, and the wind blowing strongly from that quarter, increased the violence of the flames. His so-called mother ran to the house where he was staying, and begged of him to pray to God to preserve their houses from the flames that surrounded them. Without the slightest fear, he charged his mother, saying, 'Fear nothing, for this fire will not hurt you,' and falling prostrate on the ground before the door, he prayed silently. Immediately, at his prayers, a strong wind arose from the west, and turned the fire away without doing harm to any one."† Three

---

* Minstrelsy, p. 433.   † Bede, chap. xiv.

large stones were taken away from Wranghame, and set upright upon the hill, about three quarters of a mile to the west of the town.

MACKARVASTOUN;* MALCARSTOUN;† MALKANSTOUN;‡ MACARSTOUN;§ MALKERSERTON;|| MAKERSTON.—This barony lies on the left bank of the Tweed, and originally extended northward till it met the territory of Smailholm; on the west, it was bounded by the lands of the Morvilles; on the south, the river was the boundary; and on the east, the manor of Kelso. Such was the old territory of *Mac-car;* and though the domain is not now so wide, it still is a fair barony. The mansion is seen to great advantage from the south side of the river, especially from the North British Railway, a little to the east of Rutherford station. The house has undergone considerable enlargement and improvements in comparatively modern times. It was cast down by the Earl of Hertford in 1545. It is thought to have been rebuilt in 1590, as the weather-cock, which formerly stood on the top of the house, was taken down in the course of recent improvements, contains the letters T. M. M. H., and the date 1590, and is yet to be seen near the Observatory. When Hertford destroyed the house, the ground storey,

---

* Circa, 1116, 1130, 1150.   † Ib. 1159.   ‡ Ib. 1159.
§ Ib. 1291. || Ib. 1296.

composed of massy stone arches, must have been left, and on which the house of 1590 has apparently been erected. The lower part of the house is undoubtedly far older than the other parts of it. The policy is full of valuable wood. On the north of the mansion, a number of fine wych elms are to be seen, of about fifteen feet in girth, and rising to the height of at least seventy feet. A remarkable tree of this kind stands about 150 yards north of the house; it is fully fifteen feet in circumference, and at a few feet high sends out a massy branch in a straight line from its trunk. There are also a number of fine beech-trees that raise their graceful forms to a great height. The sycamore and ash trees also abound, many of them ten and twelve feet in circumference, and rise fully sixty feet high. On the banks of the river, and in the park, are a few fine thorns mixed with the other wood, adding greatly to the beauty of the scenery, and affording, as remarked by an accomplished botanist, a favourite concealment in which the thrush seeks to build her nest:

> "Within yon milk-white hawthorn bush,
> 'Mang her nestlings sits the thrush;
> Her faithfu' mate will share her toil,
> Or wi' his songs her care beguile."

It is thought that the name was conferred on this place by some early settler of the name of *Mac-car*, but of whom no other trace exists than the name of this ancient baronial mansion. The earliest proprietor named in the records is *Walter Corbet*, who acquired the barony about the middle of the 12th century. His father was Robert Corbet, who came from Shropshire in the beginning of the 12th century, and settled in Teviotdale under Earl David. In the "Inquisitio Davidis, 1116," Robert Corbet is a witness to the charter of Prince David to the monastery of Selkirk. He also witnessed a grant of David I. to the monks of Dunfermline. Before 1159, Walter Corbet gave to the monks of Kelso the church of Malkariston, with the tithes thereof, and a piece of land, lying on the Tweed at Brockesford, which he had given to that church at the time of its dedication. This land he afterwards exchanged with them, and added, for the love of God, that piece of land called "*Gret-riges-medow*," for the safety of William his king. Walter, his son, made another grant to them of half-a-ploughgate, with toft and croft, and confirmed a grant by Michael, one of his vassals, of two acres of land, lying on the north side of the road from Langtoune to Roxburgh. He married Alice, a daughter of Philip de Valoines, the chamberlain who possessed the barony of Kingwode in Teviotdale. She bare to him a son and a daughter; the former died in the lifetime of his father, and the latter, Christian, married William, the second son of Patrick, Earl of Dunbar, carrying with her all the vast estates of her father. On the marriage taking place, Earl Patrick conveyed to his son William the manor of Foghou in Berwickshire. Christian had two sons to William, named Nicholas and Patrick, who assumed their mother's name of *Corbet*. Nicholas got Makerston, and Patrick obtained from his father the manor of Foghou. Foghou afterwards went to the Gordon family, still, holding of the Dunbars till 1400, when it was forfeited by Earl George. The monks of Kelso granted leave to Christian and her husband to celebrate divine worship in their own chapel at Malcarvistoun; in return, William, with the consent of his son Nicholas, and for the safety of his wife Christian, granted the monks a release of all claims which he might have on their estate, and, in presence of the Bishop of Dunkeld, swore to perform faithfully his promise. The last of the ancient race of the Corbets died in 1241, and was buried in the chapter-house of Melrose Abbey.* But her son, Nicholas, by Gospatric, and his heirs, inherited the lands. In 1263, on the feast of St. Lucia, in the refectory of the abbey, and in presence of the king, Nicholas Corbet granted to the monks of Melrose, for their *support* and *recreation*, all the fisheries in the river Tweed, from Dal Cove on the west, to Brockesmouth on the east, on condition that the produce thereof should be applied to the proper uses

---

* Chron. Mail. p. 153.

of the convent. Leave was given by him to the men of the convent to land their cobells and nets on part of his grounds, with passage through his lands to the fisheries, and the privilege to build a fishing-house.* But troublous times were at hand, during which it is difficult to trace the fortunes of the family. In 1296, Alexander Corbet was detained captive in Windsor.† In 1334, Edward III. commanded restitution of the lands and goods of Patrick Shartres, [Chartres], and Margaret Corbet, lady of Malkerstoun.‡ About 1390, *Archibald M'Dowell* got a grant from Robert III. of the lands of M'Carstoune, Yhethame, and Elystoun.§ In 1398, Archibald M'Dowell of M'Carstoune appeared at Melrose, and granted an obligation for the amount of his relief, granted by the Crown "to the new worke of the kirke of Melrose."‖ In 1478, Dougal M'Dowall of M'Carstoun, was ordained by the Lords of Council to pay to Robert, the abbot of Kelso, twelve chalders and a-half of victual, for the teinds of M'Carstoune, for the year bypast, in terms of the obligation by him to the abbot.¶ In the same year, M'Dowell was summoned before the Lords Auditors for one hundred merks, by Walter Kerr of Caverton.** In 1480, the Lords of Council allowed Dougal a

---

* Lib. de Melros.   † Rotuli Scotiæ, vol. i. p. 45.
‡ Ib. vol. i. p. 271.   § Robertson's Index, p. 148, No. 27.
‖ Lib. de Melros, p. 490.   ¶ Acta Dom. Con. p. 26.
** Acta Aud., p. 69.

proof that he had paid the abbot of Kelso 12 chalders 4 bolls of meal and bear, 4 bolls of wheat, for the land of M'Carstoun, at the terms of St. Andrews and Candlemass. In 1483, the Lords Auditors heard Dougal M'Dowell and Walter Kerr of Cessford, in the cause pursued by Cessford v. M'Dowell, for L.100, being the penalty contained in an agreement between them, for fulfilling of a contract of marriage between Andrew M'Dowell, the son of M'Carstoun, and Margaret Kerr, a daughter of Cessford, and continued the cause, in consequence of Dougal alleging that he was possessed of a discharge of the same. On the 17th October, 1493, Dougal M'Dowell pursued Alexander Craik, John Craik, Martine Gibsine, George Bowo, John Richardson, and Thomas Tailfor, Thomas Bowo, Thomas Donaldson, Adam Camis, James Bowo, Richard Bowo, John Tod, and Thomas Aitchison, chaplain, for the wrongous occupation of the lands of Rhynynlaws, and the Spittal Green, belonging to him, as part of the lands of M'Carstoun. The Lords adjourned the cause to the next Justiciare at Jedburgh.* In the same year, a reference was entered into between the said Dougal M'Dowell and Nichol Ormiston, to John Edmonstone, son and apparent heir of the laird of Edmonstone, William Sinclair of Moreham, Mr. Patrick Aitkinson, and Mr. William

---

* Act. Aud., p. 303.

Scott, as arbiters, and George Douglas of Bonjedworth, oversman, and, failing him, the Laird of Rutherfurd, or Walter Ker of Cessford, in regard to the withholding of 100 merks claimed by the said Laird of M'Carstoun from Ormiston, for the *gersome* of Merdane; and also as to the said Laird of M'Carstoun withholding a tack of the West Mains of M'Carstoun from Ormiston; parties to meet in the chapel of Fairningtoune on the sixth day of November next.* In 1536, Thomas M'Dowell of Macarestoune found caution of 1000 merks to underlye the law at the next Justiciaire at Jedburgh, for oppression and hamesucken done to Alexander Dunbar, dean of Murray, and his servants. In 1545, the army of Hertford visited the barony, and destroyed the town of Makerston, Manerhill, and Charterhouse, Luntinlaw, and Stotherike tower. In 1564, the Laird of M'Carstoun was one of the prolocutors for Elliot of Horsleyhill, and others, for the slaughter of the Laird of Hassendean. Alexander M'Dougall of Stodrig was also one of the defenders of the pannels. The Laird of Makerstoune was one of the assize on the trial of William Sinclair of Herdmanstone, in 1565, for the murder of the Earl Bothwell's servant; and he defended James Bog, accused of the slaughter of George Hamilton of Pardovane.† In 1590, Thomas Makdougal rebuilt the house which had been cast

---

* Act. Aud., p. 312.   † Pitcairn's Trials, vol. i. p. 477.

down by Hertford. In 1596, Thomas Macdougall of Mackarstoune was one of the assize on the trial of Robert Hamilton of Inchmauchane, Sir James Edmestoune of Duntraith, and James Lockart of Ley, accused of treason. In 1598, the Laird of Mackerstoune published an advertisement, that he would undertake to make land more valuable by sowing salt on it.* In 1604, James Macdougal succeeded his father, Thomas Macdougal, in the lands and barony of Makerstoun. In 1608, he acquired the lands and town of Danieltown, near Melrose.† In 1622, Sir William Macdougal and a number of others were fined 100 merks, for being absent from the trial of Turnbull of Belsches, and others, for perjury.‡ In 1625, the Laird of Malkerstoun was a commissioner to the Parliament for the county of Roxburgh. In 1643, Robert, Earl of Roxburgh, seems to have been possessed of the lands and barony of M'Caristoune.§ About the same time, "Ettrick Heidis, and Ettrick Medowis," part of the lands of M'Caristoune, belonged to John Veitche.|| Before 1568, Captain Robert Macdougall was in possession of part of the estates of Makerstoune, as at that time Barbara Macdougal, his niece, and spouse to Harry Macdougal, was served heir to him in the lands of Lyntonlaw, the lands of Wester Meredene,

---

* Birrel's Diary. † Retours, No. 50.
‡ Pitcairn's Trials, vol. iii. p. 539.
§ Retours, No. 181. || Ib. No. 182.

part of the barony of Makerstoune, and the lands of Townfootmains, also within said barony. In 1665, Harry Macdougal, and John Scott of Langshaw, were commissioners for the shire of Roxburgh. In 1669, Charles II. granted a charter of donation and concession to and in favour of Henry Makdougal of M'Cariston, in liferent, and of Thomas Macdougal, his only son, procreate of the marriage between him and Barbara M'Dougal, and his heirs in fee, all and haill the lands and barony of M'Caristoune, with the tower, fortalice, manor place, comprehending the lands of Luntonlaw, and the lands of Westermuirdeane, the lands of Nethermains, commonly called the Townfootmains, the ten-mark lands of M'Cariston, and the lands of Manorhill and Charterhouse. By the same charter, his Majesty annexed and erected said lands into a barony, to be called the barony of *M'Caristoune,* ordering the said tower and fortalice to be the principal messuage of the lands and barony, and at which sasine was to be taken for all the lands and barony, whether lying contiguous or not. In 1670, the charter was ratified by Parliament.*
In 1678, Henry M'Dougal, and Robert Pringle of Stitchel, were commissioners to Parliament for the county of Roxburgh. In May 10, 1689, Henry Macdougal appeared before the Convention of Estates, and bound and enacted himself, on his word of

---

* Acta Parl. vol. viii. p. 41.

honour as a gentleman, to live peaceably, and with submission to the present government of William and Mary, and appear before the Committee of Estates, when called upon or cited to appear.* In 1692, he was one of the commissioners on the annexation of the four parishes of Eskdale to Roxburghshire. In the beginning of the 18th century, the barony of M'Caristoun was carried into the family of Hay, by Barbara, the heiress of Henry Macdougal, marrying George, brother of Sir Thomas Hay of Adderstone, at whose death he succeeded to the baronetcy and estates. Sir George was Lieutenant-Colonel of the Royal North British Dragoons. He died in 1777, at the advanced age of seventy-three years; and Barbara, his spouse, died in the following year, aged seventy-four. Sir Henry succeeded, and married Isabella, a daughter of Admiral Sir James Douglas, Bart., of Springwood Park. Sir Henry died in 1825, leaving three daughters, the eldest of whom, Anna Maria, married, in 1819, Thomas Brisbane, Esq., who was created a baronet in 1836. On 14th August, 1826, Sir Thomas and his wife were authorized, by sign manual, to use the surname of Macdougal before that of Brisbane. Sir Thomas is a G.C.B., G.C.H., LL.D., F.R.S., President of the Royal Society of Edinburgh, and a General in the army.

---

* Acta Parl. vol. ix. p. 17.

In the barony of Makerstoun, the monks of Kelso had two carrucates of land, with pasture for 300 lambs, which they estimated at 40s. yearly. They had two cottages, each having a toft and half-an-acre of land, with common pasture for two cows. Four of these cottages rented for four shillings yearly, and nine days' labour; and the other four rented at 1s. 6d. each, and nine days' work. They had also a brewhouse in the town, with an acre of land, which rented for five shillings yearly. The church belonging to the monks was "*in rectoria,*" and stated by them to be usually worth 20 marks.

On the apex of the rocky bank of the Tweed, a short distance above the mansion of Makerston, are traces of a small camp, which seems to have taken in a part of the face of the crag, as one of the ditches terminates in the precipice. This camp is exactly opposite to the strong fort called Ringley Hall, on the top of the steep cliff forming the right bank of the river. From the size of the camp, it is obvious that it could only have been occupied by a small body of men, probably to watch the movements of the occupants on the other side of the river.

Within the barony is CHARTERHOUSE, which was of old a priory inhabited by a small society of Carthusians. They possessed half of the midtown and mains of Sprouston.

During the reign of William the Lion, *Adam de Malcarvestoun* was vicar of Cranstoun.

THE MANOR OF ROXBURGH.—In the days of Earl David, the manor was of great extent; and at the time he ascended the throne, the greater portion of it remained in his own hands. In 1147, a carrucate of land is described as lying within his *lordship* of Roxburgh—"*dominico meo de Rokesburg.*"* During the reigns of his successors, Malcolm IV. and William the Lion, a considerable part of the territory was held by subjects; but all that land which was necessary for the defence of the Castle of Roxburgh was kept by the kings *in demesne.* In 1232, the monks of Melrose obtained from the Earl of Oxford a grant of "four acres of arable land in the territory of Old Roxburgh, upon the Tweedflat, as they lay in one tenement along the stones placed as bounds—perambulated by him and other good men, and this grant he made in presence of the monks, and many of his own and other men, and made the oblation by placing a rod on the great altar of the monastery."† In 1250, *Walter* was steward of Old Roxburgh; and in 1264, Stephen the Fleming seems to have had the bailyerie under his charge. In 1265, Hugh de Berkeley drew from the bailierie £40, 6s. 8d. Before 1296, Nicholas de Soules was a tenant-in-chief of the king of lands in Roxburgh. In 1306, Richard Lovel and Muriel, his wife, obtained from the English king the lands and tenements in Old Roxburgh, which had belonged

---

* Reg. Glas. pp. 9, 10.　　† Lib. de Mailros, p. 228.

to John de Soules. On the independence of Scotland being regained, Lovel lost the manor of Roxburgh, but in 1347 it was restored.* In 1403, the manor was granted to Henry de Percy, Earl of Northumberland, by Henry IV.† In 1434, the Duchess of Turon was in possession, in terms of an agreement made with her brother, James I. In 1451, the barony was granted by James II. to Andrew Ker of Altonbourne, for payment of a silver penny at Whitsunday, in name of *blenche ferme*, if demanded, and with whose descendants it still remains.‡ At that time the barony was nearly co-extensive with the parish, excepting the barony of Fairnington, which lay up to the Watling-street on the west. The court of the barony was held at FRIARS, situated between the Tweed and Teviot.§ In the remains of this religious house, the family of Roxburghe occasionally resided, especially during the rebuilding of Floors in 1718. The gardens of the convent were kept up till 1780, when, it is said, the butler to Duke John ploughed them up, and destroyed several beautiful vestiges of antiquity. In these gardens there was a raised walk called the Lovers' Walk, between two rows of large elms, terminating with a remarkable wych elm, called the "*Trysting Tree*," "whither," says the informant of

---

* Rotuli Scotiæ, vol. i. pp. 697, 698.   † Ib. p. 163.
‡ Reg. Mag. Sig. lib. iv. No. 3, supra.
§ Supra, vol. ii. p. 74.

the editor of "Gilpin's Forest Scenery," "the *beaux* and *belles* of these old times used to resort to enjoy themselves on a summer evening, and to eat the fruit, which was always sold during the absence of the family. Upon these occasions, the gentlemen were often made to walk blindfolded in the alley; and if any one failed to grope his way from one end of it to the other, without diverging from the grass into either border, he was immediately fined in a treat of fruit."*
It is said, that many a courtship came to a happy termination at this antiquated Vauxhall. The *trysting tree*, one of the largest wych elms on record, stood on the margin of the Teviot, near to where that river was forded before the erection of the bridge. It died several years ago, and its remains have been entirely removed from the place where it grew. The trunk measured thirty feet in girth. Mason, in his "History of Kelso," published in 1789, calls it "the king of the woods and prince of the neighbouring trees." Several articles of furniture have been made out of the timber of this tree, and may be seen at Floors. It exists in a young tree growing in Springwood Park.† It is said by Sir Thomas Dick Lauder, that Mr. Smith of Kelso informed him, "that the most plausible tradition regarding the origin of the trysting tree is, that the

---

* Gilpin's Forest Scenery. Edited by Sir Thomas Dick Lauder. 1834.

† Postea, description of Springwood Park.

lairds of Cessford and Ferniehirst, with a number of Scottish gentry, assembled there in 1547, to meet the Protector Somerset, during his rough courtship, and to swear homage to the King of England." It is, however, obvious, that the tree could not derive its name from such a meeting. The name of the "*Trysting Tree*" means, that the tree was a place of constant meeting, where lovers told their hopes and fears:

"When winds were still, and silent eve,
Came stealing slowly o'er the lea."

Tradition bears, that it was under this tree that the Earl of Douglas and his friends met on the night of Shrovetide, in 1313, and dressed themselves in the skins of bullocks, before proceeding to recover the castle of Roxburgh by stratagem, in which they were successful; but while the locality was a likely one for the warriors of Teviotdale to assemble on such an occasion, it may well be doubted whether the trysting tree had any existence at that early period.

About thirty acres of this peninsula, called the Kelso lands, are said by several authorities to be included within the parish of Kelso, while others of equal claim to respect give the whole of the land lying between the Tweed and Teviot to the parish of Roxburgh. Before the year 1147, the churches of Roxburgh, with the lands belonging to them, were the property of the Bishop of Glasgow. On the death of the bishop, the churches reverted to David I., who conferred them, with their pertinents, on the monks of Kelso. This grant was confirmed in 1159, by his successor, Malcolm IV. It seems that a part of the church lands had not been granted by the king; for, in 1160, Bishop Herbert restored to the churches of Roxburgh that part of the parish lying without the moat of the town, between the Tweed and Teviot, towards the abbey, which he retained in his hand under an agreement with King Malcolm, "as fully as Ascellin, the archdeacon, had these churches in the time of King David and Bishop John;" and granted and confirmed the same churches, without diminution, to the monks of Kelso.* William the Lion confirmed to the monks of Kelso the same churches and lands as held by Archdeacon Ascellin. In 1180, Bishop Joceline confirmed the previous grants, and added all casualties, with lands, and titles, pertinents, and rights, and patronage of said churches, for the proper use and maintenance of the monks. King William confirmed this grant before 1199. In 1201, at Perth, an arrangement was entered into in presence of the Pope's legate, between the bishops of St. Andrews and Glasgow and the monks of Kelso, regarding all the churches of the monks situated in the two dioceses, from which the churches of Roxburgh were exempted, as being free of all synodal aids, entertainments, and corrodies, under the provision that there should be

---

* Lib. de Calchou, p. 326.

perpetual vicars in these churches, and who required to be approved of by the Bishop of Glasgow before being inducted. These grants and arrangements were confirmed by Pope Innocent IV. From this, it will be seen, that the monks of Kelso had the charge of the churches of the burgh, with the little district attached, till they were destroyed in the beginning of the 15th century. I do not see any grounds for holding that any part of the peninsula lies within the parish of Kelso. There can be no doubt that the territory was held by Ascellin, the Archdeacon of Glasgow, and included in the grant by Malcolm IV. to the church of Glasgow, Bishop Herbert, and his successors.* It is not sufficient to make this little district a part of the parish of Kelso, that it was granted to the monks of Kelso, and that they presented to the Bishop of Glasgow vicars for induction in the churches of the burgh. Whenever the monks ceased to take charge of the district, it devolved upon the mother-church of *Auld* Roxburgh, as lying within the original parish, and not upon the parson of the church of Kelso. The church of St. John, in the King's Castle, had an independent parish, as well as the churches of St. James, and the Holy Sepulchre; and if these two are to be placed within the parish of Kelso, what is to become of the parish of St. John?

---

* Reg. of Glas. p. 14.

The exact site of the *auld* church at Roxburgh has been disputed;* but I am now satisfied that it stood within the graveyard of old Roxburgh, at the east end of the present church, which was built in 1752. The old church was nearly wholly underground, having a strong arched roof of stone, with an entrance-porch of the same construction, descending by six or seven steps to the body of the church. The porch still exists, partly modernized, and is the burying-place of the family of Sunlaws.† The arched doorway into the old church is to be seen in the north gable of the aisle. On a stone in the built-up portion of the arch, are the letters raised, "A. K. M. H., Anno 1612." A small stone of about a foot square, with a pedestal, surrounded by a raised border, stands near to the walk running south from the church, bears to have been erected in

---

* Supra, vol. ii. p. 57. The town at the castle existed in the beginning of the 16th century; and, at that time, it is certain that a church and graveyard existed where the present church now is. There were no churches in this district, except the mother-church, and the churches of the burgh and castle. If, then, a church stood at this place in the beginning of the 16th century, it could only be the mother-church of *Auld* Roxburgh. There is not the slightest trace of a church and graveyard at any other spot in the parish. Had there been another graveyard, the ashes of the Kers would not have lain in the graveyard at the parish church.

† It was formerly the burying-place of the Kers. The family of Sunlaws succeeded to part of the entailed estates of Sir Andrew Ker of Greenhead.

1402, to the name of Hope, but the letters are evidently of a later date. A stone, standing against the church wall, records that it was erected in 1788, to a member of the family of Hogg, who had resided there for 600 years. Another stone bears that the ashes of Randolph Ker, son of Thomas Ker of Altonburn, repose in the neighbourhood of the church. Near to the west-end of the church, an inscription on a stone shows that William Weymess, minister of the parish, was interred there in 1658. A little to the west of the church, a tombstone points out the place where sleeps the celebrated Blue-gown, Edie Ochiltree, who died at Roxburgh New-town, in 1793, aged 106. On the back of the stone is a full-length figure of Blue-gown, with a dog at his feet, a staff in one hand, and a bag in the other, which he is holding up, and above the figure are the words, "Behold the end o't;" intended to represent a scene, which tradition says took place between Ochiltree and a recruiting-serjeant at St. Boswell's Fair. When the serjeant finished a harangue to the rustics on the glories of war, Blue-gown stepped forward, held up his "meal-pock," and exclaimed, " Behold the end o't."*

The present village consists of a row of houses

---

* This monument was erected in 1849 to Ochiltree's memory, by Mr. William Thomson, farmer of Over Roxburgh, who, in his boyhood, had seen Blue-gown when he visited his father's house.

on the side of the road which leads to the passage of the river. A number of these householders are called *cotlanders*, from possessing, with their house and yard, about two acres of land.

In a field adjoining the manse, are the ruins of a tower, formerly of considerable strength, and popularly known as *Wallace's Tower** and Merlin's Cave. The writer of the "Old Statistical Account" says that old people " remember its having various apartments; the windows and doors secured by iron bars and gates, and the lintels and door-posts, especially those of the great porch, highly ornamented by grand Gothic sculpture. They speak also with rapture of the fine gardens, the fruit trees, and various works of decoration, whereby they have seen this mansion surrounded."† While an examination of the ruins does not induce the belief that the tower warranted the description given by the old people to the minister of the parish, it shows that it has been a well-built strength, of the size and form common in the 15th and 16th centuries. The ruins contain no sculptured stones; indeed, the building

---

* It is said by Blind Harry, that Wallace built a tower within a little space of Roxburgh; but it is probable that the name of Wallace's Tower was conferred upon the building on account of its strength. In the Borderland, everything strong or powerful is named after the patriot, whose fame will ever live in the memories of the people. In this part of Scotland, no monument is needed to his memory.

† Old Statistical Account, vol. xix. p. 129.

has not been of that kind on which much ornament was expended; but the stones forming the sides of the door and corners of the walls, have all been removed. The ground-flat still exists, about 30 feet in length, and 20 feet in breadth, strongly arched over with stone. An entrance from this apartment leads into a circular space in the corner, also arched with small slits in the wall for defence. Part of the stair is still to be seen. The walls are fully six feet thick, and strongly built. On the summit of the wall, I noticed a thorn-tree in full blossom, and several small ash-trees nodding silently in the breeze. At a short distance to the north of the ruins is an ash-tree, nearly 10 feet in circumference, and about 50 feet in height. All around the ruins the ground bears evidence of the existence of building, which formed, in times long bygone, a part of the town of old Roxburgh. In September, 1545, this tower was destroyed by the Earl of Hertford, and is entered in the list of places rased as *"the toure of Rockesborough."* It is occasionally called Sunlaws Tower, and North Sunlaws Tower.

SUNLAWS.—This estate lies on the right bank of the river Teviot. The situation of the mansion, naturally beautiful, has been improved as far as possible by art. This estate formerly belonged to the Kers. In 1588, William Ker of Cessford possessed this property, as part of the barony of

Roxburgh.* It afterwards belonged to the Kers of Greenhead; and, at the death of Christian Ker, commonly called Lady Chatto, who was lineally descended from William Ker of Greenhead, brother-german to the Earl of Ancrum, the entailed estates of Sunlaws and Chatto passed to William Scott of Thirlestane, who assumed the name and arms of Ker. In 1661, James Scott, brother-german to Sir William Scott of Harden, acquired the lands of Thirlestane, Heaton, and others, from Sir Andrew Ker of Greenhead. Alexander Scott, the grandson of James Scott, married Barbara Ker of Frogden, by whom he had the said William Scott, first of Sunlaws. He died in 1782, and was succeeded by his eldest son, who was a lieutenant in the army, and died, unmarried, at Philadelphia, in 1790. Robert Scott Ker, his brother, then succeeded to the estates, and married Elizabeth Bell, daughter of David Fyffe of Drumgarth, Forfarshire, by whom he had issue, the present proprietor, William Scott Ker, and five daughters. There was formerly a tower at Sunlaws, and it is supposed that it was the strength referred to by Lord Dacre in his letter to the Earl of Surrey, in July, 1523. He states, that after the burning of Kelso, he "proceeded to a great towre called Synlaws, three miles within Kelsoo, and kist it doune." It is said, that while Prince Charles was

---

* Reg. Mag. Sig. lib. xxxvii. p. 125.

on his way to Jedburgh, in 1745, he passed a night at Sunlaws.

RINGLEY HALL.—This place is on the south side of the Tweed, on the top of a high cliff which overhangs the river. According to old maps, it is several hundred yards within the parish of Roxburgh, the boundary line between Maxton and Roxburgh being exactly opposite to Makerston Mill. The name is obviously derived from the British *Rhin*, a point, and *ley*, a fortified place, a *court or manor house;* i.e., *Ringley*, a fortified place on the point or nose of the promontory.* I have no doubt a fort at this place was first constructed by British hands, and at a very early period. There are good grounds for believing that the territory of Boadicea extended to the Tweed. The name of the river would at least indicate that it formed a boundary line, when the name was imposed. Tweed is the ancient British *Tuedd*, signifying *"the state of being on a side the border of a country."* There can be no doubt, however, that when the Romans left the country, to defend their own homes and altars, the

---

* The Saxons added *Heal* or Hall, meaning the same thing as the British *ley*, a court-house or principal place. It is likely that *Ringley* was at one time the residence of one of the great men of the country, whose name has been lost in the sands of time, while the ruins of his house remain a memorial to future ages of the state of the district in early days.

RINGLEY HALL.
BIRDSEYE VIEW TAKEN IN 1776.

Tweed formed the boundary between the Saxon people of Lothian on the north, and the Romanized Britons on the south of the river. The whole south bank of the Tweed has been bridled with forts and strengths of every kind. This fort now forms part of a plantation, the eastern fence of which has encroached upon the strength. Like all the early forts, it takes in all the naturally strong points of the cliff. The crown of the fort is an exact circle, and level with a rampart of earth of about six feet high from the inside. Within the rampart, the level top measures about 180 feet in diameter, and the entrance thereto has been from the east about 36 feet wide. In the south-west side of the upper circle are traces of a stone building of about 40 feet square. From the top of the upper rampart to the next terrace or level, is 18 perpendicular feet, and has been made as steep as could be done with soil or turf. This level is nine yards wide, with a rampart on its edge which ends on the brink of the cliff. From this rampart to the next level is 15 perpendicular feet, and as steep as the one above it. This level is 18 feet wide. The rampart to this level forms the outer defence to the fort, and is six feet high, composed of dry stones, both ends terminating, like the middle rampart, on the edge of the precipice. When entire, the height, measuring from the plain ground on the outside, must have been about 34 feet perpendicular. It is said by several writers, that it is a Danish fort, by others, Roman; but I do not think there are any grounds for attributing its formation to either of these people. The writers of both old and new statistical accounts refer to a tradition in regard to this locality, which relates, that during the Border wars, an English army occupied Ringley Hall, and the Scots lay on the opposite side, in a place called the "*Scots' Hole.*" The English, being superior in numbers, resolved to pass over to the enemy at a ford a little above this place; but the Scots, creeping out of their hole, attacked them while part of the army was in the dangerous passage of the river, and, after an obstinate battle, the English were beaten; and many of them slain and interred in the burying-ground at Rutherford. From this battle tradition tells us, that the place was called *Rue-the-ford*, on account of the great loss sustained by the English. Such is one tradition; but there exists another, which says, that it was a *ford* through which *Ruther*, king of Scots, was conducted while on an expedition against the Britons, and was from that circumstance named *Rutherford*. I have no doubt that this important passage of the river has been often well-contested; but it is clear to me, that the traditions, so far as the name of the place is concerned, are not correct. In the second volume, I have endeavoured to show that the name of *Rutherford* is derived from the *red colour* of the land, and the cliffs of red freestone peculiar to that part of the river. Unfortunately for the traditions, the name is British, and must have been imposed at a period when that race inhabited the district. It is right, however, to mention, that there is a British word, "*Rhuthyr,*" which signifies "*assault,*" and assuming it to be the correct word, *Rutherford* would mean the "*assault ford,*" or the "*ford*" of "*assault.*"

To the eastward of this fort, and exactly in front of Makerston House, is a large *tumulus,* or mount, said to be an exploratory mount to Ringley Hall; but this view cannot be maintained. It has the appearance of an ancient mote-hill, and is popularly known by the name of the Pleahill. A careful examination leads to the conclusion that it is partly natural. The lower part of it seems to be one of the sand or gravelly knowes which abound on that part of the river, and the top composed of soil taken from the ground around. It seems to have been surrounded by terraces, or levels ascending above each other, which, on the south and north, are yet distinct. The access to the summit has been from the east. The diameter of the top, which is level, is about 34 feet. It may have served the purposes of a mote, as its name would lead one to believe, but it appears to me to have been used as a place of strength, to protect the weak part of the Tweed at this particular spot. As such it must have been powerful. The minister of Roxburgh, who wrote the old statistical account* of the parish, says, that a well of several streams issued out of its base, was called St. John's, and from the salubrity of the water, and remains of nice building, must have been of great repute. It was planted with trees about the middle of last century, but from the exposed situation, they have made but little progress; the trees, however, add to the picturesque appearance of the locality. It is a conspicuous object to travellers by road or rail.

The river, when in a very low state, may be forded in front of Makerston Mansion; but excepting at that place, it cannot be forded between Rutherford Mill and Brochesford.† At a little below Makerston, the bed of the river is composed of large rocks, rising here and there above the water, and among which the river rushes wildly. Before 1797, the rock was divided into four slits, which contained the whole water when the river was not flooded. Two of these were 34 feet deep, and so narrow, that a person might easily have stepped across them. In summer, people on foot often passed the river by stepping from one rock to the other; but Sir Henry Hay M'Dougall caused the middle rock to be blown up, and thus stopped the dangerous passage. An active person can step it at the present day, when

---

* Vol. xix. p. 137.

† Brochesford means, the ford at the Burn, or the Burnford.

the river is in a low state; and it is said, that Kerse, the fisher, who lived at this part of the river, stept across with one of his children on his back. As the river passes through these rocks it makes a loud noise, at all times; but at the breaking up of the ice, the noise resembles the sea breaking upon a rocky shore. In winter, the various fantastic shapes made by the frost are very remarkable. Amidst these rocks are deep pools, which whirl with great rapidity. Great numbers of salmon frequented these rocks, and to such an extent sixty years ago, that it was not uncommon for three or four cart-loads of fish being caught there in a morning.* The locality is called *Trows* at the present day, evidently derived from the British " *Thor,*" signifying, " a perpendicular rock or height;" changed into *Tor* by the Saxons, into *Tower* by the English, and corrupted into *Trows* by the people of the present day. The name of *Tors*, then, means a number of perpendicular rocks; and, at the time the name was imposed on this place, would aptly describe the bed of the river Tweed. From a careful examination of the channel, and the banks on each side, I am satisfied that the *Tors* have at one time formed almost a complete bar across the river, so as to flood the low-lying ground to the south below *Stodrig* to the *wastes* of Eden-

---

* Old Statistical Account, vol. xix. p. 133. It is said that Kerse the fisher knew the reason why the salmon were found in such numbers below the *Tors*, and not above that place.

ham. The names of places in that direction evince that they stood in the midst of mosses and moist meadows, when they obtained their appellations. *Stodrig* is derived from the Saxon *Strodre, Strother*, signifying a moss, marsh, or any watery place, *i. e.*, Strodrig, the ridge in the marsh. In like manner, *Mus-rig*, the rig in the moss. On the north margin of the Tweed, the name *Strodre* or *Strother* is used to describe a marsh or wet meadow. In the days of Malcolm IV., and William the Lion, the word was in common use in the southern districts of Scotland.

While treating of this locality, I may refer to a tradition of the Church of Rome, which relates, that the body of St. Cuthbert, the saint of Tweedside, floated down the river in a stone boat from Old Melrose to Tillmouth. St. Cuthbert was buried in Lindesfarne, and, on the monks being forced by the Danes in 875 to leave the monastery, they carried the corpse of the holy man along with them, in all their wanderings through the north of England and in this district of Scotland. The monks visited Norham, Carham, and Old Melrose on the Tweed; but after staying there for some little time, the remains of the saint showed the same signs of restlessness and agitation as had occasioned former removals. The attendants were ordered, in a vision, to pacify the impatient spirit, to construct a boat of stone, into which they were to place the said relics, and commit it to the river.* The monks formed a boat ten feet long, three feet and a-half broad, eighteen inches deep, and four and a-half inches thick, out of the stone of that sacred place in which the remains of the saint were put, launched it upon the waters of the Tweed, and sailed down to Tillmouth, where, on a peninsula formed by the meeting of the waters, a small chapel was erected, called St. Cuthbert. Wherever the monks rested in their flight with the sacred remains of the saint, a chapel was erected in after-times, dedicated to St. Cuthbert. *Cavers,* in Teviot, was hallowed by being the temporary resting-place of the body. About the end of last century, an attempt was made by a peasant of Northumberland to feed his hogs out of the boat, and also to use it for pickling pork; but the spirits of darkness broke it in two during the night, leaving the fragments near the chapel. The learned Hutchinson, who repeats this strange traditional story, seems to have no doubt that the coffin of stone floated down the Tweed, as by some hydrostatical experiments it had been found

---

* "They rested him in fair Melrose:
   But though alive he loved it well,
Not there his relics might repose;
   For, wondrous tale to tell,
In his stone coffin forth he rides,
A ponderous bark for river tides,
'Yet light as gossamer it glides
   Downward to Tillmouth cell."
—*Marmion,* ii. 14.

capable of doing, and carrying the remains of the saint, observing that these philosophical exhibitions, in ages of profound ignorance, were always esteemed miracles and food for superstition. I am sceptical as to the floating of the stone ark and the body of the saint from Melrose to Tillmouth. I think it impossible; and had Hutchinson known the Tweed as well as I do, he would not have needed the aid of philosophy to explain to the people that a miracle had *not* been worked. The raft of wood, and coffin of stone, could not have passed the rocks at Makerston; and all the monkish and philosophical skill in the world could not have floated it over the *Tors*. If the stone coffin sailed down the Tweed from Melrose to Tillmouth, it could only be by a miracle, and not by the aid of philosophy.

FARNINDUN;* FARINGDUNE;† FARNEDAN;‡ FAIRNINGTON.§—This BARONY appears in record as early as the 12th century, in possession of the family of Burnard, from whom the Burnets are descended. In 1200, the monks of Melrose obtained from Richard Burnard thirteen acres and a rood of his land of Faringdun, adjoining, the land of Simon of Farburne, on the east side, below the king's road which

---

* Circa, 1196, Reg. Glas. p. 55.
† Ib. 1208, Reg. Glas. p. 99.
‡ Ib. 1370, Reg. Mag. Sig.
§ Ib. 1791, Valuation Books of the County of Roxburgh.

led to Roxburgh. To the same monks he also granted a right to a part of his peatry in said territory, as bounded by great stones, with leave to them to make a ditch of six feet in diameter, and granted as much land and moor adjacent as was necessary to dry the peats, with right of passage over the territory of Faringdun, for the purpose of carting the peats.* Between the years 1208 and 1232, Walter, Bishop of Glasgow, obtained from Ralph Burnard a grant of fuel from the two peatries of Faringdune, for the house of Alncrumbe, with liberty to the bishop's servants to select the most convenient place for digging the peats next to the place in the moss where he got his own peats.† The grant to the monks of Melrose was confirmed by Alexander II., between 1214 and 1249. Sir Richard Burnard of Faringdune, and his steward of said barony, Symon of Fard, appear as witnesses to a charter granted in 1250. Two years after, the monks of Melrose bought from Richard Burnard, for thirty-five merks, which they paid him beforehand, the east meadow of Fairningdun, consisting of eight acres within the ditch, which the monks caused to be made around the same, with free ish and entry to the same through his land; and in the event of the meadow being injured through his fault, or that of his servants, he bound himself to give them value

---

* Lib. de Melros, pp. 75, 76.   † Reg. of Glas. pp. 99, 100

out of his best and nearest meadows, at the sight of honest men to be chosen for the purpose.* This grant was confirmed by Alexander III. In 1296, William, lord of the manor of Faringdun, swore fealty to Edward I. About the middle of the 14th century, John Burnard appears as lord of this manor.† In 1372, Robert II. granted to Wawayne a ploughgate of land, forfeited by John Scampe, and half of which lay in the territory of Farnyngdon.‡ Richard II. claimed the whole barony of Farnyngdon as his own property. James VI. conferred the lands and hospital on Francis, Earl of Bothwell, which was ratified by Parliament in 1581.§ In 1606, the Earl of Morton was proprietor of the monklands of Pharningtoune.‖ In 1634, the lands of Fernington, with the hospital thereof, belonged to Francis, Earl of Buccleuch.¶ About 1647, George Rutherfurd appears as proprietor of Fairnington.** He was a cadet of the house of Rutherfurd of that ilk. In 1686, George Rutherfurd, younger of Fairnington, married Barbara Hallyburton, daughter of John Hallyburton of Newmains, by Margaret Rutherfurd of Edgerstone. They had a son, George, born in 1691, who "proved a plague to his own family;"

---

* Lib. de Melrose, p. 299. † Ib. p. 300.
‡ Reg. Mag. Sig. pp. 92, 124.
§ Acta Parl. vol. iii. pp. 225-227.
‖ Retours, No. 43.   ¶ Ib. 154.
** For the origin of the Rutherfurds, see vol. ii. p. 274.

and slew his brother-in-law, Thomas Hellyburton of Muirhouselaw, in the beginning of the 18th century. The two brothers-in-law had been attending a county meeting at Jedburgh, and in returning home, quarrelled, it is said, about the right to a well situated upon the line of march between the estates of Fairnington and Muirhouslaw, which join on the north. Rutherfurd followed Hallyburton to this spring, forced him to fight, and there slew him. The place where this fatal encounter occurred is popularly known as the "*Bloody Well*," and is on the Muirhouselaw side of the march fence, nearly on a line with the road leading north from the farm cottages at Fairnington. After this sad event, the family went to the West Indies. About the end of the last century, the manor passed into the hands of Robert Rutherfurd, fifth son of Sir John Rutherfurd of Edgerstone, by Elizabeth Cairncross, daughter of William Cairncross of Langlee.* He was a man universally esteemed. On the 15th October, 1777, Catherine, Autocratrix of all the Russias, by a charter under her own hand, conferred on him and all his posterity and descendants, the title and dignity of a Baron of the Russian empire, in consideration of the peculiar services rendered by him as her agent at

---

* The race of the Border Rutherfurds seems to have been singularly prolific. The couple here mentioned had 19 children; another had 22; and others, 14 and 15.

Leghorn and Tuscany. The manor was greatly improved by the baron. He kept it in his own hands, and cultivated and planted the lands with great skill. No place was more distinguished for growing potatoes. At this time potatoes were not considered a crop, and were only planted in small quantities around the chief towns. The baron, in the belief that it was the best crop for bringing in and improving the land, planted annually about 12 acres. The produce was in some parts of the land 400 firlots per acre, and, when sold, brought one shilling per firlot.* Both the spiritual and temporal interests of those who lived on the estates were attended to by the baron. In the village, which then contained 100 souls, he established a school, paid the salary of the teacher, granted an additional allowance for keeping a Sunday school, where all were "instructed in the principles of religion and morality." There were no poor on the manor, as the baron supplied all the wants of the families of his labourers. He afforded them medical assistance; and inoculation of the small-pox was successfully practised, *gratis*, within the bounds of the estate.† At the death of this truly estimable man, the estate went to his nephew, John Rutherfurd of Edgerstone, at whose death, in

---

* Ure's View of the Agriculture of Roxburghshire, published in 1794.

† Old Statistical Account, vol. xix. p. 127.

1834, the next male heir, Charles Rutherfurd, son of John Rutherfurd of Mossburnford,* descended from

---

* This gentleman was born at Scarborough, in Yorkshire, in 1746. His father having died at Barbadoes, while yet an infant, he was sent to Scotland, to the care of his grandfather, Sir John Rutherfurd of Edgerstone. When he had attained the age of fifteen, it was determined to send him out to New York, to his uncle, Walter Rutherfurd, who had settled there, and amassed a considerable fortune by commerce, besides being proprietor of a large tract of country, which still bears his name, "Rutherford County." Soon after his arrival in America, he was sent by his uncle to Fort Detroit, in charge of military stores, with supplies for the garrison; and having executed his commission, was about to return to New York, when he was prevailed upon to accompany an exploring party to the Lakes, which set out on May 2, 1763, under command of Captain Robson of the 77th Regiment. Sir Robert Danvers also accompanied the expedition. The object of it was to ascertain whether the lakes and rivers between Detroit and Michellematana were navigable for vessels of a greater burden than the small *batteaux* then made use of. Whilst sounding about the mouth of the river Huron, they were surprised by a large party of Indians, and Captain Robson, Sir Robert Danvers, and a number of the party killed. Mr. Rutherfurd and several others were taken captive, and remained for some months with the Indians, when he made his escape, and, after a perilous flight, reached Detroit. He wrote a very interesting narrative of his captivity and hairbreadth escapes, a MS. of which is in my possession. He afterwards joined the 42nd Regiment, in which corps he obtained an ensigncy at a time when they were preparing an expedition against the Shawnessee and Delaware Indians, to the westward, under the command of General Bouquet. In that regiment he served thirty years, during which time he was engaged in both American wars. On quitting the army, he

Thomas Rutherfurd, the immediate elder brother of Baron Rutherfurd, succeeded to the barony. It is now possessed by Thomas Rutherfurd, brother of the said Charles, lineally descended from the Rutherfurds of that ilk. He married Caroline Sanderson Ball, daughter of William Ball and Lydia Wivell, London; and had issue, 13 children, of whom 12 are alive.

The mansion is pleasantly situated on the right bank of a rivulet, running in an easterly direction. There are a few old trees in the park; but the greater part of the wood was planted by Baron Rutherfurd, of which the fir is said to be of excellent quality. On the west end of the estate, near to the Watling-street, is Downlaw, or Dunlaw, a round eminence of several hundred feet high, on the summit of which are the ruins of an observatory or summer residence, built by the baron, where he spent much of his time.* The view from this spot is extensive and beautiful. About a hundred yards to the west of the Watling-street, on the summit of a ridge, is a stone column, about twelve feet in cir-

---

retired to his estate of Mossburnford, on the right bank of the Jed. At this place the poet Burns enjoyed the hospitality of the old soldier, in June, 1787. At a subsequent period, he was appointed Major of the Dumfries Militia, under the command of the Earl of Dalkeith. He died at Jedburgh, on 12th July, 1830, in the 84th year of his age.

* This building is popularly known by the name of the "*Baron's Folly.*" He had no doubt selected this place on account of its beautiful prospect.

cumference, and five feet high, called the Stanan Stane. It is upon the farm of Heriotsfield, on the estate of Ancrum, and, taking every circumstance into consideration, it seems probable that this place was the scene of the battle of Ancrum Moor, and the fair maid Lilliard's exploits. The ground further to the north, where the modern stone stands, cannot be made to suit the description given of the battle-field by ancient chroniclers, but the locality of the Stanan Stane answers in every respect. A field to the east of Fairnington village is called *Harlaw*, from a circle of large stones which stood within it, but which have been removed to serve farm purposes. The old road from Jedfoot to Maxton and Rutherfurd ran through the middle of the estate. Traces of an old ditch, referred to in the charters of the 13th century, as the boundary between Maxton and Roxburgh parishes, may still be seen where the two estates of Muirhouselaw and Fairnington join.

The *Chapel* or *Hospital* of *Fairnington* stood on the right bank of the rivulet, near to the mansion. The exact site of it may be found on a careful examination of the ground. It existed as the property of the Bishop of Glasgow before 1186. At that period, Pope Urban III. confirmed the chapel of Fairnindun, with pertinents thereof, to the bishop.[*]
About 1200, Allan the chaplain was witness to a

---

[*] Reg. of Glasg. p. 55.

charter of Roger Burnard, the son of Fairnindun.*
A charter of Ralph Burnard, son and heir of Roger,
to the house of Alnecrombe, is witnessed by Pauli-
nus, the chaplain of Faringdun.† In 1476, Duncan
of Dundas was curate to William Mateland of Leth-
ington, of the chapel of Fairningtoune.‡ At this
chapel, the arbiters, in a dispute between the laird
of Makerstoun and Nicholl Ormiston, in 1493, were
appointed by the Lords of Council to meet.§ The
hospital of Fermington was granted by James VI.,
and ratified by Parliament in 1585. In 1634, it
was the property of the Earl of Buccleuch. In 1656,
Andrew Ker was owner of the lands pertaining to
the hospital of Fairnington, with common of pasturage, and liberty to dig peats in the moss. The hospital lands form now a part of the estate of Fairnington.

MACCHUSWEL; MACCUSWELL; MACKESWEL; ||
MACCUSVILLE;¶ MAXWELL; MAXWEILLE.**—The
first time this territory appears on record, is in the
days of David I., by whom it was granted to an attached follower of the name of *Maccus*. He is a
witness to the *Inquisitio Davidis*, in 1116, and is

---

* Lib. de Melros, p. 75. † Reg. of Glas. pp. 99, 100.
‡ Act. Dom. Aud. p. 44. § Ib. p. 312, supra, p. 146.
|| Circa, 1159, 1300; Lib. de Calchou, pp. 176, 316, 470;
Chron. de Mailros, pp. 154, 319; Reg. of Glas. p. 102.
¶ Circa, 1200. ** Circa, 1354; Lib. de Calchou, p. 382.

in that document styled, "*Maccus Filius* UND-WEYN."* He built a town, church, and mill, and called the whole territory after his own name, *Maccuswel*. It is said by Chalmers, that *wel* is a corruption of *vil*, and that the name denotes the ville, or dwelling, of *Maccus;* but the earliest form in which the name appears, terminates in the Saxon *wel*, and the Norman *ville*, so far as I am aware, is only seen in a charter of William the Lion, granting to Robert, the son of Maccus, that part of Lessudden, in Roxburghshire, which was comprehended in the barony of Maccus*ville*, and which had formerly belonged to Herbert Maccus*ville*, the sheriff of Roxburghshire.† The barony is situated between the rivers Teviot and Tweed, and was co-extensive with the parish of the same name, now united to Kelso. Edmund Liulphus and Robert, said to be the sons of Maccus, witnessed several charters of David I., Malcolm IV., and William the Lion.‡ Between 1159 and 1180, Herbert of Maccusville was sheriff of Teviotdale, and his son, John, filled the same office. He was also chamberlain to Alexander II.|| Between 1258 and 1266, Aymer of Makuswell was sheriff of Dumfries, justiciar of Galloway, and

---

* Reg. of Glas. p. 5.
† Charter quoted in Burke's Peerage, p. 668.
‡ Lib. de Calchou, p. 145; Lib. de Mailros, pp. 56, 57, 141.
|| Lib. de Calchou, p. 309. He was buried in Melrose in 1241.—Chron. de Mail. p. 206.

chamberlain to Alexander III. He acquired lands in the shires of Renfrew and Dumfries. In 1290, Herbert of Maccuswel was appointed one of the commissioners to treat with Edward I., in regard to a marriage between his son and the heiress of the crown of Scotland.* In 1292, he was named by John Baliol, to maintain his claim to the crown of Scotland.† In 1296, Herbert swore fealty to Edward I. at Montrose.‡ In the same year, John, his son, took the same oath to the usurper. Eustace of Maxwell was celebrated for his defence of Caerlaveroch Castle against the English. He was one of the conservators of truce with the English in 1336.§ At the battle of Nevilles Cross, his brother John was taken prisoner, and committed to the tower of London. In 1343, Herbert had a safe-conduct to London, and John was one of those appointed to treat as to the liberation of David Bruce. In 1374, Robert of Maxwell got a safe-conduct from Edward III., to visit the tomb of St. Thomas of Canterbury. Richard II. granted to the same Robert, a safe-conduct to England; and in 1414, Henry V. granted him leave to enter England. In 1471, John, the son and heir of Robert of Maxwell, received a grant of the baronies of Maxwell and Caerlaveroch, and of the lands of Mearns.‖ In 1484, John, lord Maxwell,

---

* Rymer's Fœdera, vol. i. P. 111, p. 66. † Ib. p. 98.
‡ Ragman's Rolls, p. 87. § Rotuli Scotiæ, vol. i. p. 397.
‖ Reg. Mag. Sig., lib. viii. No. 74.

was keeper of the Western Marches. Four years after, he got a safe-conduct from Henry VIII.* In 1491, John, lord Maxwell, and his wife, Agnes Stewart, possessed the lands of Wodden, and the lands of St. Thomas' Chapel, in conjunct-fee and liferent. In 1534, a charter was granted to Robert, lord Maxwell, of the baronies of Maxwell and Caerlaveroch.† In 1548, Robert, lord Maxwell, in presence of the Governor and the Lords of Articles, gave in a writing to be passed into a statute, to the effect that, "it shall be lawful to all our sovereign lady's lieges, to have the Holy Writ, both the New Testament and the Old, in the vulgar tongue, in English or Scots, of a good and true translation, and that they shall incur no crime for the having or the reading of the same," which was agreed to, as there was no law "*to the contrary;*" the Archbishop of Glasgow, for himself, and in name and behalf of the prelates of the realm, dissenting.‡ In 1550, Robert, lord Maxwell, was served heir to his father, and the said Robert Maxwell, of the barony of Maxwell and Caerlaveroch. John, lord Maxwell, obtained a grant of the Earldom of Morton, in 1581, after the execution of Regent Morton, his grandfather, but which reverted to the lawful heir of the Regent, on the attainder being rescinded by Parliament in 1585.

---

* Rotuli Scotiæ, vol. ii. 1488.
† Reg. Mag. Sig., lib. xxv. No. 145.
‡ Acta Parl. P. 11, p. 415, No. 12.

In 1581, John, earl of Morton, lord Maxwell, appeared before Parliament, and protested that he had a right to hold the lands of Pendiclehill, Wester Wooden, St. Thomas's Chapel, the half of the haugh, the half mill of Maxwell, with their pertinents lying within the barony and lordship of Maxwell, belonging to the said earl, free of any claims, at the instance of Sir Thomas Ker of Ferniehirst, Thomas Ker of Cavers, and Adam Turnbull of Billerwell, which protestation the King, with advice of Parliament, admitted.* In 1593, Lord Maxwell was killed in a battle with the clan Johnstones in Anandale. Spottiswoode says, that he was a nobleman of great spirit, humane, courteous, and more learned than noblemen generally were in these times. John, lord Maxwell, his eldest son, succeeded, and being of a vindictive spirit, put to death Sir James Johnstone of that ilk, in revenge for the slaughter of his father by the Johnstones. He escaped to France, where he remained five years. On his return in 1613, he was arrested, and immediately tried for the slaughter of Johnstone, and for fire-raising, for which he was attainted, condemned, and executed. In 1617, his forfeiture was reversed, and as he left no issue, his estates and honours were restored to his brother Robert. In 1619, Robert was served heir to his brother John, of the barony of Maxwell.†

---

* Acta Parl. vol. iii. p. 282. † Retours, No. 98.

He was created Earl of Nithsdale in 1620. The earls of Nithsdale were strongly attached to the royal family during the civil war. Robert, his son, the second earl, was imprisoned by the Parliament in 1646. Before 1663, the lands were in possession of Sir Andrew Ker of Greenhead. In 1676, William, lord Ker, was served heir of his brother, Sir Andrew Ker, of Greenhead, *inter alia*, of "the lands of Maxwellheugh, with the half of the valley, or haugh, called "Maxwellhaugh," with half of the mills; the lands of Wodin, in the barony of Maxwell; the lands called St. Thomas Chapel, half of the lands of Maxwellhauch, with meadows; half of the mills of Maxwellheuch, half of the multures and lordship of Maxwellfield, and lands of Brigend; portions of the town and lands of Heiton; the town and lands of Softlaw and fishings.*

In 1750, the estate of Bridgend, comprehending a great part of the barony of Maxwell, was purchased by James Douglas, a naval officer, from Sir William Ker of Greenhead. He was the second son of George Douglas of Friarshaw, in the parish of Bowden, whose predecessors had possessed the estate since the middle of the 16th century, when they branched off from the family of Douglas of Cavers. He was captain of the ship *Alcide*, which brought over Colonel Hale, with an account of the victory

---

* Retours, No. 270.

and surrender of Quebec in 1759. The news created the greatest joy among the populace; and the king expressed his satisfaction by conferring the honour of knighthood on Captain Douglas, and gratified him and Colonel Hale with considerable presents. In 1761, Sir James commanded in the Leeward Islands, took Dominica, and had a broad pendant at the siege of Martinique in the same year. In June 27, 1786, he was created a baronet, as a reward for his gallant services rendered to the country. He married, first, Helen, daughter of Sir Thomas Brisbane, and by her had two sons, George and James. He died in 1787. Sir George, who was born in 1754, succeeded, and married Elizabeth, daughter of David, earl of Glasgow, by whom he left an only son, John James, who married, in 1822, Hannah Charlotte, only daughter and heiress of Henry Scott of Belford, on the Bowmont Water, and in consequence assumed the name of Scott by sign-manual, in addition to that of Douglas.* By this lady he had one son and three daughters. Sir John James Douglas was a captain in the 34th Hussars, and served at Waterloo, for which he got a medal. He was succeeded, in 1836, by his only son, George Henry Scott Douglas, born June 19, 1825. Sir George was a captain in the 34th Regiment, and

---

* This lady was descended from the ancient family of Scots of Horsliehill in Teviotdale.

married, in 1851, Maria Juana Petronella, eldest daughter of Senor Don Francisco Sanches Senano di Pena, of Gibraltar, and has issue, three children.

The old mansion of *Brigend* stood in the haugh, where two silver-trees grow, and near to the old ford in the Teviot. From the place being called Brigend before 1545, it may be inferred that the river was crossed by a bridge at this place. The name could not refer to a bridge over the Tweed, as no bridge existed over that river till 1754. The *Brigend* was destroyed by Hertford in 1545.* In 1718, the house was burned by accident while it belonged to Sir Andrew Ker of Greenhead. Timothy Pont places a tower at the confluence of the two rivers, which probably was the original stronghold of the Maxwells.† The mill stood, within the memory of man, a little farther up the river Teviot.

On the family of Douglas acquiring the property, the old house was taken down, the present elegant mansion built in 1756, and the name changed to SPRINGWOOD PARK. The archway was designed by Gillespie Grahame, and erected by Sir John James Scott Douglas in 1822. The house occupies a very

---

* Hayne's Statistical Papers, p. 53. May not this place be the Berton of King Robert's Charter? Robert the Bruce granted to Hugh de la Vikers the lands and villages of Roxburgh, *Berton*, and Maxwell, which had belonged to Ade Mindrum and William Dalton.—Robertson's Index, p. 5.

† Blaeu's Atlas.

lovely situation on the right bank of the Teviot, nearly opposite to the ruins of Roxburgh Castle. At this place the ground begins to rise, and gradually increases in height till it reaches Maxwellheugh, when it becomes the south bank of the river Tweed. On the north of this bank is an extensive haugh, bounded by the rivers Teviot·and Tweed. From the house, several fine views are obtained. On the north are the ruins of Roxburgh; and beyond, the palace and dark woods of Floors; while looking eastward, Kelso and its ruined abbey forms a lovely picture. Although the woods are comparatively young, there are a number of fine trees in the park. It is interesting to notice a wych elm growing at the side of the easter approach, measuring five feet nine inches at the ground. This tree is a slip from the celebrated trysting tree, which grew at Friars, and was planted by James White, forester. An elm near the Teviot lodge is 13 feet 7 inches in girth; another tree of the same kind near the garden, 14 feet 11 inches. A plane-tree, near the same place, measures 14 feet 4 inches. A crab-tree in the chapel park, at two feet from the ground, measures 10 feet 8 inches, and rises 40 feet high. A poplar at Maxwellheugh is 92 feet high; the height of the main stem is 26 feet 6 inches; its girth at the ground measured, in 1828, 31 feet 8 inches; in 1859, 32 feet 6 inches; the smallest girth of the stem measured, in 1828, 16 feet 10 inches; in 1859, 18 feet 8 inches. At the height of 12 feet, 19 feet 6 inches in 1828; and at the present day, it measures 24 feet. It contains above 760 feet of wood, and is worth about £63, 6s. 8d.

Higher up the river Teviot stood the *Maisondieu*, or Hospital of Roxburgh, for the reception of pilgrims, the diseased, and the indigent—every stone of which has been removed: the very foundations have been digged out. It is said by Morton, that garden flowers run wild mark the spot of its garden; but a farm onstead having once occupied the site of the hospital, it is impossible to say whether the flowers to be seen in the locality indicate the garden of the Maisondieu or that of the farmhouse.*

Near to the hospital there are very distinct traces of a mill and dam-dyke across the Teviot. It is said that this was the mill of Old Roxburgh, but there is no information existing to enable any one to fix with any degree of certainty the name of this mill.

The village of Maxwellheugh is situated at the summit of the right bank of the Tweed. It is doubtful whether this was the ancient town of the barony of Maxwell, as it is clear that another town in the haugh existed near to the present mill. It is, however, certain that the Earl of Morton had a house at this place before 1581, and it may be presumed to have been at the chief town of the barony. The

---

* Vol. ii. p. 76.

site of the old town is said to have been in the field lying between the present village and Pinnaclehill, and the appearance of the ground would warrant the belief that considerable buildings have existed at that place. Within the grounds of Pinnaclehill, close to the entrance gate, is a considerable tumulus, which might, without any stretch of imagination, be held to be the motehill of Maccus, the original settler. The tumulus is about 35 feet high, having a slope of about 33 yards. Maxwellheugh is in the list of places destroyed by Hertford in his wasteful inroad of 1545. From the top of the cliff forming the bank of the Tweed, but especially on the summit of the ridge to the west of the village, extensive views are obtained of scenery unrivalled in the Border land. Many of the houses are old, but the proprietor, Sir George Douglas, is in the course of taking all the mean houses down, and building in their stead tasteful and commodious cottages.

The lands of *Softlaw* formed a part of the barony of Maxwell. In 1296, these lands were possessed by Adam de Softlawe. In the 14th century, a family of Sadler was proprietor of Softlaw. In 1354, Robert Sadler gave to Roger of Auldton, Wester Softlaw, with the privilege of grinding corn at the mill of Softlaw "roumfre," on condition of giving annually, at the feast of St. John the Baptist at Maxwell, the head mansion of the lord, the fee of a pair of gold spurs, or 12 pence sterling.* John, the lord of Maxwell, when he confirmed the grant, did so without the condition. Roger of Auldton conferred the lands on the church of St. James at Roxburgh, for the support of a chantry and the minister thereof. This grant was confirmed by David II., Edward III., and William, bishop of Glasgow. In 1374 the lands of Softlaw were granted by Robert II. to John of Maxwell, forfeited by William Stewart. Richard II. granted the towns of Maxwell and Softlaw to Richard Horslie. In 1534, Elizabeth Fallaw, one of the heirs, wife of John Bredin, Selkirk, sold to Andrew Ker of Primsydloch her half of the lands of Softlaw. In the seventeenth century the lands passed into the families of Ker and Kene.†

The church of Maccuswel was situated in the haugh near to the junction of the rivers Teviot and Tweed. It was dedicated to St. Michael. Before 1159, Herbert of Maccuswel, sheriff of Teviotdale, granted the church to the monks of Kelso. The grant was confirmed by Malcolm IV., in 1159; by Jocelin, bishop of Glasgow, in 1180; by William the Lion, before 1199; and in 1232, by Walter, bishop of Glasgow.‡ The church was held, *in*

---

* Lib. de Calchou, p. 302.
† Retours.
‡ Lib. de Calchou, pp. vi. 111, 316, 319, 229.

rectoria, by the monks, and was estimated at £11, 16s. 8d. yearly.

The graveyard of the church is marked by a clump of trees in the haugh near to the mill. There are still a few tombstones sufficiently legible to tell the names of those who rest in this sacred spot, but the inscriptions on many of the stones have been defaced, and no doubt numbers carried away. The oldest inscription that I could read is on a stone raised to a family of the name of Cadonhead, and dated 1680. Another bears the name of Refal, dated 1692. One, Waugh of Windywals, was buried in 1703, and the latest inscription is on a stone erected to a family of Broomfields in 1748. This little graveyard is now carefully preserved.

When Herbert the Sheriff gave the church of the territory to the monks, he erected an oratory within his court of Maccuswel, dedicated to St. Thomas the Martyr, and which he appended to the gift to the monks with a toft. Considerable diversity of opinion exists as to the site of this chapel. In Stobie's old map, it is marked to the south of the present mansion, in a field still called St. Thomas' Lands, near to the *Maisondieu*. The writer of the New Statistical Account follows Stobie, and conjectures the site to have been at the place pointed out by the chorographer. On the other hand, Morton states that it stood at *Harlaw*, near to the head of Woodenburn, about a mile from Maxwell, and that stone coffins have been found on the spot supposed to have been the cemetery of the chapel, but no authority is given for the statement.* There can be little doubt of the *toft* which Herbert annexed to the chapel being correctly marked by Stobie, as the name has been continued till the present day; still it does not follow that the chapel was planted there by the Sheriff. In the grant by Edward III. to Sampson Hauberger, of the chapel of St. Thomas, in November, 1361, it is described as *in* Maxwell, opposite to Roxburgh.† Next year, the same king granted the chapel to St. Thomas of Middleton, which he calls *of* Maxwell, and as standing opposite or near to Roxburgh.‡ In the list of places given by Hertford as destroyed by him in 1545, "St. Thomas' Chapel" is placed between Brigend and Maxwellheugh. But may not the name of *Pendicill* not fix the site of the chapel, which was a *pendicle* to the church of Maccuswell? A number of chapels granted under similar circumstances are called *pendiciles*, which signifies the chapel appended to the Mother Church. If this view be correct, then the site of the chapel of St. Thomas the Martyr must be looked for near to the little *law* or tumulus at the entrance gate to Pinnaclehill—a corruption of *Pen-*

---

* Monastic Annals, p. 110, Note.
† Rotuli Scotiæ, vol. i. p. 857.
‡ Ib. p. 865.

*dicillhill.** The grant of this chapel and toft was confirmed by Bishop Josceline in 1180, and by William the Lion. In 1232, Walter, bishop of Glasgow, confirmed the grant at Alnecrum, and Pope Innocent IV. before 1254. At the time the grant was confirmed by the bishop, an agreement was entered into between the lepers of Alnecrum and the monks, that the latter should hold it in connexion with their church of Maccuswil.† As already seen, when the territory was in the hands of Edward III., he presented Sampson Hauberger and Thomas de Middleton to the chapel of St. Thomas of Maxwell.‡

SPROSTON; SPROUISDONE; SPROUISTON; SPROUSSTONE; SPROUSTON.—The name of this place is first seen in the foundation charter of David, Prince of Cumberland, to the monks of Selkirk, in 1114. The origin of the name cannot be traced with any degree of certainty. Chalmers conjectures that the territory " may have derived its singular name from some person called *Sprous*, who cannot now be traced, whose *tun* or dwelling it may have been. The same name may, however, be derived from the qualities of the place. *Sprus*, in the Cornish speech, signifies grain, and seems to be connected with the Saxon *Sprote;* and

---

* In former times, the entire farm was known as Wester Wooden. *Pendicill* appears in the 13th century.

† Lib. de Calchou, pp. 229, 316, etc.

‡ Rotuli Scotiæ, vol. i. pp. 857, 865.

hence Spruston, or Sproteton, may denote, the place fruitful in grain."* I think the conjecture, that the name denotes a place fruitful in grain, is untenable. It occurs to me that the name may be derived from *Sprossen*, signifying to shoot out, descriptive of the shape of the territory. The *manor* of Sprouston was the property of Earl David, and remained in the hands of the Crown till about 1193, when it was granted by William the Lion to Sir Eustace de Vescy, on his marriage with Margaret, the bastard daughter of that king by a daughter of Sir Adam Hutchinson. It seems to have included all the parish, with the exception of Redden and Haddon. Eustace de Vescy was the possessor of the barony of Alnwick and Malton, in Northumberland. He was the great-grandson of Ivo de Vescy, one of the followers of William the Conqueror, who gave to him in marriage Alda, daughter of William Tyson, proprietor of the barony of Alnwick, and who fell at the battle of Hastings in defence of his king. The issue of this marriage was an only daughter, Beatrix, who carried Alnwick, Malton, and other possessions, to Eustace St. John, the one-eyed lord of Knaresburgh, in Yorkshire, who, with consent of his wife, founded the abbeys of Alnwick and Malton. The issue of this marriage was William, who assumed to himself and posterity the surname and arms of De Vescy. About

---

* Caledonia, vol. ii. p. 191.

1150, he witnessed a grant by Robert, bishop of St. Andrews, of the church of Lohworuora, to Herbert, bishop of Glasgow.* He was Sheriff of Northumberland from 1154 to 1158.† He married Burga, the daughter of Robert Esto Hevil, and by her had Eustace de Vescy, who became Baron of Alnwick, Malton, and Sprouston. In 1207, Eustace and Margaret his wife confirmed to the monks of Kelso all their possessions, rights, and liberties, within the barony, and compounded the tithes of the mill of Sprouston by an annual payment of twenty shillings for lights to the church of Kelso, to be paid by the tenant of the mill, at two terms in the year, Martinmas and Whitsunday, on condition that the monks would receive him and his wife and their heirs into the society of the House, and absolve the souls of his father and mother, and make them partakers of all the spiritual privileges of the monastery for ever.‡ In the same year, the monks granted leave to Eustace and his wife to erect a chapel in their court of Sprouston, where they might hear divine service, provided that the priest should obey the abbot and convent of Kelso, and the mother church should not be injured to the amount of fourpence yearly; that the chaplain of the mother church

---

* Reg. of Glas., p. 13.
† Hutchinson's Northumberland, vol. ii. p. 452.
‡ Lib. de Calchou, pp. 172, 173.

should receive all the offerings of the lord of the manor and parishioners of the district, whether their master should be present or not, and also of all the guests there, so long as the master and mistress were present, except those who resided in the parish.* In 1212, being accused of a conspiracy against the life of the king, Eustace de Vescy took refuge in Scotland. In 1216, he did homage to his brother-in-law Alexander II., which so displeased King John, that he marched into the north with a large army, and destroyed Felton, Mitford, Morpeth, Alnwick, Wark, and Roxburgh. Whilst John made his wasteful inroad into Northumberland, Eustace de Vescy, with Alexander II., entered England, and proceeded as far as Bernard Castle, the seat of the Baliol family in the county of Durham, to which they laid siege; and Eustace, approaching too near the fortress, with the view of planning an assault, was killed by an arrow from one of the outposts. His son William succeeded to the great possessions of his father. He married Isabel, daughter of the Earl of Salisbury, but had no issue: afterwards, he married Agnes, a daughter of the Earl of Derby, and had by her John de Vescy, who, dying without issue, was succeeded by his brother William de Vescy, who died in 1297, without leaving any legitimate children. It was this William de Vescy who gave in a claim

---

* Lib. de Calchou, p. 172.

to the crown of Scotland in 1292. He was the last Baron de Vescy. On the death of William de Vescy, King Edward issued a command that the lands and tenements in Scotland held in dowry by Isabella, the wife of John de Vescy, and all the land and tenements assigned to Clemence, the wife of John, the son of William de Vescy, who had been scised in these lands on the death of said William de Vescy, should be restored.* Robert Bruce conferred the barony on his son Robert I.† David II. granted the barony of Sprouston, before 1371, to Thomas Murray, and afterwards to Maurice Murray.‡ In 1402, Henry IV. conferred the barony on Henry Percy, earl of Northumberland. In 1451, the barony of Sprouston was given to William, earl of Douglas.§ In 1591, the lands of Sprouston were given to Sir Robert Kerr of Cessford. In 1629, Lord John Cranston was served heir to his father William, lord Cranston, of the lands of Sprouston, and of the office of baillie of the whole regality. In 1644, Henry, lord Ker, and his wife received a grant of the demesne lands of Sprouston. In 1675, Robert, earl of Roxburgh, was served heir to his father William, earl of Roxburgh, in the town and

---

* Rotuli Scotiæ, vol. i. pp. 45, 46.
† Robertson's Index, p. 12, No. 62.
‡ Ib. p. 45, No. 17, p. 54, No. 3.
§ Reg. Mag. Sig., lib. iv. No. 148.

demesne lands of Sprouston.* Within the barony of Sprouston, a number of persons held lands as vassals of the lord of the manor. At the end of the war of independence, King Robert I. bestowed the twenty-pound lands of Sprouston on William Franceis, forfeited by persons of the names of William Rict, Henry Drawer, Thomas Alkoats, John, Thomas, and William, the sons of Allan and Hugh Limpitlaw. The same king also gave to Aymer of Hauden eleven husbandlands of Sprouston, extending to twenty-merk lands, which Robert Sprouston and others forfeited by serving the English king during the war.

The monks of Kelso possessed considerable property in Sprouston. Before David ascended the throne, he conferred on the monks of Selkirk a ploughgate of land in *Sproston*, and ten acres of arable land and a measure pertaining to a ploughgate.† After he became king, he added three acres of meadowland, the pastures of Sprouston, and moor for making turf. Malcolm IV. granted, in 1159, two oxgangs of lands near Prestrebridge in said territory, in exchange for two oxgangs in Berwick. In 1165, Serlo, the king's clerk, granted the monks half a ploughgate in the territory of Sprouston. Ralph de Veir, or Weir, during the reign of William the Lion, gave to the monks an oxgang of land next to the lands of his man Umford. About 1300,

---

* Retours.   † Lib. de Calchou, pp. 4, 5.

they had in Sprouston two ploughgates, with right of common pasture for 12 oxen, 4 work horses, and 300 year-old lambs. An oxgang of land held by Hugh Cay yielded them ten shillings yearly. They had also six cottages, one of which, near the vicar's house, had a brewhouse and six acres of land attached, let for six shillings yearly; the other five, which lay at the other extremity of the village called Latham, had each an acre and a-half, and let each for six shillings and six days' work in the year.

David I. granted to the monks of Kelso the church of Sprouston, which was confirmed by John, bishop of Glasgow; by Bishop Josceline, in 1180; by Bishop Walter, in 1232; and by Pope Innocent IV. before 1254. The grant was also confirmed by William the Lion. The church was dedicated to St. Michael. The present church was built in 1781.

The village of Sprouston is situated about 200 yards south of the Tweed, and consists of about 100 cottages. It was at one time of considerable extent, and defended by a strong tower. In 1790, there were 30 weavers in the town. The locality is remarkable for the advanced age of many of its inhabitants. About 1790, a number of persons were living from 70 to 100 years old. There is here a ferry on the Tweed.

The priory of Charterhouse possessed half of the Midtown and Mains of Sprouston, which are now the property of the Duke of Roxburgh.

In 1256, the king and queen of England, accompanied by a numerous retinue of knights, earls, and barons, took up their residence for some days at Sprouston, till their son-in-law, Alexander, king of Scotland, and his nobles, prepared and delivered a deed into the hands of the English king, for the peace and government of Scotland. In 1418, the town was destroyed by Sir Robert Umfraville. In 1522, it was burned by Ross and Dacre. In the same year, it was burned by the Duke of Norfolk's army, in its progress up the Tweed. Two years after, it shared the fate of other towns and villages, in an inroad by Sir Ralph Eurie. It was again destroyed by the Earl of Hertford in 1545.

The lands of Easter Softlaw were, before 1514, possessed by Elizabeth Fawlay. At that date they were granted to Thomas Ramsay, with the office of common sergeant of the county of Roxburgh.

REVEDEN; REDDEN.—This territory lies to the east of Sprouston, and before 1140 was mostly in the hands of the king. At that time King David I. granted the domain to the monks of Kelso, with rights of water, pasture, and peatry, excepting a ploughgate, which belonged to the hospital of Roxburgh.* This grant was confirmed by William the Lion. In 1210, the monks got from Bernard of

---

* Lib. de Calchou, p. 297.

Hauden, the mill of Redden, with its pond, part of the meadow lying near the rivulet, which of old formed the boundary between Haudon and Redden. In 1258, John of Redden appeared in the abbot's court at Ettrick Bridge, and resigned to the monks a place called Floris, in the territory of Redden, admitting at the time that the lands belonged to the convent, and that he had long unjustly kept them out of it. The monks purchased from Hugh, his son, all the lands held by him and his ancestors in the towns of Redden and Home. In the year 1300 the monks had the grange of Redden, with the town, which they laboured with five ploughs. In the grange they kept 24 score of ewes, and cattle in proportion. They had also eight husbandlands and a ploughgate let to tenants, for which services were rendered by the respective occupants. In summer, each husbandman was bound to go to Berwick, weekly, with one horse cart, carrying three bolls of corn, and returning either with three bolls of salt or one and a half firlots of coals; in winter, two bolls of corn, and returning with one and a half bolls of salt or one boll and a firlot of coals. The husbandman who did not go to Berwick gave two days' work in summer and three in autumn. The stock of the farm was steelbow, and consisted of two oxen and a horse, three chalders of oats, six bolls of barley, and three bolls of wheat. The mill of Redden rented for nine merks yearly. Two brew-houses rented at two merks yearly. The monks had nineteen cottages at Redden, eighteen of which rented for 12 pence yearly, six days' labour in autumn, with their victuals. The cottagers also assisted at the shearing of the sheep of the grange. The nineteenth cottage rented for 18 pence and nine days' labour. David II. erected Kelso, Bolden, and Redden into a regality in favour of the monks, with exclusive jurisdiction. Robert III. confirmed the grant.

The territory of Redden passed to a family of Kene at the Reformation. In 1609, the lands were held by Richard Kene. In 1634, Mary Ker, Lady Carnegie, succeeded to a third part of the lands as heiress of her brother the Master of Roxburgh. In 1675, Redden was the property of Robert, Earl of Roxburghe. Andrew Ker of Greenhead possessed, about the same time, the lands of Thankless.

In the New Statistical Account, Origines Parochiales, and other works, it is mistakenly stated that Reddenburn in this territory was one of the places where commissioners met to settle Border disputes. The court met at Reuedenburne, one of the upper sources of the Jed. It is called Jedwart *Overbourne*.*

HAUDEN; HAWDEN; HADDEN.—This manor was granted by William the Lion to Bernard, the son of Brian, an Anglo-Norman, who assumed Hauden

---

* Acta Parl., vol. i. p. 84.

as his surname. He witnessed many charters of King William the Lion and Alexander II.* Ralph, Peter, Sir Almyer, and William of Hawden, witness many charters of Alexander II. and Alexander III.† Before 1211, Bernard of Hawden, nephew of the first Bernard, was sheriff of Roxburgh. In 1281, William Sulis, the sheriff of Roxburgh, paid Ralph of Haudin eighteen pounds for himself and his men, for losses sustained by the English, from his lands lying on the marches near Reddenburn. In 1292, Edward I. commanded John Twynham, tacksman of the customs of Dumfries, to pay the same sum to Ralph of Hauden, for loss sustained by English inroads, and which it was his wont to receive from the kings of Scotland.‡ Bernard was lord of Hawden in 1354.§ In 1357, Edward III. gave Peter Tempest the manor of Haudin, because the lord thereof had adhered to his enemies of Scotland.|| In 1407, John of Haudene received a grant of the lands of Hawdene, Yetholm, and Brochton.¶ William of Hawden possessed the barony in 1523. In 1624, John Halden was possessed of the 20-pound lands of his barony of Hauden. The lands are now the property of Sir William Elliot of Stobs

---

* Lib. de Calchou; Lib. of Mail.; Reg. Glas.   † Ib.
‡ Rotuli Scotiæ, vol. i. p. 13.
§ Lib. de Calchou, p. 337.
|| Rotuli Scotiæ, vol. i. p. 817.
¶ Reg. Mag. Sig., p. 238, No. 39.

and Wells. The monks of Kelso had a ploughgate of land in Hawden, before Bernard obtained a grant of the territory from William the Lion. This land was confirmed to them by Bernard, who added to it a toft free from all services and customs. In 1170, he gave them ten acres on the west side of the village. When his nephew Bernard confirmed these gifts during the reign of William the Lion, he added eight acres and a rood which lay contiguous to their property on both sides of the road to Carram, between the two fountains called Blindwelle and Croc. In return for these gifts the monks granted leave to Bernard to have a private chapel at Hawden, where he and his guests might hear divine service all the days of the year except on Christmas-day, Easter-day, and the Feast of St. Michael, when they were bound to attend the mother church at Sprouston. The officiating priest was to swear fealty to the abbot, and the offerings of the private chapel were to belong to the parish church.* The monks kept their land in Hawden in their own hands. In 1609, Richard Kene possessed the plew lands of Hawden. In 1675, these lands were in possession of Robert, earl of Roxburghe. During the reign of Alexander II., Bernard of Hawden granted to the hospital of Soltre, which had been erected on the Lammermoors for paupers and pil-

---

* Lib. de Calchou, pp. 174, 175.

grims, four bolls of wheat yearly out of Hawden, at the feast of St. Nicholas.*

HADDENSTANK was one of the places where the commissioners of England and Scotland met to settle disputes. In 1410, the commissioners of the Duke of Albany met the deputies of Henry IV. at this place. In 1542, Sir Robert Bowes, warden of the east marches, accompanied by Angus and his brother, Sir George Douglas, entered Scotland with the design to ravage Teviotdale and sack Jedburgh, but they were met on Haddonrig by the Earl of Huntly and Lord Home, and repulsed. The town of Haddon is situated on Haddonrig, and commands a beautiful and extensive prospect of the valley of the Tweed and a great portion of the Merse. The town was destroyed by the Duke of Norfolk. The manor, owing to its situation on the marches, shared in the full miseries of Border warfare.

LEMPEDLAWE; LEMPEDLAW; LIMPITLAW; LEMPETLAW.—This barony was granted by David I. to Richard Germyn. During the reigns of William the Lion and Alexander II., Richard Germyn witnessed several charters.† In 1222, he granted to the house of the Holy Trinity of Soltre the church

---

* Chart. of the Holy Trinity of Soltre; MS. Advocates' Library, No. 28.

† Lib. de Mail. pp. 127, 154, etc.

of Lempitlaw, with all the lands and rights pertaining thereto.* Sir Adam Quinton was in possession of the arable land called Wellflat, with toft and croft belonging to it in the territory of Lempitlaw, which had been granted by Sir Richard Germyn to Floria, spouse of Sir Adam, during the end of the reign of Alexander III. After Sir Adam's death, his relict, Floria, granted the subjects to the house of Soltre.† In 1463, James III. granted to David Scott, son of Sir Walter Scott of Kirkurd, a charter, erecting into a free barony the lands of Branxholm, Langtown, *Limpitlaw*, Elrig, Rankilburn, Eckford, and Whitchester, to be named the barony of Branxholm.‡ In 1624, Andrew Young was in possession of the five-merk lands of Lempitlaw called Cowenshill.

Geoffrey of Lempitlaw, chamberlain to William the Lion, appears on record about 1190.

The barony of Lempitlaw was originally a separate parish, but it is now united to Sprouston. The church, which stood in the graveyard, has entirely disappeared. The graveyard is still used by the parishioners and those who wish their ashes to lie with their ancestors.

The village consists of about twenty cottages and

---

* Chart. No. 4, Advocates' Library.
† Ib. No. 44.
‡ Retours.

three farmhouses. In the days of Pont a tower stood at Lurdenlaw.*

LINTUN;† LYNTOUN; LYNTON;‡ LINTON.§—This manor appears on record about the beginning of the twelfth century, under the name of *Lintun*, which is thought to be derived from the British *Lyn* and the Saxon *tun* or *ton*, signifying the dwelling on the lake, a name very descriptive of its position in early days. Chalmers, in his "Caledonia," says that Richard Cumyn, a nephew of William Cumyn, chancellor of England, got a grant from David I. of Lintun Manor, then known as Linton Roderick, and that Richard Cumyn afterwards gave the church of this manor to the abbey of Kelso for the soul of his lord, Earl Henry, who died in 1152, and for the soul of his son John, who had been buried in the cemetery of the house. The Rev. James Brotherstone, who wrote the New Statistical Account of the parish, takes the same view, and refers to the chartulary of Kelso as his authority for the statement made by him. But both are mistaken, as the church of Linton Roderick, granted by Cumyn to the monks of Kelso, was the parish church of that

---

* Blaeu's Atlas.
† Circa, 1160, 1249; Reg. Glas. p. 17; Lib. de Melros, p. 129.
‡ Circa, 1275; Reg. Glas. p. 15.
§ Circa, end of 16th century.

name in Peebleshire. Richard Cumyn may have obtained a grant of the manor from David I.; but if so, he must have parted with it previous to his death, in 1189; for, in 1160, William de Sumerville gave three acres of land in the territory of Linton, with the tithes thereof, to the church of Glasgow.* It is certain that Cumyn was in possession of Linton in Peebleshire before 1153, and it is equally certain that he granted the church thereof, with half-a-carrucate of land in the township, to the monks of Kelso, for the soul's rest of his lord, Earl Henry, and of his son John, whose bodies were buried at Kelso, on condition that he himself and Hextild his wife, and their children, should be received into the brotherhood of the convent, and made partakers of its spiritual benefits.† This gift was confirmed by Malcolm IV.; by William the Lion; by Josceline, bishop of Glasgow, before 1199; by Bishop Walter in the year 1232, and by Pope Innocent before 1254.‡ It is obvious that Linton in Teviotdale has been taken for Linton in Peebleshire. The first person whose connexion can be traced with the manor, is William de Sumerville, about 1160. He is said to be the second son of Sir Walter de Sumerville, who was the son of the first Walter de Sumerville, who came over with William the Conqueror, and

---

* Reg. of Glas. p. 17.
† Lib. de Calchou, p. 226. ‡ Ib. pp. vi. 316, 319, etc.

obtained from him the lordship and territory of Whichenour in Staffordshire.* William de Sumerville followed David I. into Scotland, who conferred upon him the lands and barony of Carnwath, in the county of Lanark. He is a witness to the foundation charter of Melrose Abbey in 1136. In 1147, he witnessed a grant made by David of the church of Kylrmont to the bishop of St. Andrews. He is a witness to a charter of Earl Henry, confirming the endowments of his father to the church of St. John in the castle of Roxburgh, dated at Traquair, 1150.† In the same year he witnessed a grant of Robert, bishop of St. Andrews. He witnessed the confirmation charter of Malcolm IV. to the church of Kelso in 1159. He also witnessed the grant of Malcolm IV.,

---

* The eldest son, Sir Walter, succeeded his father in the lordship of Whichenour, and carried on the line of the family in England. From him descended Sir Philip de Somerville, so noted for his hospitality in the reigns of Henry IV. and V. It was this Sir Philip who held the lands of Netherton, Cowlee, Ridware, &c., by the celebrated service of furnishing a flitch of bacon to the married pair who could, on their consciences, declare that they had not once had a difference during the first twelve months of wedlock. The male line of the Whichenour branch terminated in a daughter, who was the wife of the Duke of Buckingham, beheaded in the reign of Henry VIII. From Roger, the third son of the first Sir Walter, sprang William Somerville, born in 1677, author of "The Chase," and other poems. He was the friend of Shenstone, and a correspondent of Allan Ramsay.

† Reg. of Glas. p. 10.

in 1160, to Herbert, the bishop of Glasgow, of the church of Old Roxburgh, with its appurtenances, and the chapel of the castle of Roxburgh.* It is uncertain when he died, but it is thought to have been before 1162. WILLIAM DE SUMERVILLE, his eldest son, succeeded. He was in great favour with Malcolm IV. and William the Lion, and witnessed many of their charters. This William de Sumerville is thought to have been the first of Linton. Tradition relates that he obtained the barony from William the Lion, on his destroying a monster which inhabited a glen in the territory of Linton, about a mile from the church, known at the present day as the Worm's Glen. The monster was in length three Scots yards, and about the thickness of an ordinary man's leg, with a head more proportionate to its length than thickness; in form and colour it resembled a moor adder. When this monster sought after its prey, it usually wandered a mile or two from the glen; creeping among the bent heather, or grass, it was not discovered till it was master of its prey, which it instantly devoured. So great was the destruction of the bestial, that the country people were forced to remove themselves and their cattle to a distance. Neither durst any person go to church or market in that direction, for fear of the worm. Several attempts

---

* Reg. of Glas. p. 14.

were made to destroy it, by shooting arrows and throwing darts from a distance; but as no one durst approach near to it, to use a sword or lance, it only received slight wounds. So terrified were the country people at last, that they imagined that the monster was a judgment sent by God, to plague them for their sins. While the people were in such fear and terror, William Sumerville, who was in the south, hearing such strange reports of the beast, resolved to see it. On his arrival at Jedburgh, where the court was at the time, he found the whole inhabitants in a panic, owing to the stories told by the country people, who had fled to that place for shelter. He was told that it had wings; was full of fire, which blazed out of its mouth at night; and so venomous, that its breath killed the cattle at a considerable distance. However, Sumerville was curious to see this monster, whatever might happen. Having learned that the animal usually left its den at sunrise or sunset, and wandered the fields in search of prey, he went on horseback to the glen by dawn of day. He was not long there, till the beast crawled out of his den, and observing him at a little distance, lifted up its head, with half of the body, staring him in the face, with open mouth, but not offering to advance, on which he took courage and went nearer, that he might examine its shape, and try whether it would attack him or no; but the beast turned in a half-circle, and entered its den. Being informed of the means already used to kill the animal, and being satisfied it could not be destroyed by sword or dagger, owing to the hazard of approaching so near to it as these weapons required; for several days he watched the animal to ascertain the manner of its leaving and entering the den; and finding that it did not retire backwards, but always turned in a half-circle, so that there was no way of killing it but by a sudden approach, by a long spear on horseback; a mode by which, if the body was impenetrable, he might endanger not only the life of his horse, which he loved well, but also his own, to no purpose. At last, he caused a long spear to be made, plated with iron about six quarters from the point upward, on the top of which he placed a lighted peat, and accustomed his horse to the smell of smoke and fire. Having the horse well trained, he made a slender wheel of iron, and fixed it near the point of his lance, that the wheel might turn round on the least touch, without a risk of breaking the lance. All things being ready, he proclaimed to the gentlemen and commons of Teviotdale, that he would, on a certain day, kill the monster, or die in the attempt. Many looked upon the offer as a boast, others as an act of madness on the part of the youth, and endeavoured to advise him to forego the attempt; but no argument could turn him from his purpose. Accordingly, on the appointed day, he placed himself, with his servant, a stout, resolute fellow, within half-an-arrow shot of the mouth of the den, which was no larger than easily to admit the monster, whom he watched with a vigilant eye on horseback, having some small, hard peats, bedaubed with pitch, rosin, and brimstone, fixed with a small wire, on the wheel, at the point of the lance, so that, on being touched with fire, they would immediately burst out into a flame. The proverb, that the fates assist bold men, was verified in this enterprise, for the day was calm, with only as much air as served his purpose. About the rising of the sun, the beast appeared, with its head and part of its body out of the den; on which, the servant, as previously arranged, set fire to the peats on the wheel at the top of the lance, and instantly, Sumerville, putting spurs to his horse, advanced at a full gallop, the fire still increasing, placed the same, with the wheel, and nearly the third part of his lance, directly in the monster's mouth, which went down the throat into the belly, and the lance breaking by the rebounding of the horse, was left there, causing a deadly wound. So great was the strength of the animal, that, in attempting to get back into the den, the whole ground above was raised up and overturned, which aided in its destruction. The body of the serpent, or dragon, was taken from under the rubbish, and exposed for many days to the sight of a great number of people, who came far and near to look on the dead carcase of the creature, which was so great a terror to them while it was alive.* For this gallant action, Sumerville obtained universal applause from the people, and his gracious king honoured him with knighthood, conferred upon him the whole barony of Linton, and

---

* The celebrated poet of Teviotdale, while singing of the scenery of Cayle, alludes to this tradition:

"Pure blows the summer breeze o'er moor and dell,
Since first in Wormiswood the serpent fell:
From years, in distance lost, his birth he drew,
And with the ancient oaks the monster grew,
Till venom, nursed in every stagnant vein,
Shed o'er his scaly sides a yellowy stain,
Save where, upreared, his purfled crest was seen,
Bedropt with purple blots and streaks of green.
Deep in a sedgy fen, concealed from day,
Long ripening, on his oozy bed he lay;
Till, as the poison-breath around him blew,
From every bough the shrivelled leaflet flew,
Grey moss began the wrinkled trees to climb,
And the tall oaks grew old before their time.

"On his dark bed the grovelling monster long
Blew the shrill hiss, and launched the serpent prong,
Or, writhed on frightful coils, with powerful breath,
Drew the faint herds to glut the den of death;
Dragged, with unwilling speed, across the plain,
The snorting steed, that gazed with stiffened mane;
The forest bull, that lashed, with hideous roar,
His sides indignant, and the ground up-tore.
Bold as the chief, who, 'mid black Lerna's brake,
With mighty prowess quelled the water-snake,
To rouse the monster from his noisome den,
A dauntless hero pierced the blasted fen:
He mounts, he spurs his steed;—in bold career,
His arm gigantic wields a fiery spear;

appointed him Royal Falconer. The grateful people of Teviotdale perpetuated the gallant exploit, which freed the territory of Linton from such a monster, by cutting out in stone the figure of young Sumerville, as he performed the deed, and placed it above the principal door of Linton church, with an inscription referring to the event.* The inscription has

---

>   With aromatic moss the shaft was wreathed,
>   And favouring gales around the champion breathed;
>   By power invisible the courser drawn,
>   Now quick, and quicker, bounds across the lawn;
>   Onward he moves, unable now to pause,
>   And fearless, meditates, the monster's jaws,
>   Impels the struggling steed, that strives to shun,
>   Full on his wide unfolding fangs to run;
>   Down his black throat he thrusts the fiery dart,
>   And hears the frightful hiss that rends his heart;
>   Then, wheeling light, reverts his swift career.—
>   The writhing serpent grinds the ashen spear;
>   Rolled on his head, his awful volumed train
>   He strains, in tortured folds, and bursts in twain.
>   On Cala's banks, his monstrous fangs appal
>   The rustics, pondering on the sacred wall,
>   Who hear the tale, the solemn rites between,
>   On summer Sabbaths, in the churchyard green."

* In the memoirs of the Baronial House of Somerville, written by James, the eleventh Lord Somerville, who died in 1690, it is stated that *John* was the destroyer of the *worme;* that he was the first of Linton, and the first of the name who acquired lands in Scotland. But the noble author is mistaken. There was not a *John* in the descent of the Scottish branch, till the middle of the fourteenth century; and the John of that time was a third son; besides, it is undoubted

long been effaced, but tradition says it was as follows:—

> "Wode Willie Somerville
> Killed the worm of Wormandaill,
> For whilk he had all the lands of Lintoune,
> And six miles them about."

The monument was to be seen above the door of the little church of Linton, till the summer of 1858; when, in consequence of repairs upon the edifice, it was taken down, and placed outside a newly erected porch. The sculpture presents a rude representation of a horseman, in full armour, with a falcon on his arm, in the act of charging his lance down the throat of a large four-footed animal, not in the least resembling a worm or serpent. Several writers imagine that there is no foundation for the legend, and that the sculpture above the church door gave rise to the legend, and not the legend to the sculpture. But I have no doubt that the legend is in substance true, and that a monster of one kind or

---

that the tradition relates to William Somerville. It is also certain, that William Somerville arrived in Scotland, as a follower of David, Prince of Cumberland, before 1124, and obtained from him the manor of Carnwath, in Lanarkshire. It is said by Chalmers, and several Peerage writers, that the first William Somerville died in 1142, and was buried in Melrose Abbey; but this is also a mistake, as the only entry of a Somerville being buried in that cemetery, is William Somerville, who died in 1242, no doubt, the grandson of the first William.—Chron. Mail. p. 155.

another existed in that place, which made it dangerous to dwell in the locality, and that it was killed by young Somerville. It is very easy to account for the improbable statements as to the power and dimensions of the animal. At that time the old faith would be in the full remembrance of the inhabitants of the district, and no doubt, secretly believed by many; and when such a destructive animal made its appearance, it is not surprising that they should connect it with the obscene spirits, that infested the hills, mosses, and fens, and attribute to it a portion of their power. According to the Gothic mythology, there existed flying dragons, who floated on their wings over the plains, and carried away corpses. One of these is alluded to in the fine Saxon poem of Beowolf, under the name of Grendel:

> "There was a more grim spirit, called Grendel;
> Great was the mark of his steps,
> He that rules the moor,
> The fen, and the fastness."

The place where this *worme* is said to have had its abode would, in former days, be entirely surrounded by lakes, mosses, and fens peculiarly adapted for such a reptile. At that time the Cayle valley, from Marlfield to Crookedshaws, would be almost an entire lake or marsh. Another fen extended from the Bowmont river, by Cherrytrees and Thirlestane, to within a very short distance of a large flow moss, which existed on Greenlees farm, forming a circle of lakes and mosses around Wormesglen.* But Linton was not the only place which was infested at that early day by such animals. Duncan Fraser, an old bard, who lived upon the Cheviot mountains about 1270, sings of a Laidley worm which existed at Spendleston heugh—

> " For seven miles east and seven miles west,
> And seven miles north and south,
> No blade of grass nor corn could grow,
> So venomous was her mouth."

Within the bishopric of Durham, two MANORS were obtained, under nearly the same circumstances as Linton was gained by Somerville. The manor of Sockburn, in Northumberland, originally belonging to the ancient and powerful family of Conyers, is

---

* About 1826, the skull of a beaver was found in Linton loch by Mr. Purves, the tenant, who was in the course of making operations in the morass, so as to get at a very extensive deposit of marl. After penetrating about eight feet of moss which covered the marl, the skull was found on its surface, in an excellent state of preservation. The remains of deer and other animals were also found on the surface of the marl, about twenty yards from the margin of the loch. At other places, horns of the red deer, with bones of animals of the same species, were found at a depth of twenty-two feet from the surface of the moss. At a depth of seven feet within the marl was found the left tibia of an ox, *bos primogenius*, which was computed to have belonged to an animal measuring at least six feet, or, with hoof and soft parts entire, fully half-a-foot more to the summit of the shoulder. Near the margin of the loch, and about seven feet deep in the moss, were found an arrow-head, and two or three small horse-shoes. The moss was divided into three layers, the upper

held by the service of presenting a falchion to every bishop on his first entrance into his diocese, and the use of an ancient form of words when he does so, to the effect that the presenter " represents the person of Sir John Conyer, who, on the fields of Sockburn, with this falchion, slew a monstrous creature, a dragon, a worm, or a flying serpent, that devoured men, women, and children. The then owner of Sockburn, as a reward for his bravery, gave him the manor and its appurtenances, to be held for ever, on condition that he meets the lord Bishop of Durham, with this falchion, on his first entrance into his diocese after his election to that see." It is said that

---

layer about three feet in thickness; the second, measuring about two feet, was not so firm as the upper layer, and changed its colour, of a greenish brown when moist and newly exposed, to almost a white when dry; the third extended to four feet, but in some places to a greater thickness, and of a black colour, holding embedded, in various grades of preservation, the trunks of hazel and birch trees, with an occasional oak, measuring from two to four feet in diameter; large quantities of hazel nuts, in masses, as if gathered and swept from the upper woodlands by the mountain freshets. The stratum of marl was eighteen feet in thickness.—Paper by CHARLES WILSON, M.D., late of Kelso, in the *Edinburgh New Philosophical Journal*, July, 1858.

In Linton loch grew a species of reed, which the inhabitants of the neighbouring villages and onsteads used in the roofing of their houses. With these reeds they also made "bennils" for laying above the joists of their cottages, instead of deals. While the workmen were taking out the marl, they found a strong and copious mineral spring issuing from the sand beneath the marl.

the animal slain was venomed and poisoned, which overthrew and devoured many people, for the scent of the poison was so strong that no person was able to abide it; yet he, by the Providence of God, overthrew it. But, before he entered upon his enterprise, he went to the church in full armour, and offered up his son to the Holy Ghost. This took place before the Conquest. The monument, says a writer of the end of last century, is still to be seen, and the place where the serpent lay is called Graystone.* Pollardslands, in the same county, are held by the same tenure.† In the Cathedral of St. Andrews, the tusks of a boar long hung in the choir, in gratitude for the destruction of the enormous and savage animal to which they belonged.

In the memoir of the family of Somerville, it is said that the destroyer of the *worme* married Elizabeth, daughter of Sir Robert Oliphant of Cessford, whose lands lay next to his own barony of Linton, the water of Cayle being the boundary, and by her had several children.‡ Between 1180 and 1189, he confirmed to Joscelin, bishop of Glasgow, the church of Carnwath, which he had, by the advice of his father and other friends, previously granted to Bishop Englram.§ WILLIAM, his son, succeeded,

---

* Harleian MSS., No. 2118, p. 39.
† Tennant, vol. iii. p. 341.
‡ Memoirs, vol. i. p. 60.
§ Reg. of Glas., p. 46.

and married Margaret, daughter of Walter Newbigging of that Ilk in Clydesdale. In 1239, William, baron of Linton, attended Alexander II. at Roxburgh Castle, on his marriage with Mary of Picardy.* He died in 1242, and was buried in the cemetery of Melrose.† WILLIAM, his son, succeeded, and was knighted by Alexander III. In 1263, he attended the king at the battle of Largs, where he greatly distinguished himself. In 1270, he witnessed a charter of Henry of Halyburton to the monks of Kelso. In 1289, THOMAS of Somerville was one of the commissioners appointed to consult the king of England as to a marriage between his eldest son and the heiress of Scotland.‡ JOHN, his second son, swore fealty to Edward I. in 1296.§ Sir WALTER Somerville of Linton, with his son, Sir David, joined Wallace, and commanded the third brigade of horse at the battle of Biggar, fought in the end of May, 1297. WALTER Somerville followed Robert Bruce to the battle of Methven Wood, near St. Johnstone. His son, Sir David, who was also present, was taken prisoner. In consequence of the Somervilles adhering to the interests of Wallace and Bruce, the barony of Linton was given by Baliol to Walter Cumyn of Kilbride. On

---

* Hailes's Annals, vol. i. p. 185.
† Chron. de Mail. p. 155.
‡ Rymer, vol. i. P. iii. p. 66.
§ Ragman's Rolls, p. 139.

the independence of Scotland being won on the field of Bannockburn, the lands were restored to the lawful owners. In 1348, two years after the unfortunate battle of Durham, where king David was taken prisoner, Edward III. charged the sheriff of Roxburgh to restore the lands forfeited by William of Somerville, in Lynton and Carnwath, to Richard Cumyn of Kilbride, son of Walter Cumyn, to whom the lands had been granted by Baliol.* On King David Bruce regaining his liberty, he granted two charters, one in 1365, and the other in 1369, confirming and ratifying all former rights and charters granted by himself, or father, to and in favour of Walter Somerville, of the barony of Linton and Carnwath, to be held ward of him and of his successors. He died in 1380, at Kelso, on his way to Linton, in the house of William Somerville, his natural son, from whence his remains were conveyed to Linton, and buried in the "queir of the church." JOHN Somerville, his son, was served heir to his father, at Jedburgh, April 10, 1381, before Robert Ker of Cessford. In 1396, he sat as one of the barons of Scotland, in the parliament of Perth, called by Robert III. In 1426, THOMAS Somerville lived at Linton for some time, and while there, repaired the tower, church, and queir of Linton, with the ancient monument to the destroyer of the

---

* Rotuli Scotiæ, vol. i. p. 723.

worme, which, by length of time, and the perpetual incursions and burnings of the English, were much decayed. In 1434, James I. confirmed Thomas of Somerville in the barony of Linton. WILLIAM of Somerville witnessed a confirmation by James II. of charters by David I. and Robert III., to the canons of Holyrood. He died in 1456, and was succeeded by his eldest son, JOHN. During the siege of Roxburghe Castle, in 1460, he was of great service to the king and the army, in furnishing provisions from his own barony of Linton, and adjacent country, which he the more easily accomplished owing to his being nearly allied to the Kers of Cessford and Fernieherst. On the breaking up of the siege, he retired to his tower of Linton. In 1476, WILLIAM of Somerville was infeft in the barony of Linton, confirmed by James III. in the following year. Between 1486 and 1538 the family of Somerville seems to have sold the barony of Linton to the Kers. In 1594, William Ker of Littleden had a grant of the barony, with the patronage of Linton kirk.* In 1608, John Ker of Hirsel, son and heir of Walter Ker of Littleden, obtained a charter of the baronies of Maxton, Linton, and Town Yetham.† In 1619, Linton and Maxton were granted to John Ker, son of Sir John Ker of Jedburgh. In 1670, Elizabeth and Anna

---

* Reg. Mag. Sig., lib. xi. No. 90. † Ib. lib. xii. No. 35.

Scott were served heirs portioners to their father, George Scott, who was the brother of Walter Scott of Whitslaid, in the land and barony of Linton, with the patronage of the church.* In 1686, Janet Pringle was served heir to her father, Robert Pringle of Clifton, of parts of the barony of Linton, viz., the lands of Park, Hindlaw, Burnfoot, Easter and Wester Howden, Glendelhaugh, Ladywelbrae, Swinesclos, part of the lands of Linton, now called Southquarter, and Yaitt, on the south side of the town of Linton, which is the southern division of the lands of Linton; part of the lands of Linton, called Bankhead, and Shielscrocerig, on the north side of the town of Linton, which is the northern division of the lands of Linton, which extend the 22-pound lands with the astricted multure and privilege of the common in Shielscrocemoor, Woolstruther bog, and Wormeden, within the parish and barony of Linton; parts of the lands of Priorlaw, lying runrig, with the privilege of pasture in the parish of Linton.† At the death of Robert Pringle of Clifton and Haining, the lands passed to the present owner, Robert Elliot of Harwood, who, after his accession to the estate, erected an elegant mansion, within a well-wooded park, called CLIFTON Park.

The Kers retained GRADEN to a later period. Andrew, or *Dand* Ker, the laird of Graden, was a

---

* Retours, No. 253. † Ib. No. 290.

man of note on the Borders, in the beginning of the 16th century. He held the lands under Walter Ker of Cessford, who, in 1551, confirmed him anew in the lands, Graden tower, fortalice, and pertinents, in consequence of the old writings being destroyed by the English. In 1679, Henry Ker was laird of Graden, and one of the justices of the peace for the county of Roxburgh for the purpose of suppressing conventicles. Three days after the battle of Bothwell-brig, the Council ordered him to secure Sir Henry Hall of Haughhead, Turnbull of Bewly, Turnbull of Stanehill, and Archibald Riddell, brother of Riddell of that Ilk, as being either at or accessary to that battle. The infamous laird of Meldrum was ordered to assist. In 1680, Archibald Riddell, Turnbull of Knowe, and the laird of Down, were apprehended by Henry Ker, and imprisoned in Jedburgh. The Council ordered Meldrum to carry the prisoners to Edinburgh, and recommended the laird of Graden to the Lords of the Treasury for the reward offered by the Council's proclamations for taking Riddell.* In 1699, he was served heir to his father in the lands of Wester Hoselaw, *alias* Place Graden, and in the lands of Falside, in the

---

* In these doings a key is furnished to the way in which the Kers acquired a number of small properties in various parts of the counties of Roxburgh and Selkirk. It is curious to notice that the descendants of the clan Turnbull, and other Border thieves, lost their properties for non-conformity.

parish of Linton.* William Dawson, the agriculturist, possessed part of Graden till a few years ago. George Humble of Kelso is the owner of another part of Graden. The lands of Fauside were possessed at a very early period by a person who had assumed the name of the place as his surname. Robert Bruce granted to William de Fauside the lands of Greenlees, which adjoined Fauside, forfeited by Sir James Torthorald.† In 1372, John de Fauside and John of Linton witnessed a notarial copy of a confirmation, by Pope Gregory IV., of gifts to the canons of Holyrood. In the middle of the 17th century, Greenlees was the property of William Bennet, son of the rector of Ancrum.‡

BLAKELAW, which formed a portion of the barony of Linton, was the property of Mark Ker, portioner of Cliftoune, in 1655. It now belongs to Robert Oliver. On this property was born Thomas Pringle, the author of "The Excursion." He emigrated to Africa, and established a newspaper at Cape Town; but the measures he supported were deemed too liberal for that day, and the journal was suppressed by the governor. In returning to his native land, he devoted himself to literature, published

---

* Retours, No. 324. † Robertson's Index, p. 6.
‡ Retours, No. 195.

"African Sketches," and edited "Friendship's Offering." When about to embark for Africa, he thus took leave of his native land:—

> " Our native land—our native vale—
>   A long and last adieu ;
> Farewell to bonny Teviotdale,
>   And Cheviot's mountains blue."

He died in December, 1834. Dr. Clarke, who was celebrated as the first physician of Newcastle-upon-Tyne, was also a native of this barony.*

Of the old town of Linton, which was formerly of great extent, there are now no remains, excepting the church and mill. A number of the old buildings have been removed within the memory of man, and the foundations of others are occasionally exposed by the plough. Tradition fixes the site of the baronial cross opposite to the farm-house, and near to the butts, where the inhabitants were trained to archery. The tower stood on an eminence to the south of the church, and between it and the mill. The site is now covered with trees. In 1522, it was destroyed by the English warden. Next year it was again visited by the Earl of Surrey, who razed it to the ground. Linton was again destroyed by the Earl of Hertford, in 1545.

There are traces of the church of Linton as far back as 1127. In 1160, Edward was parson of the

---

* New Statistical Account.

church.* Patrick was parson in the reign of Alexander II. In 1304, Richard was pastor. Edward III. appointed Richard of Skypton and Richard Prodham to the church, between 1358 and 1360.† In 1459, William Blair was parson of the church. The "queir" of the church was the burying-place of the Somervilles. In 1214, Roger Somerville of Whichenour, who had joined in the rebellion against King John, fled to Scotland. He died in the "*toure*" of Linton, at the age of 94, and was buried in the queir of the church, where his descendants continued to be buried for nearly 200 years. The present church is situated on the top of a considerable *law* or knoll of pure sand.‡ Tradition bears that this little hill was sifted by two sisters, to save the life of their brother, who had slain a priest; but it is not easy to believe in the legend, as the hill, at a moderate computation, must have a solid content of about half a million of cubic feet. It is probable that the legend owes its origin to the early Catholic priesthood, with the view of impressing upon the rude people of the locality of that day the sacredness of their persons. The legend is, however, implicitly believed in by the people of the district at this day.§

---

* Reg. of Glas. p. 17.   † Rotuli Scotiæ, vol. i. p. 852.
‡ Vol. i. pp. 40–42.
§ Sir Walter Scott, in his "Minstrelsy," says that the hill was sifted by two beautiful sisters, as a penance on them for

Although there is no certain information to show that the present site occupies the position of the old church which existed during the days of David, Malcolm, and William the Lion, it may be inferred that it does, from the Somervilles being buried within it for nearly 200 years.* In repairing the church, sometime before 1792, there was found a large grave, containing fifty skulls, all equally decayed, and from several of them being cut, it is supposed that they had fallen in battle. The minister of Linton, who drew up the last statistical account, conjectures that the skulls belonged to individuals who had fallen at Flodden-field, the remains of many of whom were consigned to a common grave in the cemeteries of the nearest Border parishes; but this conjecture is very improbable, from the distance, and several graveyards lying between it and Linton. It is more likely that the skulls belonged to individuals who had fallen on one of the English visits to Linton. When the English warden destroyed the town in 1522, he had with him an army of 2000 men, which may sufficiently

---

the blood shed on their account by the gallants of the district. The legend, as given in the text, is as related by the people living in the locality, and implicitly believed.

* The interior of the church was taken out in 1858, and entirely renewed. The beautiful Norman font was used for years by a blacksmith for the purpose of holding small coal. It is now in the possession of the owner of the barony.

FONT OF LINTON

account for the remains, without including the raids of Surrey and Hertford.

A chapel, dependant upon Linton, is said to have stood at Hoselaw, probably for the convenience of the eastern part of the parish; but the plough has now passed over it and its little graveyard.*

YETHAM, YHETAM, JETAM, JETHAM;† ZEDON;‡ YETTAM;§ YETHOLM.‖—The name of this ancient place is thought to be derived from the Anglo-Saxon

---

* No district in all the Border land has undergone so much improvement as the barony of Linton. I remember when nearly all the land lying between the Softlaws and Thirlestanes was moor, moss, and loch, with scarcely a fence to be seen. Now it has all been brought under the plough, and produces excellent crops. All the flat ground between Greenlees and Fauside was a large flow moss within my day. Not a tree was to be seen excepting an ash or two at the onstead of Greenlees. The onstead at the roadside between Fauside and Easterstead was called "*Patie's* on the *Moor*," from its situation on the top of a wild ridge. The locality is now full of fruitful fields. From the top of this ridge, where the road crosses it a little above Easterstead, is obtained one of the most extensive and beautiful views in the district. It is well worth going many a mile to see.

† 1165–1230,· Lib. de Calchou; Ragman's Rolls; Reg. Glasg.; Lib. de Dryburgh; Rotuli Scotiæ.

‡ Circa, 1388; Froissart's Chronicles, vol. iv. p. 3.

§ Circa, 1545—Account of Hertford's expedition into Scotland.

‖ Circa, 1797; Old Statistical Account; Old Valuation Book of the County of Roxburgh.

Zete, gait or road, and *ham*, a dwelling; the dwelling or hamlet at the *yet* or road. At present there are two towns bearing the name of Yetholm; the one at which the church is situated is called Kirk Yetholm, and the other, Town Yetholm. Originally there was only one village, that which is known as *Kirk* Yetholm; and *Town* Yetholm is not seen till near the middle of the 15th century. The prefix *Kirk* does not appear on record till the beginning of the 15th century.

The early history of this territory is involved in the haze of antiquity. The bounds of the manor cannot be exactly ascertained; but it is probable that it was at first co-extensive with the parish, and continued so till about the end of the 15th century, when nearly all the lands lying to the north of the River Beaumont were erected into a barony in favour of the Earl of Bothwell, and called the barony of Town Yetholm. After that period, the lands of Kirk Yetholm and the lands of Town Yetholm appear to have remained as separate baronies. About the middle of the 17th century, the manor of Kirk Yetholm was annexed to the barony of Grubet. About the end of the 12th and the beginning of the 13th centuries, occasional glimpses are obtained of persons connected with the locality. *Ralph Nanus*, who seems to have possessed the manor, granted to the monks of Kelso three acres of land in Yhetam, opposite the lands which the monks held in Colpinhopes, and near to the rivulet which divides England from Scotland, as bounded by a ditch, with right to them to build houses for themselves, their men, and animals, on the said lands, with free passage for themselves, their men, and cattle, from the lands of Colpinhopes to the lands of Yetholm. Ralph also bound himself and his heirs not to build any houses on the road lying between the foresaid lands and the rivulet dividing England from Scotland, nor suffer any person to do so to the injury of the monks.* This property is thought to be the same as that called by the name of the Half-husbandlands at the present day, and on which there are houses still named the *Halfland Houses*. The monks had also the right of common pasture in Yetholm, and which they let to the miller of Colpinhopes. Colpinhopes lay within the English border, and was granted by Walter Corbet, the laird of Makerston, to the convent. William, the son of Patrick, earl of Dunbar, with the consent of his wife Christian, daughter of Walter Corbet, confirmed the grant, and added the mill of Colpinhopes. In the chartulary of the abbey of Kelso, the boundaries of the grant are said to extend "from Edredsete to Greengare under Edredsete, and to the bridge at the head of the brook which divides England from Scotland, and down this brook towards

---

* Lib. de Calchou, pp. 307, 308.

the chapel of St. Edeldrida* the virgin, to another brook which runs down by Homildun, and then up this brook to a glen where the brook comes to Homildun, across the way which comes from *Jetam*, and along this way to the two great stones.† No person was to plough on the west side of Homildun. The monks laboured the grange of Colpinhopes in winter with two ploughs, and they had there pasture for 20 oxen, 20 cows, 500 ewes, and 200 other sheep. They had also five acres of land in Shotton or Scotton, which lay on the west side of the road beside the burn which divides England and Scotland, near Yetham, with pasture for forty sheep

---

* ETHELRIDA was the daughter of Ina, King of the East Angles, and was married to Egfrid, King of Northumbria, with whom she is said to have lived for twelve years in a state of continency. She then, with leave of the king, retired to Coldingham, where she took the veil. On the king repenting granting her leave to retire to the convent, and threatening to take her therefrom, she, with two companions, fled to the summit of a rock called St. Abb's Head. When Egfrid attempted to take her from the rock, the tide suddenly surrounded the rock, so as to make it inaccessible. The rising of the waters was attributed to a miracle, and Egfrid took to himself another wife. I think I came upon the foundations of the chapel a little way below the ruins of the Shank, and I was told by an old man in Yetholm that he had seen its Font. He also stated to me that a person in Yetholm, who died several years ago at an advanced age, had, while he was a boy, at a place called Marchlaw, worshipped in the little chapel of the Virgin.

† Are these the stones now called Stob stones?

and forty cows everywhere in Shotton, excepting in the cornfields and meadows. They had also common pasture and fuel, and a right to grind without paying multure at the mill of Schotton. In 1296, William of Yetham swore fealty to Edward I.* In the same year, Mestre Walran, the parson of Yetholm, swore fealty to the same king at Berwick.† On the 23rd of August, Edward I. arrived at Yetham, and remained two days. In 1320, William of Yetham, Sir William de Soulis, and Sir Robert de Keith got a safe-conduct from Edward II. to enter England. In 1375, Edward III. gave Parkfield, with other lands in Yetham, to Thomas Archer, for good service done to England on the Scottish border, for a payment of £4 annually. In the same year, Robert II., the Scottish king, granted the barony of Yetham to Fergus M'Dougal, on the resignation of Margaret Fraser, his mother.‡ Archibald M'Dougal obtained from Robert III. a grant of Yetham, Mackerston, and Elystoun, between the years 1390 and 1406. The manor of Yetham passed to William de Hawden, by grant of the Duke of Albany, in 1407. Before 1432, Andrew Ker got a gift of the lands of Yetham from the governor, but the Estates of Parliament found that the governor could not gift from the crown any land that fell to the crown through

---

* Ragman's Rolls, p. 128.   † Rotuli Scotiæ.
‡ Reg. Mag. Sig., p. 191, No. 33.

the decease of any bastard, and therefore the gift to Ker was of no avail.* In 1491, James IV. granted to the noted Sir Robert Ker the superiority of the tenandry of the lands of *Kirk* Yethame. In 1523, George Rutherfurd, son and heir of John Rutherfurd of Hundolee, got a charter of the ten-pound lands of Yetham and Hayhope. In 1629, the lands and mill of Kirk Yetholm were held by Andrew, Lord Jedburgh.† In 1647, William Bennet was served heir to his father, William Bennet, rector of Ancrum, in the lands of Kirk Yetham and mill annexed to the barony of Grubet.‡ The family of Nisbet of Dirlton next possessed the barony. The greater portion of these lands are now the property of the Marquis of Tweeddale.

HALTERBURNHEAD, a portion of the old manor of Yetholm, formed at one time part of the estate of Cherrytrees, belonging to a family of Murray, from whom it passed to Wauchope of Niddrie, and is now the property of Charles Rae of Middleton, Northumberland. This estate is situated on the sources of a brook of that name, which runs eastward, past the half-land-house, till it meets the burn that divides England and Scotland, from whence its course is in a northerly direction, forming the boundary of the two kingdoms till its confluence with the Beaumont.

---

* Acta Parl. vol. ii. p. 20. † Retours. ‡ Ib.

The name of Halterburn is thought to be a corruption of *Edeldrida,* and so named from the chapel of the Virgin which stood in that locality. The brook, which descends from the mountains on the west of the Shank, is stated in the grants of the 13th century to be the boundary of England and Scotland, but which is not so at the present day. The foundations of many ruined houses speak of a numerous population which once inhabited the well sheltered hopes of the mountains. It is interesting to notice the close proximity of the buildings to the border line on each side, as if the inhabitants in either kingdom had always lived at peace with each other.

The whole territory of Kirk Yetham, with the exception of the vale of Beaumont, and part lying near Shotton, is mountainous, affording fine pasture for sheep. Many of these hills bear marks of having been cultivated, at a former period, to near their summits. All the accessible lands on the slopes of the hills is being brought under the influence of the plough. Part of the hill sides, to the west of Kirk Yetham, is planted, but in a manner that does not add to the beauty of the scenery.

The church and graveyard are at the west end of the town. The present church, which is a very handsome building, was erected in 1836, on the site of the old church, which was a long low building, thatched with reeds, with the floor below the level of the ground. The earliest notice of the church is about 1233. At that time, Nicholas de Gleynwin, rector of the church of *Jetham,* is a witness to Mariote, the daughter of Samuel, quit-claiming the land of Stobhou in favour of the church of Glasgow.* In 1295, on a dispute arising between William Folcard and the monks of Kelso, the rector of Yetham was commissioner for the abbot of Dunfermline, who was chosen arbiter.† In 1368, Edward III. presented John of Alnewyk to the church of Yetham, and on the bishop of Glasgow refusing to induct, the king charged the sheriff of Roxburgh not to allow any other person to be inducted. Six years after, the same king presented John Walays to the church of Yetham. In the same year, Edward III. issued a writ for the exchange of Minto for Yetham.‡ In 1379, Richard II. presented Robert Gifford to the church of Yetholm.§ In 1406, William de Hawdin, laird of *Kirk* Yetholm, gave the monks of Kelso the advowson of the church of Yetham, and imprecated the curse of the Almighty upon whomsoever of his heirs should dispute their right to it; binding himself and them, if he or they molested the abbot in his right, to pay £20 to the church of St. Lawrence at Merebotyle for each offence.‖ In 1495, Patrick,

---

* Reg. de Glas., p. 111.   † Lib. de Calchou, p. 169.
‡ Rotuli Scotiæ, vol. i. pp. 963, 965.   § Ib., vol. ii. p. 19.
‖ Lib. de Calchou, pp. 415, 416.

earl of Bothwell, obtained the advowson of the church of Yetham.* About the beginning of the 17th century, the family of Buccleugh was possessed of the advowson of the church of Yetham.† About the middle of the same century, the advowson passed into the family of Wauchope, with whom it now remains. In 1662, the Presbytery of Kelso was discharged by the Privy Council from proceeding to ordain a minister to Yetham. Tradition tells that the bodies of a number of the Scottish nobles who fell at the battle of Flodden were buried in the cemetery of Yetham, as the nearest consecrated ground to the battle-field, seven miles distant.

The town of the manor stands on the right bank of the Beaumont River, on the base of one of the Cheviot mountains. The inhabitants are all rentallers, under the family of Tweeddale. The feu consists of a house, garden, about a quarter of an acre of land in the loaning, privilege of turf and peat, and pasture for a horse and cow on an extensive common that runs into the heart of the mountains. A number of the rentallers farm each a few acres of land in the vicinity of the town, at rents from £2 to £3, 10s. per acre, which is considered extremely high; but as the occupiers are mostly tradesmen and day labourers, who work the land at leisure hours or when unemployed, they manage to

---

* Reg. Mag. Sig. † Retours.

make the land pay and prove a source of health and comfort to themselves and families. The town has been greatly improved within the last twenty-five years. The houses look better, the streets are cleaner, and last year an abundant supply of the purest water was introduced from the springs on the sides of the mountain above the town. For some years past a number of Irish have taken up their abode in the town, contrary to the wishes of the native population, and are employed generally in labouring on the farms around. Hitherto, the conduct of these people in Teviotdale has been exemplary.

There is a manufactory here, driven by the waters of the Beaumont, confined exclusively to the working up of pure Cheviot wool into Tweeds, &c., in which a considerable trade is carried on. It was originally a fulling mill, of which there are notices extending back several centuries. The same stream drives a corn and flour mill of nearly equal antiquity.

The territory is governed by a baron baillie, appointed by the Marquis of Tweeddale. The town has right to two fairs in the year, one in July, the other in October, for sheep and cattle, both well attended. The market cross, a large block of whinstone, may be seen lying in front of the Cross Keys Inn.

Yetholm, so far as I am aware, is the only place in this part of the kingdom where a remnant of the old mode of keeping SHROVETIDE is still to be seen. In the early days of the Roman Church, Shrovetide was strictly observed. The people were particularly enjoined to forgive all offences, and be reconciled to each other before entering upon the solemnities of Lent. With the Roman Catholics it was a day of mutual intercourse and friendship. Many families opened their kitchen, and every neighbour and passenger permitted to enter and fry a pancake, for which the necessary provision was made ready. In all religious houses the table was spread for travellers and visitants. The diversions of the day consisted in fighting cocks, in some places handball, and in other places foot-ball, foot-races, &c. In Yetholm, cock-fighting used to be one of the amusements of the day, but it has been given up, and foot-ball is now the chief diversion.* The game is

---

* Although ball-playing is connected with the Shrovetide of the Romans, it is thought by several writers to be a vestige of the worship paid by the ancient Britons to the sun. In Brittany the same game is played, and there the ball is called *Soule*, derived, it is said, from the Celtic *heaul*, the initial letter of which was changed into S by the Romans, and signifies *Sun*. It is probable that cock-fighting on that day was at an early period part of the sun worship. The cock was the bird that proclaimed the rising sun, and is thus alluded to in the "Voluspa:"—

"Crow'd his Æsir call,
Cock with the glistening crest:
He in Odin's hall
Wakes the brave from rest."

The crest of the helmit of the image which represented Odin, was a cock, a device emblematical of vigilance, one of the attri-

played between the married men and the single, the one party playing east, and the other west. At two o'clock the ball is thrown up at the cross, and then a scene ensues that baffles description. Old and young join in the contest as keenly as if a kingdom were the prize of the victor. Will Faa, who long reigned as gipsy king, was a celebrated ball player in his day, and never failed to turn out with his tribes on the occasion of the annual game. The sports are continued till night puts an end to the match, and then the combatants retire to the various inns in the town, to partake of dumplings and pancakes, prepared by the hostess, and served up *gratis*. After the feast is over, the players and others who may have joined them dance and drink till morning. Foot-ball was a game very common on the Border during the wars with England. When a foray was

---

butes of Odin. The nations which worshipped the sun sacrificed this bird to that deity, because it was "sunnie, swifte, and very prompt of flight and course, and so consequently an acceptable offering to the sunne, the fountaine of light; admirable for his three qualities; his luminous beauty; his force and efficacy of heat, and his promptitude of course." The bird is mentioned by Solomon in his Book of Proverbs, as serving for the symbol of power and strength. The cock mounted on his spurs, says a learned writer, "chanteth victoriously by preference over all creatures of the earth, so say the philosophers and naturalists, God having given him such light and power; as we learn from the wise king of Edom, and mirror of patience, the patriarch Job." Pythagoras speaks of the cock as sacred to the *sun* and *moon*.

contemplated into the neighbouring kingdom, a match at foot-ball was got up, and under cover of it, great numbers were assembled without suspicion near the place where the Border line was intended to be crossed. It was also usual for persons not friendly to their own government to meet at foot-ball, and talk treason without being suspected.

The Christmas festivities were many years ago celebrated at Yetholm, much in the manner as in Northumberland and Durham. Dancers, with hat, sleeves, and buttonholes decorated with ribbons, went in companies of sometimes a dozen, to exhibit their skill in dancing, accompanied by a person called BESSY with the besom, dressed in petticoats, and disguised as an old woman; and another called the Fool, in grotesque costume. These two collected donations from the bystanders, while the others danced.

Kirk Yetholm has long been the abode of several gipsy tribes. Various opinions are entertained as to the origin of this race of people, who were once so formidable, and infested most countries of Europe and Asia. The exact year that the gipsies made their appearance is not precisely known. In Turkey they were seen about the beginning of the 15th century, and so formidable were they, that the Turks were glad to enter into a treaty with them, and admit them to the same privileges which the subjects of the Sultan enjoyed. They, however, having been so long accustomed to a vagabond rapacious life, and being unacquainted with the arts of industry, began to have recourse to their former mode of subsistence. For some time their outrages were overlooked by the Turks, for fear of another insurrection, but proving irreclaimable, they were banished the land, and a power given to every man to kill a Zingance or gipsy, or make him his slave, if found in the territory of Egypt after a limited time. Finding it impossible to maintain their liberty at home, they resolved to disperse into foreign countries. About 1420, they appeared in Germany, in various bands, under chiefs bearing the titles of Dukes and Earls. They travelled as smiths and tinkers, and others dealt in earthenware. Out of this country they were banished in 1500. In Bohemia and Hungary they assumed the character of pilgrims, and received passes from the princes through whose territories they travelled; but their morals not corresponding to the sanctity of that character, and their numbers increasing by fresh swarms from the east, they were banished out of these kingdoms under severe penalties. They also appeared in Spain at an early period, but were banished therefrom in 1492. They were also driven out of France in the years 1561 and 1612. In England they appeared about the time they were banished from Spain, and to such an extent did they impose upon the credulity of the public by palmistry or fortune-telling, that an act was passed in the reign of Henry VIII., banishing them out of the country, and any Egyptians found within the realm after the space of a month, were to be adjudged felons, and every person importing such Egyptians, should forfeit for every offence forty pounds. But this severe enactment not having the desired effect, an amendment of the act was passed five years after Elizabeth ascended the throne. In 1549, a search was made through the county of Suffolk for "vagabonds, gipsies, conspirators, players," and such like.

In Scotland these people are seen about the middle of the 15th century, under the leadership of a person sometimes styled King, Prince, Earl, and Captain. In July 17th, 1492, there is an entry in the treasurer's books of a payment made to Peter Ker of four shillings, to go to the king at Hunthall, to get letters subscribed to the "*King of Rowmais.*" Two days after, a payment of twenty pounds was made at the king's command to the messenger of the "*King of Rowmais.*" In 1502, the "*Earl of Grece*" was paid 14s. at the king's command. In May, 1529, "*King Cristal's*" servant was paid £20. In 1532, the "*King of Cipre*" got, at the command of the king, £100. About 1506, the tribe was under the government of Anthony Gawin, in whose favour James IV. wrote a letter under his own hand to the king of Denmark.* In the letter Anthony is styled Earl of Little Egypt. After Anthony Gawin left, the power seems to have fallen into the hands of Johnnie Faa, also called Earl of Little Egypt. They appear as dancers and minstrels, and as such often performed before the court. In April, 1505, an entry in the treasurer's books bears that 6s. were paid to the Egyptians, at the king's command. In May, 1529, another entry shows that they danced before the king at Hallyrudhouse. It would appear also, that the queen chose her handmaidens from the gipsy bands. It is probable that the reason of the gipsies rising to such high favour with James IV. and his successor was on account of their skill in dancing and music. When the kings of that period travelled from one place to another in their kingdom, or even on a pilgrimage to the shrine of a saint, they were always accompanied by minstrels and dancers, to beguile the way. James V. granted special protection to Johnnie Faa, and power to him to administer justice upon his people, "*conform to the laws of Egypt.*" Several of the tribe having rebelled in 1540, James V. interposed his authority in support of the gipsy king.† In May, 1540, a

---

* Pinkerton's Hist. of Scotland, vol. ii. p. 444. Lond. Ed.

† "James, be the Grace of God, King of Scottis: To our Sheriffs of Edinburgh, principal and within the Constabulary of Haddington and Berwick, Provestes, Aldermen, and Baillies of our burrowes and cities of Edinburgh, &c., greet-

precept was granted in favour of John *Wanne*, son and heir of the said Johnnie *Fall*, to hang and otherwise punish all his Egyptian subjects within the kingdom of Scotland. In 1541, the lords of

---

ing. Forasmeikle as it is humblie meanit and schewin to us be owre lovite Johnnie Faa, Lord and Erle of Little Egypt, that quhair he obtainet our Letters under our Grette Seele, direct to zou, all and sindry our said Sheriffs, Stewartes, Baillies, Provestes, Aldermen, and Baillies of burrowes, and to all and sindry ayris havand autorite within our realme, and to assist in the execution of justice upon his company and folkis *conforme to the laws of Egypt;* and in punishing of all yame that rebelles against him; neveryeless as we are informet, Sebastiane Calow, Egiptiane, of the saids John's company, with his complices and partakeris underwrittin, yat is to say, Anteane Dorea, Satona Fingo, Nova Tineo, Philip Hatfeyggow, Jowla Bailzow, Grafto Neyn, Geleys Bailzow, Bernard Beige, Demer Macskella, Nolfaw Cawlour, Martin Zemine, rebelles and conspires agains the said Johnnie Faa and has removit yame all uterly out of his company, and taken fra him divers soumes of money, jevelles, claiths, and oyrs gudis, to ye quantite of ane grete soume of money and on na wyss will pass hame with him; howbeit he has bidden and remainet of lang time upoun yame, *and is bunding and obest to bring hame with him all yame of his company yat are on live, and ane testimoneale of yame yat are deed;* and also ye said Johnnie has the said Sebastiane's obligatioune maid in Dunfermling befor our maister housald yat he and his company suld remane with him, and on na wyss depert fra him, as the samin beiris incontrar ye tennor of ye quhilk, ye said Sebastaine be sinister and wrang information fals relatioun and circumventioun of us, hes purchest our writings, discharging him, and ye remanent of the personis above written, his complices and partakeris of the said John's

council, on considering the complaints given in by Johnnie Faa and his brother, and Sebastiane Lowlaw, Egyptians, to the king, each against the others, were ordered to depart the kingdom within thirty

---

company, and with his gudes takin be yame fra him, causus certane our lieges assist to yame and yair opinionis and fortify and take yair part agains ye said Johnnie, yair lord and maister, sae yat he on nae wyss can apprehend nor get yame to have yame hame againe within yair owin countre, after the tenour of his said band, to his heavy dampnage and skaith, *and in grete perell of tynsall of his heretage,* and expres agains justice. Our will is heerfor, and we charge you straitlie, and commans, yat incontinent yir our letters ze and ilk ane of zou, and within ye bouns of zour offices command & charge all our lieges yat nane of yame tak upoun hand to reset, assyst, fortify, supple, mainteine, defend, or take pairt with the said Sebastiane and his complices above written, for na buddies, nor oyr way agains the said Johnnie Faa, yair lord and maister, bot yat yai, and ze in likwys tak a lay handis upoun yame quharevir yai may be apprehended, and bring yame to him to be punist for yer demeretis, conforme to his laws, and help and fortify him to punish and do justice upoun yame for yair tresspasses; and to yat effect len to him our personis, stokis, fetteris, and all oyer things necessar yerto as ze and ilk ane of zou and all oyers our lieges will answer to us yerupoun and under all hieast penc and charge yat efter may follow; swa yat the said Johnnie have na cause of complaynt heirupoun in tyme cuming, nor to resort to us agane to yat effect, notwithstanding ony our writings sinisterly purchest or to be purchest be the said Sebastiane in the contrar. And als charge our lieges yat nane of yame molest, vex, enquiet, or truble ye said Johnnie Faa and his company *in doing yair lefull bessynes* or oyerwaiyes within our realme, and in yair passing, remanyng, or away-days after being charged so to do, under pain of death.* In 1553, Queen Mary renewed the writ granted in 1540 in favour of the gipsy king, and in the end of the same year granted a respite to Andrew Faa, captain of the Egyptians, George Faa, Robert Faa, his sons, for the murder of Ninian Smaill, one of his subjects, committed within the town of Linton.† King James VI. thought very differently of the subjects of John Faa: he declared them to be vagabonds and thieves, and to be punished as felons. In 1609 they were ordered out of Scotland under the description of sorcerers, vagabonds, and common thieves, commonly called Egyptians, with the penalty annexed, that if any of them were found within the kingdom they might be punished with death. In 1610, Elizabeth Warrock was convicted of being a follower of the gipsies or

---

ganging furth of ye samin under the pane above written: and siclike, yat ze·command and charge all skippers, maisters, and merinaris of all schippes within our realme at all portes and havyns quhair the said Johnnie and his company sal happen to resort and cum to resavi him and yame yrin upoun yair expenses for furing of yame furth of our realme to the portes beyond sey; as zou and ilk ane of yame sicklike will answer to us yereupoun, and under the pane forsaid. Subscrivit with our hand, and under our Privie Seele at Falkland the fiveteene day of Februar, and of our reign the 28 zeir."

* Acta Dom. Con. xv. 155.
† Reg. Sec. Sig. xxvii. 3.

jugglers. Next year, Moyses Faa, David Faa, and Johnnie Faa, were indicted and accused for remaining within the kingdom contrary to the statute expelling them from the country. At the trial, Moyses Faa produced a licence to her by the Privy Council; but owing to the conditions under which it was granted not being fulfilled, the court refused to give it effect. They were all found guilty, and taken to the Burrow Moor and hanged.* In 1616, Johnnie Faa, James Faa, his son, Moyses Bailzie, and Helen Brown, spouse to William Bailzie, Egyptians, were charged with abiding within the kingdom contrary to the laws. They were found guilty, and because they could not find caution, were ordered to be taken to the Burrow Moor and executed; but the king granted them a respite during pleasure. In 1624, Captain Johnnie Faa,† Robert Faa, Samuel Faa, Johnnie Faa,

---

* Pitcairn, vol iii. p. 99.

† This is the celebrated Captain John Faa, whom tradition says ran away with Lady Jean Hamilton, spouse of John, the sixth earl of Cassillis; but, before the gipsy and his band could reach the Border fastnesses, the earl overtook them, and a battle ensued, in which he was victorious. It is said that he carried back his frail spouse, and afterwards confined her in a tower at Maybole, where eight heads carved in stone below one of the turrets represented eight of the luckless Egyptians. It is thought there is no truth in the tradition, at least in so far as it relates that the lady of "*the grave and solemn Cassillis*" eloped with the gipsy chief, who was hanged in 1624. The lady was born in 1607, and at the time of the

Andrew Faa, William Faa, Robert Brown, and Gawin Trotter, were convicted for remaining in the kingdom contrary to the laws, and hanged on the Burrow Moor.* Five days after, Helen Faa, relict of Captain Faa, Lucretia Faa, spouse to James Brown, Elspeth Faa, brother's daughter of the Captain, Catherine Faa, relict to Edward Faa, Marionne Faa, spouse to James Faa, Jeanie Faa, relict of Andrew Faa, Helen Faa, relict of Robert Campbell, Margaret Faa, daughter of the deceased Edward Faa, Isabel Faa, relict of Robert Brown, Margaret Ballantyne, relict of Johnnie Faa, Elspeth Faa, daughter of the deceased Henry Faa, were tried and found guilty of contravening the same act as their unhappy relations, and were condemned "*to be taken to some convenient pairt and drowned till they be deed.*" This barbarous sentence was not put into execution, the king having granted a respite, on condition that they should leave the king-

---

alleged elopement could not be more than fifteen years of age. But about that time a family of the name of Faa lived at Dunbar, whose progenitors, by industry in trade and commerce, became wealthy and respected. It seems a member of this family was knighted. With this family the Faas of Yetholm claimed relationship. One of the Faas of Dunbar contested the election of the Jedburgh district of burghs, in 1733. If an elopement really took place, as to which there are grave doubts, it is more likely that the offender was the rich, gay, and handsome Knight of Dunbar, and not a tatterdemalion gipsy.

* Ib., vol. iii. p. 559.

dom by the following April.* In 1636, Sir Arthur Douglas of Quettinghame having taken some of the vagabond and counterfeit thieves, called Egyptian, he delivered them to the Sheriff of Edinburgh, within the constabulary of Haddington, where they remained for a month. The Privy Council, considering that the keeping of them longer within the tolbooth was a burden on the town of Haddington, and fostered the thieves in the opinion of impunity, and encouraged the rest of the infamous "byke" to continue in the thievish trade: "Thairfoir the Lords of Secret Counsell ordens the Sheriff of Haddington, or his depute, to pronunce *doome and sentence of death* aganis so manie counterfoot theivis as ar men, and aganis so manie of the weomen as wants children, ORDANING the men to be *Hangit*, and the weomen to be *Drowned;* and that suche of the weomen as has children to be *Scourgit* threw the burgh of Hadinton, and *burnt in the cheeke:* and ordanis and commandis the provost and bailies of Hadinton to cus this doome to be execute upon the saidis persons accordinglie." After the punishment of death inflicted on Captain Faa and his gang, the records are silent upon the transactions of these unhappy creatures for many years. The next person that appears as a chief of the tribe is Alexander Faa, who was killed at Romano, Peebleshire, in a fight between

---

* Pitcairn's Trials, vol. iii. pp. 560, 561.

his tribe and that of the Schawes. Of the Fawes there were four brothers and a brother's son; of the Schawes, the Captain, with his three sons; and several women on both sides. Old Faa and his wife were killed on the spot, and his brother George dangerously wounded.* For these murders, Robin Schawe and his three sons were tried, found guilty, and executed at the Grassmarket in 1678. In 1714, William Walker, Patrick Faa, Mabel Stirling, Mary Faa, Jean Ross, Elspeth Lyndsey, Joseph Wallace, John Fenwick, Jean Yorkstone, Mary Robertson, Janet Wilson, and Janet Stewart, were tried at Jedburgh, and found guilty of wilful fire-raising, and of being notorious Egyptians, thieves, vagabonds, and sorcerers; when they were banished to the plantations in America, with the exception of Janet Stewart, who was scourged through Jedburgh, and afterwards stood a quarter of an hour with her left ear nailed to a post at the cross. They were conveyed from Jedburgh to Glasgow in carts, with a guard, and in the burgh books there is a receipt for their bodies by the jailor of the tolbooth at Glasgow.† About the same time, three men and two women of the tribe were hanged at Edinburgh. In 1727, Geordie Faa, husband of the notorious Jean Gordon, was killed at a clan meeting at Huntlywood on Leader, by Robert Johnstone. Johnstone was apprehended, and lodged

---

* Old Statistical Account. † Burgh Records.

in Jedburgh prison. He was afterwards tried, and condemned to death, but, while lying under the sentence, he contrived to break the prison, and escaped. A traditionary tale is told of Jean Gordon, the relict of the murdered man, that when the murderer escaped out of jail, she followed him to Holland, and from thence to Ireland, where she had him seized and brought back to Jedburgh. But the tale is not true, for, whatever revenge she felt against the slayer of her husband, she had no share in his apprehension. Rewards having been offered by the magistrates, the officers of the law were on the alert, and in some places too active, for in York a man was seized as answering Johnstone's description, and lodged in jail till a person could be sent from Jedburgh to identify him. One of the magistrates accordingly went to York, when he found the person detained upon suspicion not Johnstone. The right person was, however, detained at Newcastle, brought to Jedburgh, and from thence carried to the Justiciary Court at Edinburgh, where the identity was established, and he was transmitted to Jedburgh to carry into effect the original sentence. He was executed on the Gallahill. In 1731, John Faa, William Faa, John Faa *alias* Faley, Christian Stewart, and Margaret Young, were tried at Jedburgh, and convicted of house and shop-breaking, and of jail-breaking. In the summer circuit of 1732, the celebrated Jean Gordon, commonly called "Dutchess," presented a petition to the justiciary court sitting at Jedburgh, setting forth that she was indicted as an Egyptian, common vagabond, and notorious thief; that she was old and infirm, and had lain long in jail, and was willing to enact herself to leave Scotland never to return. "Her grace," says the reporter, " was banished accordingly, with certification to be imprisoned for twelve months, and scourged once a-quarter, in case of return."* After being liberated, Jean left Scotland, and wandered upon the English side of the Border. Being at Carlisle on a fair-day, after the rebellion of 1745, she was seized by the mob for declaring her partiality to the Jacobite cause, and ducked to death in the river Eden. The murder was not easily accomplished, as Jean was a very powerful woman; and whenever she got her head above water during the struggle with her murderers, she screamed, "*Charlie yet! Charlie yet!*"† The year following Jean's sentence of banishment, John Faa, William Faa, John Faa, William Millar, Christian Young, and Elspeth Anderson, were tried at Jedburgh for theft, and, with the exception of Millar, received sentence of death.

From the rigorous enactments already noticed, and the unrelenting severity with which they were applied, the gipsy settlement at Yetham is sufficiently

---

* Hume, vol. i. p. 474.

† Jean is the *Meg Merrilees* in "Guy Mannering:" Introduction, p. xix. et seq.

accounted for. Being close to the Border, and in the immediate neighbourhood of the Cheviot fastnesses, rendered it a peculiarly eligible locality for the residence of these unfortunate people. On the executors of the law of either kingdom attempting to enforce obedience to the statutes, it was easy for the gipsies to retire across the ideal line to the friendly side, or penetrate the recesses of the Cheviot mountains, in which they might mock the utmost efforts of their pursuers. In these wilds they could have no difficulty in procuring provisions from the numerous herds of deer and other animals with which these mountains then abounded. Following the range of the Cheviot fells, they could make incursions into the very heart of Northumberland, and, under cover of the same wilds, they might travel to the west seas. But although these people, from an early period, concealed themselves near the Borders, it does not appear that they had any fixed residence at Kirk Yetham till a late period. Tradition bears that the tribes became house-dwellers at this place in consequence of one of their number saving the life of Captain Bennet, proprietor of the barony of Yetham, at the siege of Namur. The captain, while mounting a breach, was struck to the ground, and his supporters slain, with the exception of a gipsy of the name of Young, who defended his officer with the utmost gallantry till he gained his feet, then rushed past him, mounted the wall, and seized the flag, which so encouraged the troops, that the attack was renewed, the breach gained, and Namur taken. In gratitude for this gallant act of the gipsy, it is said, that David Bennet built cottages at Kirk Yetham, and feued them out to the tribe, and from that time they have continued to make the place their headquarters. Nisbet of Dirleton, the successor of Bennet, showed particular attention to the wanderers by building additional cottages; and so highly did he esteem them, and so certain was he of their support, that he named them his bodyguard. After the death of their patron and protector, the estate was purchased by the trustees of the Marquis of Tweeddale, under whom they enjoy their cottages in peace. While such kindnesses were heaped upon the gipsies by the possessors of the barony of Grubbet, they were not allowed to place the soles of their feet upon the barony of Town Yethom, belonging to Wauchope of Niddrie.

The present strength of the various tribes in Kirk Yetholm is about 80, consisting of the Blythes, Ruthvens, Taits, and Douglases. The strong tribe of the Faas, from whom the king was selected, is now extinct. At the death of Will Faa, several years ago, the throne was seized by Charles Blythe, husband of Etty Faa, sister of the king. Before the death of the late king, the revenue of the tribes had decreased to such an extent, that his majesty was forced to lay aside the diadem, and become, for a time, the protector of game on several farms belonging to the Marquis of Tweeddale. He was an excellent fisher, well acquainted with every pool and stream in the Beaumont, Cayle, and Colledge waters. By game-preserving and fishing, he contrived to scrape together as much as supported life, and he was well supplied with drink by visitors from every part of the country, anxious to see those people who had been rendered so interesting by the pen of the mighty magician. But times are changed; visitors are few to the present king, and but for the generosity of a noble Lord who occasionally resides in the neighbourhood, his majesty would often be without supplies. The king is about 85 years old, possesses a fair share of health, but complains that living in houses subjects him to colds which he never had while he dwelt in tents.

The chief employment of the gipsies was travelling in the summer season in promiscuous bands. They generally left their settlement at Kirk Yetholm in the end of March, and did not return till driven back by the storms of winter. Most of the men assisted in the operations of the harvest, and in the winter carted coals to Jedburgh. When out on the rout, they lay beneath their carts, or upon straw under wicker frames, with a cover which resisted the weather. During their progress through the country, they laid the farm-yards, corn, and potato fields, under contribution to a great extent. They had a perfect knack of thieving, and carried off everything that came in their way—corn, hay, hewn stones, wheels, and axletree. They may be said to have lived in a complete state of ignorance, "without God and without hope in the world," till the Rev. John Baird was inducted into the pastoral charge of the parish, when, through his efforts, they were induced to attend church and school; and he obtained from the Edinburgh Bible Society a grant of Bibles and Testaments, which enabled him to place a copy of the Scriptures in every gipsy dwelling.

A few of the gipsies still travel the country, dealing in earthenware, horn spoons, baskets, heather brooms, and mats; but the strictness with which they are watched by the police, prevents any exercise of their thieving talents. From the improved state of the district, there are few waste places for them to pitch their camp, and the raising of a fire on the roadside is certain to be visited with a fine and imprisonment. They cannot now remain in idleness, and are forced to apply themselves to some occupation to procure daily bread. A number of the men have become labourers, and, mixing with the population, acquire better habits, and marry out of their tribe. The gipsy girls, too, are beginning to leave their tribe, and to engage as domestic servants and bondagers, and occasionally marry farm-servants. The houses are now more comfortable; instead of the stone and straw beds, stools, chairs, tables, and the ordinary country beds are to be seen in many of their dwellings. There can be little doubt that the original race is fast falling off, and that ere many years run their course, the oriental blood will have ceased to flow. The days of the gipsy have passed away.

THE BARONY OF TOWN YETHOLM.—With the exception of a small portion of land on the south of the Beaumont Water, this barony lies on the north of the beautiful vale through which this stream flows. In 1495, the Earl of Bothwell got a charter of Town Yetham, with the patronage of the church. In 1523, George Rutherfurd, heir-apparent of John Rutherfurd of Hundolee, was possessed of the ten-pound lands of Town Yetham. At the close of the 16th century, Gilbert Ker of Primsideloch, Elizabeth Edmonstone, his wife, and their third son, got a charter of the *demesne* lands of Town Yetham.* In 1585, James VI. and his parliament ratified an infeftment in favour of Francis, Earl of Bothwell, of " all and haill the landis and baronie of Town Yethame, with towns, pairtis, dependencies, pendecilis, annexis, outsettis, mylnis, tennetis, tenandriis, etc."† In 1608, John Ker of Hirsel obtained

---

* Reg. Mag. Sig.   † Acta Parl., vol. iii. p. 409.

a charter of the baronies of Maxton, Linton, and Town Yetham.* Three years afterwards, Gilbert Ker of Lochtour, his eldest son, was in possession of Lochtour.† In 1624, John Ker of Lochtour succeeded his brother Robert in the lands of Town Yetham.‡ Ten years after, the barony passed into the family of Buccleuch.§ In 1643, John Wauchope of Niddrie got a charter of the tennandrie of Town Yetham.|| In 1662, Sir John obtained a new charter of all and haill the town and lands of Sunnyside, Wideopen, Stankford, and Boghouse, with houses, yards, tofts, and crofts, which formerly belonged to Sir John Ker, and formed part of the barony of Lochtour, " of late called Town Yetham;" also all and sundry the town and mains of the barony of Town Yettoun, milne and milne lands, and the patronage of the kirk of *Town Yettoun;* the lands of Bennetsbank; the lands of Shirrietrees; the lands of Hayhope; half of the husbandland called the Closs and Butterbrae, being a pendicile of the land of Hayhope, with pasturages and privileges according to wont, in the bounds of Town Yettoun; the haugh called Little Roughhaugh; the lands of Easter and Wester Rysides; four husbandlands of Baltrees; which charter contained an erection of said lands,

---

* Acta Parl., vol. iii. p. 409.
† Ib.; Pitcairn's Criminal Trials, vol. iii. p. 538.
‡ Retours, No. 123.   § Ib., No. 154. || Reg. Mag. Sig.

town, mains, and barony of Town Yettoun, Shirrytrees, and Little Roughhaugh into one barony, to be called in all time coming the barony of Lochtour, for the yearly payment of thirty pounds. In 1672, the charter was ratified by Parliament.* In 1683, James Wauchope, born of the marriage between his father and the widow of Sir John Ker of Lochtour, claimed the estate of Lochtour in right of his mother.† The family of Wauchope is still in possession of the barony of Yetham. The principal messuage of the barony was Lochtour, built on an island in Yetholm Loch, connected with the land by a causeway. This was the Avenel Castle of the " Monastery," described as occupying "a small rocky islet in a mountain lake or *tarn*, as such a piece of water is called in Westmoreland. The lake might be about a mile in circumference, surrounded by hills of considerable height, which, except where old trees and brushwood occupied the ravines that divided them from each other, were bare and heathy. The surprise of the spectator was chiefly excited by finding a piece of water situated in that high and mountainous region, and the landscape around had features which might rather be termed wild than either romantic or sublime; yet the scene was not without its charm. Under the burning sun of summer, the clear azure of the deep unruffled lake refreshed the eye, and im-

---

* Acta Parl., vol. viii. pp. 106, 107.   † Burke, vol. ii. p. 1539.

pressed the mind with a pleasing feeling of deep solitude. In winter, when the snow lay on the mountains around, these dazzling masses appeared to ascend far beyond their wonted and natural height, while the lake, which stretched beneath and filled their bosom with all its frozen waves, lay like the surface of a darkened mirror around the black and rocky islet and the walls of the grey castle with which it was crowned."* The fortress is now removed, and in its place is a comfortable house for the farmer of the baronial lands. Although the lake has been greatly lessened by drainage since the day Sir Walter Scott penned the above description, it is still an extensive and lovely sheet of water. In its northern margin, a beautiful mansion has in the course of the present year been erected by Robert Oliver, owner of the estate of Lochside.

Town Yetholm, now the principal place of the barony, stands on the left bank of the Beaumont, forming the southern base of Yetholm Law. It is a regularly built village, containing the parish school-house, a ladies' school, a Free church, and a dissenting meeting-house. The village was at one time deemed unhealthy and liable to epidemic diseases, owing to an extensive morass on the east of the village, and which encircled Yetholm Law; but a drain

---

* "Monastery," vol. ii. p. 85.

was carried up the middle of the marsh, and the stagnant pool is now converted into excellent land. Last year, a good supply of water was brought to the town from a neighbouring height. There is little trade in the town. It has two fairs in the year, and what is termed a high market after each term of Martinmas and Whitsunday. It formerly had a market on the Wednesday, but it has long ceased to exist. It is governed by a baron baillie.

CHERRYTREES, the property of Adam Brack Boyd, occupies a very lovely situation on the east side of the vale, which extends from Beaumont, round Yetholm Law, to Primside. The house is small but handsome, and the grounds around are adorned with wood. Part of this estate seems at one time to have formed part of the barony of Lochtour. In 1523, it was the property of George Rutherfurd, son and heir of John Rutherford of Hundolee. A family of Tait seems to have possessed part of the estate before 1605. At that time, William Tait is designed "of Cherrytrees," in a criminal libel at his instance against James Tait of Kelso, for the murder of his son on the green at Cherrytrees. The charge was, that the said James Tait of Kelso, with his accomplices, armed with swords, steel bonnets, lances, and pistols, came to the green of Cherrytrees, where the deceased was, and slew him. The jury found the said James Tait to be "cleane innocent and acquit of airt and pairt of the said slauchter." The jury consisted of John Mow of that Ilk, who was chancellor; Thomas Ker of Pryoraw; Thomas Tait of Hoill, and John Riddell, younger, of that Ilk, and the remainder of feuars. According to the practice of that period, the jury were taken from the neighbourhood where the panels dwelt, however distant, that they might be tried by their neighbours. In 1624, it belonged to John Ker of Lochtour. In 1665, it was the property of William Ker. In 1684, Ker, the laird of Cherrytrees, was accused, along with the lairds of Brodie and Grant, Craufurd of Ardmillan, Elliot of Stobs, and others, of conspiring against the succession of the Duke of York. In 1672, part of it was granted to Wauchope of Niddrie. In the end of last century it was the property of a family of Murray. The estate has been greatly improved since the present owner came into possession. The small estate of THIRLESTANE is now included in the estate of Cherrytrees. This property appears to have belonged to the Kers of Lochtour; at all events, it was the property of Sir Andrew Ker of Greenhead before 1661, when it was purchased by James Scott, brother-german of Sir William Scott of Harden. One of the lairds of Thirlestane was a physician to Charles II., and distinguished as a chemist. The old mansion-house of Thirlestane stood near Lochtour, in the centre of the vale where it bends around Yetham Law; but it was pulled down above

twenty years ago. One of the rooms in the house was called the "Warlock's room," and is supposed to have been the laboratory of the learned doctor.*
In this family was long preserved a prototype of the *Poculum Potatorium* of the Baron Bradwardine, in the form of a jack-boot. "Each guest was obliged to empty this at his departure. If the guest's name was Scott, the necessity was doubly imperative."†
The family is now represented by William Scott Ker of Sunlaws. In the beginning of the present century, Thirlestane was possessed by George Walker and George Douglas.

King Edward was at Yetham for two days in 1304, on his way to England. It is said by Froissart and others, that the Scottish army, under James, Earl of Douglas, assembled at Yetham in 1338, before the battle of Otterburn; but this is a mistake, as that gallant army mustered in Jedforest, at *Sudon* or *Southdean*. The army could not have met here, as the whole line of forts, from Berwick to Jedburgh, were in the hands of the English. Douglas entered England by the Watling-street, and Albany by the Maidenway.‡ In 1523, the Earl of Surrey, while on his way to destroy Linton and Cessford, razed Lochtour, near which he had lodged for the night. The two Yethams, with Cherrytrees, Barears, the Bogge,

---

* New Statistical Account.
† Note to chapter xi. of "Waverley," vol. i. p. 114.
‡ Vol. ii. p. 238.

Longhouse, Fowmerdon, and Hayhope were destroyed by Hertford in 1545. In 1745, a party of Highlanders marched through the village of Yetholm, up the Beaumont Water, to receive some supplies of money remitted from France, and entrusted to the care of Charles Selby of Earl. The minister of Yetholm, in his account of the parish, states that "an old man, lately deceased, in Town Yetholm, distinctly remembered having seen these Highlanders passing his father's house.*

A number of persons have borne the surname of Yetham. Adam of Yetham is a witness to charters in the reigns of William the Lion and Alexander II.† Reginald of Yetham appears about the same period. William of Yetham lived in 1296.‡ William of Yethame was archdeacon of Teviotdale between 1321 and 1326.§

MOLLE,|| MOW.¶—This territory owes its name to the Cambro-British people, and intended to describe a mountainous tract, abounding with hills of a round form,—*Mole* signifying a round or conical hill.

The territory of Molle is bounded on the south

---

* New Statistical Account.
† Lib. de Melrose, pp. 130, 131, 239.
‡ Ragman's Rolls, p. 128.
§ Regist. of Glasg., pp. 228, 233. Lib. de Dryburgh, p. 275.
|| Circa 1124–1500. Lib. de Mailros; Lib. de Calchou.
¶ Circa 1536; Criminal Trials; Reg. Mag. Sig.

and south-west by the march line between England
and Scotland, beginning at a place called the Black
Hag on the east, and ending where the boundary of
Hownam meets the English border on the south-
west. On the east it was bounded by the parish of
Morebattle, of which it now forms a part. The
march line left the English border near the Black
Hag, at a place where Northumberland slightly in-
dents itself into Roxburghshire, and from thence to
the source of Altonburn. The burn then formed
the boundary till it reached the water of Beaumont,
which it crossed, and then ran in a straight line by
the east side of a place then called *Hulaweshou*,* to
the base of *Hunedune*,† where it met the Hownam
boundary, and along that line to the English border.
The whole of the territory is mountainous. On the
west, a ridge of hills runs from Hownman on the
Cayle Water into Northumberland, forming the table
land between Coquetdale and the vale of Beaumont.
From this chain on the north, is a tract of hills
running eastward, and dividing the vales of Cayle
and Beaumont, and another chain of summits on
the south wends eastward, separating the vale down
which Colledge Water rushes from Beaumont. Between these two chains of mountains is the vale of
Beaumont, extending from the ridge running north
and south eastward by Yetholm to the English bor-

---

* Ellisheugh. † Hounamlaw.

der. In the centre of this vale flows the Beaumont Water, dividing the territory into nearly two equal divisions. The mountains afford the finest pasture for sheep, and the valley produces excellent crops.

This territory originally formed a part of ancient Northumbria, and was granted, with other lands and towns on the Beaumont, to Lindisfarne, during the seventh century. During the reign of Alexander I., it was possessed by a person of the name of Liulf. After his death, Uctred, his son, succeeded to the territory, and who, before the year 1153, granted to the monks of Kelso the church of Molle, with land lying adjacent, as bounded by him and Aldred the dean.* From Uctred the land passed to ESCHENA DE LONDONIIS—called Lady Eschena of Molle; but the connexion between her ladyship and Uctred does not clearly appear. She was married first to Walter, the first steward of Scotland. This Walter, the husband of Eschena of Molle, was a younger son of Alan, who was the son of Flaald, a Norman, who acquired the estate of Oswestrie in Shropshire, soon after the conquest. William, the brother of Walter, added the estate of Clune, in the same shire, to Oswestrie, by marrying the heiress, Isabel de Say, and John Fitzallan, by marrying the third sister of the third Earl of Arundel, who died in 1196 without issue, became fourth Earl of Arundel,

---

* Lib. de Calchou, p. 144.

and removed to Sussex. Both brothers espoused the cause of the Empress Maud, niece of David I., against Stephen, and after the siege of Winchester, Walter followed David into Scotland, and obtained from him large possessions in the shires of Renfrew, East Lothian, and Kyle.* Malcolm IV. granted to Walter the lands of Birchinside and Leggardewdede in Berwickshire, and also the territory of Molle by its right bounds, and with all its just pertinents, to him and his heirs in fee and heritage, for a knight's service.† The charter is dated at Roxburgh, and the witnesses are Ernald, bishop of St. Andrew; Herbert, bishop of Glasgow; John, abbot of Kelso; William, abbot of Melrose; Osbert, abbot of Jedburgh; Walter, the chancellor; William, the king's brother;

---

* A number of persons of rank followed Walter to Scotland, and obtained from him grants of land. Robert de Mundegumeri, a younger son of Roger, the Earl of Shrewsbury, got from Walter the manor of Eglesham, which is still enjoyed by his descendant, the Earl of Eglinton. Robert was the first Montgomery who settled in Scotland. The family of WALLACE were vassals of Walter. It is said the Boyds owe their origin to Simon, a brother of Walter, who had followed him to Scotland.

† Acta Parl., vol. i. p. 83. "Molle per rectas devisas suis et cum omnibus justis suis pertinentiis Tenendam et habendam sibi et heredibus suis de me et heredibus meis in feodo et hereditate ita libere et quiete plenarie et honorifice sicut aliquis comes vel baro in regno Scotie terram aliquam de me liberius quietus plenius et honorificentius tenet et possidet faciendo de predictis terris mihi et heredius meis servitium unius meletis."

Richard, the constable; Gilbert of Umphrmville; Waldevo, son of Earl Cospatric, and Jordan Riddell. Walter died in 1177,* leaving, by Eschina, a son, Alan, who succeeded to the estate and the office of Steward of Scotland, and whose lineal descendant, Robert the Steward, became king of Scotland in 1371. After the death of Walter, his widow married Henry of Molle, by whom she had four daughters, Margaret, Eschina, Avicia, and Cecilia. She died about 1200, and shortly after the De Vescis appear as over lords of the territory. Lady Cecilia married Simon Maleverer, but no information exists to show what became of her three sisters. During the lifetime of Cecilia, Sir Gilbert Avenel appears in possession of portions of the estate of Molle, upon which he had built a hall.† Chalmers states that Cecilia was married to Robert, a younger son of Gervase Avenel, and that Gilbert was the issue of that union. Morton, author of the "Monastic Annals," takes the same view, but both are undoubtedly mistaken. The charters in favour of the monks at Kelso prove that Cecilia was married to Simon Malverer, and that at the period these grants were made by her with consent of her husband, the lands conveyed are described as being bounded by the pro-

---

* Chron. Mail., p. 88. "Walterius filius Alani dapifer regis Scottorum familiaris noster deim obiit cujus beata anima vivat in gloria."

† Lib. de Calchou, p. 29.

perty of *Gilbert Avenel*. Gilbert may have been her nephew, but her son he could not be. At the death of Cicilia, about 1250, the family became extinct, and the lands not gifted to the monks devolved upon the said Gilbert Avenel, but who does not seem long to have enjoyed them, as they were in the hands of Sir John Halyburton, whose daughter, Johanna, carried the estates to Adam of Roule, whom she married after the death of her first husband, Ralph Wyschard.* About the end of the thirteenth century, those lands were possessed by Alexander Molle, and, in the beginning of the next century, by John Molle. Before 1357, the lands

---

* The Halyburtons were a Berwickshire family, and derived their name from the town, *i.e.*, *Haly-burg-tun*, signifying the holy fortlet and village. John Halyburton, who was the second son of Sir Adam, married a daughter of William de Vaus. Her father dying without issue, his great estates were carried by her into the family of Halyburton. In 1392, Sir Walter Halyburton, the grandson of that marriage, succeeded his father in the estate of Dirlton, and in the beginning of the next century, succeeded his cousin, Sir John Halyburton, in the estate of Halyburton. Sir Walter married a daughter of Regent Albany, and became a peer by the title of Lord Halyburton of Halyburton. After various transmissions, the estates and title came to Patrick, Lord Halyburton, who died in 1506, leaving three daughters, who carried the estates to Lord Ruthven, Lord Home, and to Ker of Faudenside. Patrick Halyburton was married to a daughter of Patrick, Lord Hailes, celebrated for his defence of Berwick Castle in 1482, against Albany and Gloucester. The sister of Patrick's wife, Euphemia, married Andrew M'Dougal of Makerston.

seem to have been in the keeping of John de Copeland, probably Edward's sheriff of the county, and about that date all the lands and tenements in Auldtownburn, with their pertinents, which formerly belonged to Adam of Roule, were resigned by Copeland in favour of John Ker of the forest of Selkirk. In 1358, the same John Kerr, on the resignation of William of Blackdeane, of part of the lands of Mow and Auldtownburn, obtained a charter in favour of himself and Mariote his spouse, of the said lands and others. These lands were confirmed to him by Archibald, Earl of Douglas, his superior. In 1474, the lands of Altonburne, as part of the barony of Cessford, were resigned to James III. by Andrew Ker of Cessford, and granted by that king to Walter Ker, his son. In 1481, the same Walter resigned the lands to the king, who granted them again to him in heritage, with remainder in succession to his brothers, Thomas, William, and Ralph, and the heirs of Andrew Ker.* In 1542, these lands were granted by James V. to Walter Ker of Cessford, for services against the English, and a sum of money paid to the king's treasurer.† The lands are now possessed by the Duke of Roxburghe.

In 1490, Robert Mow resigned the town and demesne lands into the hands of James IV., who granted them to John Mow, the brother of Robert.

---

* Reg. Mag. Sig., lib. vii. No. 286; lib. ix. No. 62.   † Ib.

In 1536, John Molle of that Ilk, William Douglas of Bonne-Jedburgh, Thomas MacDougall of Maccaristoune, found caution to the extent of 1000 merks each, to underlye the law at the next justiceaire of Jedburgh, for oppression and hamesucken done to the dean of Murray.* In May, 1541, at the court at Jedburgh, John Mow of that Ilk, William Stewart of Traquair, Walter Ker of Cessford, Robert Scott of Howpeslat, and Gilbert Ker of Greenhead, became cautioners for John Johnstone of that Ilk, to the extent of L.10,000.† In the same year, John Mow, and twenty-nine others, got a respite for three years, for art and part in the slaughter of William Burn, son to Robert Burn, in Primsideloch, at the Kirk of Mow.‡ In 1575, the laird of Mow fell at the raid of the Redswyre.§ In 1606, William Mow was served heir to his father, James Mow, in the lands of Mow-mains, extending to six mercat lands.‖ In 1618, John Mow was served heir to his father in the lands of Mow.¶ In 1631, Gilbert Mow was served heir to his father in the lands of Mow-mains.** In 1636, John Mow of that Ilk was served heir to

---

* Pitcairn's Criminal Trials, vol. i. p. 176.
† Ib., p. 230.   ‡ Ib., p. 257.
§ Border Minstrelsy:—
  "Scotland has cause to mak great sturt,
   For laiming of the laird of Mow."
‖ Retours, 44.   ¶ Ib., 94.   ** Ib., 145.

John Mow of the eleven-mercat lands and twenty-pound lands of Mow, called Mow-town and Mow-mains.*

About 1165, Anselm of Whitton, afterwards styled of Molle, appears to have been in possession of a part of the territory of Molle. He left two daughters, Matildis and Isolde. The former married Richard of Lincoln, and the other, Alexander, said to be the son of William, who was the son of Edgar, and between these two ladies the estate of Anselm was divided at his death. It is difficult to ascertain the portion possessed by Anselm, but so far as can be gathered by grants from him to the monastery of Kelso, it lay on the east of Ernbrandsdene, as far as the ford of the river; and upwards towards Hunedune; all Hulasheshou, Ladhladde, Thueles, Mollehope,† &c.

The monks of KELSO had at a very early period considerable possessions in this territory, independent of the land which they held in name of the church. Lady Eschina of Molle granted to the abbey the lands of Hethou, bounded, "as the water descends from the fountain called Bradestrother, between Hethou and Faveside, and as far as the rivulet which descends from Westerhethoudene; along that rivulet as far as the passage of the upper ford of the

---

* Retours, 145.   † Supposed to be the present Mowhaugh.

same rivulet, next to Crag, and so across Hathoudene, eastwards, as the crosses have been placed, and the ditches have been made, and the furrow has been drawn, and the stones have been set, as far as the rivulet of Easter Hethou; and from the ford of the same rivulet ascending as the wood and arable land meet above Halreberge, and so eastward, as far as Grenelle, near the white stone, as far as the foresaid head of the fountain of Bradestrother; with a certain portion of land beyond the rivulet of Hethou, westwards as far as Blyndwell, as the meadow and arable land meet, descending as far as the foresaid rivulet of Hethou."* This land afforded pasture for 400 sheep, 16 cattle, 2 work-horses, and 12 swine. About 1198, she also granted them "pasture for twenty cows and their calves, till the latter were grown up, and also one bull, part of a meadow which lay between Eddredesete and the rivulet of Ruhope, as far as the water of Blakepool; and that portion of land which lay above the bank of the Bolbent, opposite Blakepool; and the croft lying on the north side of the house of William the Forester, under the hill, and gave up every claim which she might have on the mill."† Before 1249, her daughter Cecilia, with the consent of her husband, gave them the toft and croft which belonged to William of Mollehope, (Mowhaugh), on the moors near to the outlet at

---

* Lib. de Calchou, p. 146.   † Ib., p. 130.

Whitelaw, on the English border; and 26 acres of the demesne lands of Molle, which were arable, viz., in Hauacres, from the land of Gilbert Avenel, eastward, nine acres, with half-an-acre near the rivulet of Altouneburne; two acres in Persouthside, and one acre next to the outlet which led to Persouth; one acre on the west side of Benlawe; nine acres and a rood in Dederig, which lay in detached portions between Altouneburne and the two crosses on the ascent to the south, and below a little hill; three acres next to the lands of the monks; one rood and all her share of the hill, and half-an-acre in Kydellawes croft: in Haustrother, eight acres of meadow, four of which lay between Hauacres and the furrow which separated the meadow from the meadow of Gilbert Avenel, and four acres of meadow below Persouthswire; thirteen acres of land in her demesnes, that is to say, her whole part of Mollestelle, which contained four acres and a half; and her part of the land which lay next the rivulet, descending from Brademedue, as far as the Bolbenth; half-an-acre called Crokecroft next the road to Persouth; two acres and a half between her sheepfold next to the outlet towards Persouth, as you ascend; and three acres in the *tilth* next to Persouth, excepting the *tilth* of Gilbert Avenel; and all her part of Brademedue, with pasture for 300 sheep, 10 cattle, 4 horses everywhere on the pasture of her lands; and her sheepfold near Aultonburne, and free passage to the monks and their men. The monks were also to have liberty to take from the woods of Persouth materials necessary to make their ploughs and fences.* Sir Gilbert Avenel, after the death of Lady Cecilia, confirmed said grants; and Eustace de Vesci, the over lord of Molle, at the request of Sir Gilbert, confirmed the monks in all their possessions.† These grants were also confirmed by Pope Innocent IV., before 1254.‡ In 1270, Henry of Halyburton confirmed all previous grants. About 1300, Adam de Roule and his wife Johanna, daughter of the said Henry Halyburton, granted the monks "four acres of land in the tenement of Molle, which lay in the upper part of Stapelaw, to be held so as they were not entitled to claim any commonty within their demesne lands of Molle, for which grant the monks received the granters into their brotherhood and participation in their prayers, and engaged to celebrate one mass weekly for their souls.§ About 1190, *Anselm* of Molle granted to the same monks "all the land and meadow and wood in the territory of Molle, which was on the east side of Erndbrandesdene—namely, from the bounds of the lands of the monks of Mailros, by the direct path as far as Erndbrandesdene, and as far as the ford of Bolbent, which

---

* Lib. de Calchou, pp. 118, 120, 141. † Ib., p. 139.
‡ Ib., pp. 351, 352. § Ib.

included all the lands and the wood and meadow which extended from these bounds to the eastward, as far the bounds of the church-lands of Molle, and upwards towards Hunedune; all Hulcheshou, in wood, plain, and pasture, except one acre of land which he gave to Walter the Mason.* From Richard, the son of the said Anselme, they got the *tilth* of Ladladde, containing eight acres and a rood. Richard of Lincoln confirmed the grant, and added an acre of land. About 1200, Isolde, daughter of Anselm, with consent of her husband, gave the monks an oxgang of land which lay on the east side near the land which Henry the *Fat* held of Richard Scott, with the pertinents thereof. In 1255, Richard, the son of Richard of Lincoln, gave them twenty acres of arable land and meadow in Mollehope, which the canons of Jedworde held of him in ferme, and pasture for sixty sheep and four cows, wheresoever they pleased, in all his lands of Molle, except corn-land and meadow, for the term of ten years after Whitsunday, 1258, for ten merks yearly. In 1260, Matildis, wife of Richard of Lincoln, in her free widowhood, "forgave to the monks all causes and complaints which she had or could have against them, their men, and their servants." She also granted the monks all the lands which they held in ferme from her late husband in Molle, to possess the

---

* Lib. de Calchou, pp. 12, 123.

same without claim or hinderance, on the condition that they should find her son William in victuals, along with the better and more worthy scholars in their poor's-house, as long as they retained the said lands in their hands.*

The monks of MAILROS also obtained valuable grants in this manor. Anselm of Molle, before 1185, granted them his whole *petary*, which was between Mollehopc, Bereop, and Herdstrete, which separated the lands of Molle from Hunum and his wood of Mollope, as much brushwood as one horse could carry to their grange of Hunedune, every year between Easter and the Nativity of St. Mary.† He granted them also the land and meadows which he and the nephew of Robert Avenel perambulated. He also granted to them that portion of land in the territory of Molle which was next their land on the south of the hill of Hunedune, and on the east bounded by the road from that hill to Molle, which road lay between the foresaid land and the church-lands of Molle, as far as a fountain on the west side of the same road—from thence along the side of Kippemoder, as far as certain large stones of the old building, which stood upon a small ridge on the south side of the land called Cruche. Afterwards, the boundary descended along the same ridge to the south side of the same Cruche, as far as the rivulet

---

* Lib. de Calchou, p. 142.   † Lib. de Mail., pp. 126, 127.

between the lands of Hunum and Molle.* Before 1218, these grants were confirmed by the over lord, Eustace de Vesci. In 1236, Walter, the son of Allan, who was the son of the first Walter the Stewart, granted to the same monks all the lands in Molle which he had in the fief of Sir William de Vesci, and all rights competent to him, in exchange for Freertun, which formerly belonged to the nuns of Southberwick, with 200 merks in boot. About the same time, Alexander II. erected the lands which the monks held in Molle into a free forest.† The monks also purchased Hungerigge, about 1258, from Adam of Hetune. About 1285, William of Sproveston gave the monks of Mailros that part of the lands of Altonburne which he had obtained from John de Vescy, his over lord.‡ They also had the lands of Uggings.

The monks of *Paisley*, about 1157, obtained from the wife of Walter the Stewart a ploughgate of land in the west part of Blackdene, according to the boundaries measured to them at her command by Eldief, provost *(prepositus)* of the town of Moll, viz., as the Stelnaburn falls into the Blackburn, and along that stream as far as two stones lying near the bank opposite the house of Ulf the steward, on the west; as far up as a certain ditch, and two stones standing in that ditch; from these stones as far as another

---

* Lib. de Mail., p. 129.   † Ib., p. 263.   ‡ Ib., p. 307.

ditch heaped with stones, to another ditch also heaped with stones, and from thence to Heselensahe, which goes as far as the ford of the torrent of Alembarke; from thence to the ford of Stelanburn, and down that stream to the Blackburn; four acres and three roods in the town of Molle, with common pasture belonging to one ploughgate. She also granted them pasture for 500 sheep.* The monks let their ploughgate to Robert Maleverer, for payment of half-a-merk of silver. At Paisley, Robert III., in 1396, granted to the monks the lands which they held in this territory, as part of the regality of Paisley.

The canons of *Jedburgh* only held twenty acres in this territory, till 1255, when they were granted to the monks of Kelso, as above stated.

ROBERT CROC, who followed Walter the Stewart into Scotland, and obtained from him Crocs-town, possessed the lands of Hungerigge in Molle, which was granted to him by Lady Eschina, with all its pertinents, liberties, and easements. The estate was given with his daughter Isabel in marriage to Robert Polloc, and about 1300, was granted by Isabel to Simon of Lyndesay, with consent of her husband and advice of her father, for payment of ten shillings yearly to herself, and " an aerie of young hawks to Lady Eschina and her heirs." The lands were afterwards granted by

---

* Regist. de Pass., pp. 24, 75.

Simon of Lyndesay to Helen, his daughter, and before 1238, the said Helen and her husband, Adam of Hetun, sold the same lands and a meadow called Holmede to the monks of Kelso, for £10 sterling and 10s. yearly, to Isabel, the daughter of Robert Croc, and her heirs.* Simon Lyndesey seems also to have been owner of other lands in Molle, which he derived from his mother.† He granted to his man Patrick six acres of land, an acre of meadow, an acre and a half in toft and croft, and one acre of meadow below *Chestres*, and above Selestede Ade ; two acres, and a half to be held of him in fee and heritage, for payment to him and his heirs of one pound of cumin, or threepence, at the Festival of St. James.‡

---

* Lib. de Mailros, pp. 257, 258.
† The surname of Lindsay is derived from the manor of Lindsay in Essex. Walter Lindsay and William Lindsay, two brothers, came into Scotland while David was Prince of Cumberland. William witnessed the Inquisitio Davidis in 1116. He is a witness to the charter of the Prince to the monks of Selkirk. They seem to have been constantly about David after he ascended the throne, and from him received grants of lands in Clydesdale and in the Lothians. Between 1189 and 1199, William Lindsay, the son of William, was Justiciary of Lothian. In the progress of time, branches of the family settled in Fifeshire and Berwickshire. A William de Lindsay held the lands of Earlston under the Earl of Dunbar. He granted land in Earlston and in Caddesley to the monks of Dryburgh, and he granted the patronage of the church of Earlston to the monks of Kelso.
‡ Lib. de Mailros, pp. 131, 132.

During the 13th century, Vedastus of Jeddeword was infeft in part of Swynesdene which he held of the monks of Melros. A person of the name of Simon possessed part of Blackdene. Before 1279, John de Vescy granted to William of Sproveston, chaplain, all the land which belonged to Amicia de Capella, in the town of Molle, the chief messuage there, and with the born slaves, their followers, and their cattle, with pertinents and services of freemen, to be held by him, his heirs, and assignees, excepting religious men, for payment of one suit thrice in the year at the head court of Sproveston. All the land belonging to William in Molle was erected into a free forest, for him and his heirs, by the same John de Vescy. About 1285, William granted these lands, half of the mill, half of the services of the lands held by Thomas Palmer, half of the services of the lands of Vedast of Jeddewood, half of the services of the land of Symon of Blackdene, and half of the services of Thomas, the son of Aucia, in consideration of which he asked only the prayers of the monks. The monks held these lands to the Reformation. They are now enjoyed by the house of Roxburghe.

COCKLAW, on the upper sources of the Beaumont, formed part of the territory of Molle. A powerful castle stood on this estate between two burns which descend from Cocklaw and Windgatehill, and near the houses now called Cocklaw-foot. Immediately after the battle of Homildon, in 1401, Henry Percy, with the Earl of March, laid siege to this castle, which was gallantly defended by John Greenlaw. At last, Percy, finding that he could not take this fortress, entered into an agreement with Greenlaw, that, if he had no rescue within three months, the castle was to be delivered up into the hands of the English. Intimation of this agreement being made to the Governor of Scotland, he assembled the lords in council for advice as to the levying of an army within the appointed time. Many of the council were of opinion that it was better to lose the castle than to hazard the lives of so many men as were necessary for the saving of it; but the Governor declared that he weighed the loss of it so much that, if none of the nobles would pass with him to the rescue, he would go himself and do what in him lay to save it. But the troubles which at that time arose in England caused Percy to raise the siege of the castle.* In 1481, the castle was ordered to be garrisoned with twenty men, to support the warden of the marches.† Before 1560, the estate of Cocklaw belonged to a family of the name of Gledstones. In 1561, John Gledstone of Cocklaw was charged with the slaughter of

---

* Hollingshed, vol. ii. pp. 48, 49.
† Acta Parl., vol. ii. p. 140.

Thomas Pebles and William Bell.* In 1569, James Gledstones subscribed the bond by the Border barons and others at Kelso, for the purpose of putting down the thieves of Liddesdale, Ewsdale, and Eskdale.† In 1606, James Gladstones, apparent of Cocklaw, was fined and amerciated in 500 merks for not entering Thomas Turnbull, younger, of Wauchope, accused of fire-raising on the lands of Harwood, and stealing from the Lady of Appotsyde 200 cows and oxen, 30 score of sheep, 30 horses and mares, and the whole plenishing of her house, worth £1000, and cutting down the trees growing on her lands.‡ In the same year, Robert, Lord Roxburghe, was served heir to his father, William Ker of Cessford, of the lands of Cocklaw, with whose descendants they still remain.§

COLRUST belonged to the monks of Kelso, as appears from their roll.‖ Before 1700, it was the property of Scott of Mangerton, and at that period Elizabeth Scott was served heir to her brother, Francis Scott, in the lands of Colruist, "comprehending the husbandlands of Adam Bell, feuar of Bellfoord, his twelve husbandlands of Belfoord, pertinents thereof, with teinds, rectorage, and vicarage,

---

* Pitcairn's Criminal Trials, vol. i. p. 414.
† Ib., vol. ii. p. 512. ‡ Ib., vol. iii. p. 396.
§ Retours, No. 36. ‖ Rent Roll of Abbey.

all united to the lands and barony of Heartrig.*
Colrust now belongs to the Society for the Propagation of the Gospel, and Belford is the property of Sir George Douglas, as heir of his mother, Hannah Charlotte, only daughter and heiress of Henry Scott of Belford.

The town of Molle was of old of considerable extent, with a peel and many fair houses in and around it, but it has entirely disappeared. In the town the monks of Kelso had fourteen cottages, each of which rented for two shillings yearly, and six days work, with the common easements of the town, and liberty to pasture cattle wherever the laird's cattle grazed. They had also one malt kiln, which rented at half-a-merk. A few scattered onsteads, with here and there a shepherd's house, are all that is now to be seen on that important territory. The church of Molle stood on the summit of a rising ground on the right bank of the Beaumont, but it also has fallen before the ruins of time, and the only evidence of a religious house at this place is its small graveyard, still used by those who love to mingle their ashes with their forefathers. Until lately, all kinds of bestial had access to this sacred spot, but the sepulchres of the dead are now protected by a fence. It is painful to observe the carelessness of landlords and tenants in protecting the little grave-

---

* Retours, No. 325.

yards of the district. As stated above, the son of Liulf gifted, in 1153, to the monks of Kelso, the church and the land lying adjacent thereto, namely, "from Houlaushau to its river, and from the river along Houlaueshau as far as the ford of Bolbent, opposite the church, and from that ford upward as far as Houlaueshau, and thence along the road as far as Hunedune, and thence as far as the head of the river of Houlaueshau common pasture, in the town of Molle, with easements."* This grant was confirmed by Herbert, bishop of Glasgow, by Malcolm IV., William the Lion, and Bishop Josceline. In 1186, Lady Eschina of Molle confirmed to the monks the previous grants of the church lands and liberties, and added, for the weal of the soul of her lord Walter, the son of Alan, of her daughter, who was buried at Kelso, and of others, that the monk's chaplain of Molle, their men dwelling in the town of Molle on the lands of the church, should have common pasture, with reasonable stock, and other privileges, in common with her men of Molle. Henry of Molle, the second husband of Lady Eschina, confirmed the grants made to the monks. About this time, a dispute arose between the monks and Henry of Molle and his lady, in regard to the extent of the rights claimed by the former in right of the church. It was at last agreed that the monks should have

---

* Lib. de Calchou, p. 144.

for ever, in the territory of Molle, pasture for 700 sheep and 120 cattle, in right of the church, with all the privileges which the parson ought to have, and also that the vicar and the men of the abbey, dwelling on the church lands of Molle, should have common pasture and easement in all things with the men of the land of Henry of Molle himself.* A like demand was made by the monks upon the lands of Anselm of Molle, which was settled by compromise. The monks gave up all claim made against Anselm in name of the parson of Molle, and he granted to them pasturage for 700 sheep and 100 cattle, over his land of Molle, with liberty to pasture over the whole of that land, except on corn and meadow, at any time of the year, except for 15 days before the 24th of June and 1st of August, during which time they were to use the pasture of Berehope only for cattle. He also gave them liberty to take wood for making sheep-cots, to allow both sheep and cattle to go at large, to give the monks room for their folds, with free passage through the lands of Molle. In consideration of the monks having given up the tithes of his mill, he gave up the multure, and granted to them the privilege of grinding at his mill at any time, whenever the hopper of the mill should be empty, unless the corn of his own demesne was lying to be ground. The monks of

---

* Lib. de Calchou, pp. 135, 136.

Kelso and Melrose disputed as to the smaller tithes and other rights belonging to the parish church of Molle, due by Melrose monks for the lands of Uggings. A reference being made to the Pope, he delegated the abbot of Paisley and the treasurer of Glasgow to act as the principal judges in the cause; and they having appointed the sub-dean of Glasgow to hear parties and pronounce judgment, the parties appeared before the sub-dean. The monks of Kelso stated that they held the church of Molle for their own uses; that the monks of Melrose had, after the fourth council of Latern, acquired lands within the parish, and withheld the tithes and other parochial rights of the church of Molle, to the injury of the house of Kelso: demanding that the monks of Melrose should pay £300 for the tithes which they withheld, and pay for the future. The sub-dean held that the monks of Melrose had unlawfully withheld the tithes and other rights claimed by the monks of Kelso in right of the church of Molle; that they should pay these tithes and rights to the monks of Kelso, as rectors of the church, as they had been accustomed to receive them from the other parishioners of Molle; and awarded 260 merks, as loss sustained by the monks of Kelso. In 1273, it was arranged before the sub-dean of Glasgow, in the presence of William Wyschard, archdeacon of St. Andrews, and chancellor of Scotland, who acted as mediator, that the monks of Melrose should pay yearly, for ever, to the monks of Kelso, thirteen chalders of good oatmeal, for the tithes of the lands of Molle, which they themselves cultivated, and for the teind sheaves of their men in Molle. The two houses of Kelso and Melrose seem to have had many differences as to this payment, till 1309, when a final settlement was agreed upon by several arbiters, in the church of St. James of Roxburgh.*

The chartularies of the abbeys contain many notices of the *woods* and *forests* in the territory of Molle. In the wood at "*the Scrogges*," the monks of Kelso got a grant of wood for making flakes for securing their sheep, and rods for repairing their ploughs. From the woods of Persouth, the monks were allowed to take material for their ploughs and for making fences. The same monks had also right to the *wood* on the east side of Erndbrandsdene. Not a trace of these woods is now to be seen, except a solitary tree, standing here and there in the mountain dells, and in the neighbourhood of the principal houses of the district.

This territory suffered severely during the Border wars. In Hertford's desolating expedition in 1545, the towns of Mowe, Museles, Colruist, Esheughe, Awtonburne, and Cowe were destroyed.

A number of persons in the 12th, 13th, and 14th centuries bore the surname of Molle.

---

* Lib. de Mail., pp. 391, 392.

MEREBODA,* MEREBOTLE,† MERBOTLE,‡ MERBOTTLE,§ MOREBOTTLE.‖—The ancient spelling of this place, which conferred a name on the parish, was Merbotle, which, in the Anglo-Saxon language, signifies the dwelling-place at the lake. The present orthography of the word did not come into use till the beginning of the seventeenth century. The territory of Morebattle, under the name of Mereboda, appears in the Inquisitionis Davidis in 1116.¶ At that early period, the church of Glasgow was possessed of the church and a carrucate of land in Merebotle. The territory seems to have been of limited extent, bounded by the lands of Whitton on the west, by Grubet, Clifton, and Primside, on the south and south-east, and by the barony of Linton on the north. Very little information exists as to the early history of this territory, further than an occasional notice in grants to the monks of Melrose, and in the Register of Glasgow. Between 1170 and 1249, charters are witnessed by Hugh, Roger, and William, designed of Merbotle.** The lands appear to have belonged to the family of Corbet. King Robert Bruce granted the lands of Marbottil to Ar-

---

* Circa 1116; Regist. Glasg., pp. 5, 7.
† Circa 1174; Lib. de Mailros, p. 58; Regist. Glasg., p. 23.
‡ Circa 1214; Lib. de Mailros; Regist. Glasg.
§ Circa 1575.   ‖ Acta Parl.; Retours.
¶ Regist. of Glasgow, pp. 5, 7.
** Lib. de Mailros, pp. 58, 152, 237.

chibald Douglas, supposed to be the brother of the Good Sir James.* In 1529, James V. granted to Robert Stewart and Janet Murray his wife, the lands of Marebottil and Middleby.† In the beginning of the seventeenth century, the lands of Morebattle were included in the barony of Minto, and possessed by Sir Walter Stewart.‡ The territory afterwards became a part of the barony of Grubet, and belonged to Sir William Bennet. It is now the property of the Marquis of Tweeddale.

The town of Morebattle stands on an eminence near to the river Cayle. The houses have been greatly improved since the end of last century. When the Old Account of the parish was written, the houses were mostly of one storey, and covered with thatch; but they are now well built, the greater number two-storied and covered with slate. After the property came into the possession of the Marquis of Tweeddale, he feued out the ground on which the town is built for the terms of nineteen times nineteen years, at the rate of £5 sterling per acre. About the end of last century, 380 acres of land adjoining the village were parcelled out into 26 small pendicles, and let to the feuars of the town. There was also a small common in the neighbourhood of the town, on which the feuars had the right of casting

---

* Robertson's Index, p. 11, No. 50.
† Reg. Mag. Sig., lib. xxiii. No. 115.   ‡ Retours, No. 73.

turfs, which, with the consent of the Marquis of Tweeddale, was divided amongst them in shares proportioned to the amount of their rentals. It is now enclosed, and bears good crops of potatoes, turnips, grass, and corn, and is a great benefit to the rentallers. The feu-duty is trifling. The church of Morebattle stands on the north of the village, on the verge of a steep bank, the base of which being formed of pure sand, gradually yielded to the operations of the river Cayle, and each flood brought down large masses of earth from the top of the ridge, so as to endanger the church and graveyard, but by embankments and planting, the stream is kept at a distance from the sand-bank.* Tradition tells of a prophet who foretold that the church and graveyard would be carried away by the stream. Unless care be taken to keep the stream from the bank, there can be little doubt that the prophecy will be fulfilled. The church was dedicated to St. Lawrence, and was

---

* There are three parallel ridges running south and north. On the top these ridges have a coating of soil, while below they are formed of sand. The middle ridge affords a beautiful specimen of the sand-bank being converted into rock. In it the lines are discernible by which the quarryman of centuries hence will be guided in his operations on the then solid rock. It is instructive to watch the progress of human events, to trace the path of man from a state of barbarism to civilization; and it is equally edifying to observe the progress of the earth on which we tread, from one state into another. The bank of sand referred to, with not one particle

confirmed to the bishops of Glasgow by successive popes—Alexander III., Lucius III., Urban III., and Honorius III., before 1216.* About 1228, a pertinacious controversy arose between Hugh de Potton, archdeacon of Glasgow, Walter, bishop of Glasgow, and Thomas, the rector of Morebattle, as to their several rights. Pope Gregory delegated the bishop of Dunkeld, the prior of Coldingham, and the dean of Lothian, to settle the dispute. The commissioners met in the chapel of Nesbit, and, after hearing parties, found that the church of Merebotle was a prebend in the church of Glasgow, yielding twenty merks; that, for the future, the archdeacon and his successors should perpetually receive thirty merks annually in lieu of a mansion, but should make no claim against the rectory of Morebattle on any ground whatever, and to submit to the conscientious determination of the bishop.† A dispute having arisen, in 1455, between the monks of Melrose and

---

larger than another, is fast being converted into a solid consistence, and which will, in after-ages, yield large blocks of stone. That lump of sand, which can now be crumpled to separate particles, will in process of time resist the steel-pointed tool of the labourer. Those lines, beautifully delineated on the face of the bank, are the places where the quarryman will insert his wedge and lever, for the raising of immense blocks for some stupendous undertaking of the yet unborn.—*Vide* vol. i. pp. 42, 43.

* Regist. Glasg., pp. 23, 30, 43, 50, 55, 95.
† Ib., pp. 125, 126.

Patrick Hume, the archdeacon of Teviotdale, regarding the tithes of Gateshaw and Cliftoncotis, was referred to Master John of Otterburn, licentiate of decrees, Master Gilbert Heryng, vicar of Innerwic, Sir Andrew Bell, a monk of Newbottle, licentiate in theology, and Alexander of Casteltaris, rector of the church of Keth, who met at the dwelling-place of Mr. Nicholas of Otterburn, in the presence of several notaries and witnesses, and decided that the tithes of the towns of Gateshaw and Cliftoncotis had been continually raised and possessed by the monks of Melrose from time immemorial, and that those tithes ought of right to belong to them, and that they were legitimately secured to them by prescription against the archdeacon of Teviotdale,—reserving half-a-merk of silver to be annually paid in lieu of the whole tithes of said towns by the monks of Melrose to the archdeacon of Teviotdale and his successors for the time being, and imposed perpetual silence on the said archdeacon and his successors as to the said tithes.* The present church was built on the site of the old church, in 1757. It underwent considerable repairs in 1839, and is now a comfortable place of worship, capable of containing about 500 sitters. A fountain below the churchyard bears the name of Laurie's Well, a corruption of St. Lawrence, to whom the church was dedicated.

---

* Lib. de Mailros, pp. 583, 587.

The graveyard, although situated on the top of the ridge, is rough and moorish. About 1812, it was infested by a numerous colony of rats, who, after feasting on the bodies of the dead, were observed going in great numbers to the well of the saint to quench their thirst. There were in early days two chapels in this parish, dependent on the mother church of Morebattle, one at Clifton on the Beaumont water, and the other at Nether Whitton. In 1186, Pope Urban III. confirmed to Joceline, bishop of Glasgow, the church of Morebattle, "cum capella de Cliftun et capella de Whittun."* There is a dissenting meeting-house in Morebattle. It stood originally at Gateshaw, which was the first settlement of the Secession in the south of Scotland. The first minister was ordained in 1739, and, until a church was erected, the people assembled during winter and summer on the brae, and the minister preached from a tent.† About 1779, the house and manse were removed to Morebattle. The pious David Morrison was the first minister of Morebattle, where he spent a long and useful life. His successor,

---

* Regist. Glasg., p. 55.

† In regard to this settlement of seceders at this place, the minister of Hounam, in the Old Statistical Account, remarks :—The people of Hounam are, "however, in general, piously disposed, and rational in their religious sentiments, which is, perhaps, somewhat the more remarkable, as Gateshaw is bordering on this, where there has been from the beginning of the Secession a meeting-house of the wildest

Mr. Cranstown, is at present pastor of the congregation. The wife of Mr. Morrison introduced the double-handed spinning-wheel into the district; but it was a long time before it came into general use, owing to the women of the locality being at that period chiefly engaged in agricultural labour, and sat down with reluctance to the spinning-wheel. There is also a Free Church in the village, under the charge of an excellent pastor, and which is well attended. About twenty years ago, a new school-house was erected, said to be, without exception, the finest in the county. It is attended on an average by 100 scholars.

Owing to the proximity of this village to the Border, it was often destroyed by the predatory bands of England. In 1523, it was destroyed by the Marquis of Dorset, Sir William Bulmer, Sir Anthony Darcey, and others, who carried out of Teviotdale about 4000 head of cattle. In 1544, it was burnt by Sir Ralph Eurie, Sir Brian Laiton, and Sir George Bowes. Next year, it was destroyed by the Earl of Hertford's army.

---

kind of seceders, the Antiburghers, who are zealous in disseminating their principles—not supposed very favourable to morals and true piety. These people were formerly numerous in the parish; they are now dwindled much away, and there are not twenty of all the different denominations, and of that number there is but one small tenant."—General Appendix to the Old Statistical Account, vol. xxi. pp. 19, 20.

WHITTON.—The name of this ancient place is thought to be derived from an early proprietor of the name of *Hwite*, who conferred his name on the place: *Hwites-tun*, i. e., White's dwelling or tun. The family of Riddel acquired this territory from King David I. before 1153, with whose descendants it remained until the beginning of the present century. The monks of *Mailros* had considerable possessions in this territory, which they obtained from the vassals of the over-lord, Patrick Ridel. A tenant of the name of Bernoldebi gave to the monks Rauensfen, as perambulated and bounded by him and the monks. It consisted of twenty acres, and extended from the head of Harehoudenc as far as the land which William of Ridel gave to Matildis Corbet, his wife, and thence towards Whitton, and thence towards Harehou as far as a little thorn, and thence as far as Harcar, and thence by an ancient ditch to Harehoudene. He also gave to the monks a gift of the land from the top of Harehopdene, ascending westward by a syke; and thence across southwards along a furrow which bounded the lands let to William, the parson of Hunum, as far as the old ditch, which was the boundary of the lands on the south; and thence downwards towards the east as far as the head of Harehopedene. Geoffrey, the son of Walter of Lilliescliue, gave three oxgangs of arable land, as they lay together above Rauensfen, next to the lands of Heuiside, which the monks held by the grant of

Patrick the over-lord: also thirteen acres and half-a-rood at the same place. Ysabel, the wife of William of Ridel, granted to the same monks an oxgang of land which lay between Hordlawe and Tockesheles, which oxgang had previously been granted by Geoffrey, the cook of Whitton, to the hospital of Jerusalem, afterwards purchased by Ysabel's father, and given to her. These grants were confirmed to the monks by Patrick of Ridel and his son Walter, by Robert de Brus and William the Lion. On Eustace de Vesci becoming over-lord of Whitton, he confirmed all the grants which had been made in favour of the monks before 1218. King Alexander II. also confirmed all the grants as defined in the charter of confirmation of Patrick of Ridel. In 1454, the charter of Patrick was confirmed by James II. At the beginning of the present century, Over and Nether Whitton, with the mill thereof, were possessed by Sir John Buchanan Riddel of that Ilk. They are now the property of Sir John Warrander, John Ord, and Christopher Douglas. The town of Whitton must have been of old of considerable extent. The ruins of the fort of the town are still to be seen. The fort of Whitton was cast down by Surrey when he besieged Cessford, and both Over and Nether Whitton were destroyed by Hertford in 1545.

Before 1306, several families and individuals bore the surname of Whitton.

PRENWENSETE,* PRONEWESSETE,† PRENWEN-
SETH,‡ PROMSET,§ PRIMSIDE.—This territory was
granted by Earl Henry, the son of David I., to one
of the family of Ridel.|| It is believed to have been
the earliest possession of that family in Scotland.
About 1180, Geoffrey Ridel granted to the monks of
Kelso, for the weal of the soul of Earl Henry, who
gave the town to his father, two oxgangs of land,
with toft and croft, free from multure; pasture for
1000 sheep; the common easements of said town, as
well in fuel as in other things; a portion of meadow
on the east of the town, with liberty of pasture
everywhere without the meadow-land and corn-land,
except on one ploughgate of demesne reserved for
the pasture of his own cattle.** He granted them
also a haugh lying near the waters of Bolbent, next
the march of Cliftun, on the west side of the road
from Cliftun to Primside. In 1208, on the settlement of the dispute between the monks of Kelso and
Melrose, the former, in accordance with the judg-

---

* Circa 1153; Lib. de Calchou, p. 294.
† Circa 1180; Lib. de Mailros, pp. 134, 135.
‡ Circa 1213; Ib., p. 154. § Circa 1300; Ib., pp. 110, 111.
|| Primside is thought to be the first settlement of the
family of Riddel in Scotland, which, with Corbet and King-
horn, are the oldest surnames in this country. The lineage
of Riddel will be given along with the account of the barony
of Riddel.
** Lib. de Calchou, p. 294.

ment of the king, conveyed to the latter two oxgangs of land and two acres of meadow, and pasture for 400 sheep in Primside. This grant was confirmed by Geoffrey Ridel, the lord of the territory. In 1215, Alexander II. confirmed to the monks of Melrose those two oxgangs, and pasture for 400 sheep. In the beginning of the 14th century, the house of Kelso had, in the territory, seven acres of land, and common pasture for 300 dinmonts.

There is difficulty in ascertaining the exact boundaries of this estate, but it is thought to have comprehended the present Primside, Primside Dykes, Cruickedshaws and Primside Mill. In the 15th century, Primside belonged to a branch of the family of Cessford, said to be now represented by Ker of Gateshaw. It belongs to the family of Benburghe. Primside shared the same fate as the other towns and villages in the district when Hertford paid his destructive visit in 1545.

CROOKEDSHAWS, the *Crukehou* or *Croucho*, of the charters, stands at the east end of Linton Loch. It has been at one time nearly surrounded by the waters of the loch. At this place, a high ridge or bar of sand runs from near the onstead, almost across the neck of the loch. It is not easy to account for the formation of this remarkable bar of sand; but the probability is that it has been made either by the burn of Cruikedshaws bringing down sand and gravel from the mountains,* or by the deep waters of the lake drifting sand round the turns of the hill. The ridge of sand appears as if bent by the action of the waves. The turnpike road to Yetholm passes over the end of the ridge.

CLIFTON, which derives its name from its situation at the cliffs, belonged to St. Cuthbert, at the end of the seventh century. At the end of the 12th century, it belonged to Walter of Wildleshoures. At that early period, the monks of Melros had land in the territory of Clifton. Walter granted to the said monks land in Clifton, described as follows: —" From the two stones projecting from the rock above the small rush-bed on the east side of Crukehou, close by where the lands of Prenwensete and the lands of Grubbheued meet together; along that rush-bed and the stone lying below it; along a certain ridge, according to the marches and bounds which he and Ernald, abbot of Melros, and Symon, the archdeacon, perambulated, and made as far as the Bireburn, and thence across the Bireburn in a

---

* It is hardly possible to imagine the immense quantities of sand which are brought down from the mountains in a storm of rain. Last summer, Primside Hill, which is steep and high, was under a crop of turnips, and, while the crop was yet young, a thunder-storm broke upon the locality, and brought down such a quantity of sand and gravel as filled the turnpike road at the base of the hill several feet deep, and lay like wreaths of snow.

southern direction towards Molle, as far as the rock next the road eastwards, above the Cukoueburn as the Cukoueburn descends as far as the same great road, namely, that which leads from Rochesburgh to Molle; and from thence along that road as far as the Mereburn, which separates the land of Cliftun from the land of Molle; and thence along the Mereburn to the boundaries of Hunum; and thence as the boundaries run between the land of Hunum and the land of Cliftun, as far as the boundaries of Grubbeheued; and thence along the marches and boundaries which he perambulated between the lands of Cliftun and the land of Grubbeheued; and thence above the foresaid Cruikehou, along the boundaries which he perambulated between the land of Cliftun and the land of Prenewensete; and thence as far as the foresaid two stones on the rock above the foresaid rush-bed."* The family of Corbet seems to have been the next proprietor of Clifton, and who also purchased, in 1241, the land which belonged to Roger Lardenar and his wife Matildis, in the territory of Cliftun. Before 1306, John of Sumerill had lands in Cliftun. The family of Rutherford was possessed of lands in Cliftun, which were forfeited, and granted by Robert Bruce to Roger Finlay. Roger Aillermere had a portion of the lands of Cliftun, and which were granted by Richard II. to William Badby. In the beginning of

---

* Lib. de Mailros, pp. 107, 108.

the 16th century, William Pringle of Torwoodlee obtained a charter of the lands of Clifton. In the 17th century it was divided among four families. James Tweedie of Drummelyier possessed the half of the lands and barony; in 1615, John Pringle of Tofts, a descendant of the Torwoodlee family, was proprietor of two portions thereof; and, in 1616, Thomas Pott was possessed of one mercat land of old extent, within the under half of the barony of Cliftun.* The situation of the town of Clifton was on the right bank of the Beaumont, at a place where the water of Cliftun joins that river. A farm-house and a few cottages occupying the same position, are all that remains of the once important town of Clifton, and one of the most ancient towns of Northumbria. It was destroyed by Hertford in 1545.

GRUBBEHEUED,† GRUBESHEUED,‡ GRUBHEUED,§ GRUBET.—The etymology of this name is doubtful. It may be intended to describe hills on which dwarf shrubs grow. About the middle of the 12th century, the territory was the property of Uctred, who, before 1181, adopted the name of Grubbeheued as his surname. In 1181, the said Uctred, and Symon, his son and heir, granted to the monks of Melrose Elstaneshalche, which lay on the west side of the old course of the water of Cayle, near to the

---

* Retours, Nos. 79, 82, 84.   † Circa 1180; Lib. de Melros.
‡ Circa 1180, 1189; Lib. de Melros.   § Circa 1300.

monks' lands of Whittun, on condition that they were to be admitted into their fraternity, and participate in all the privileges of the church.* The land contained in this grant was afterwards quit-claimed for ever to the monks, in presence of Joceline, the bishop of Glasgow, and the archdeacon of that church, Huctred and his heirs vowing by the holy church of St. Mary of Melrose, "that they should never claim anything within the boundary of the lands conveyed by them to the monks, but defend and maintain everywhere the house of Melros and everything belonging to it." Uctred and his heirs also granted to the monks right of road across the lands of Grubbesheued for the carriages belonging to the abbey passing to their grange of Hunedun without challenge. This family was in possession of the territory about the end of the 13th century. At this period the De Vescis were over-lords of this territory, and about the beginning of the 14th century, Robert Bruce granted the lands to Archibald Douglas. About 1426, Nichol Rutherford of that Ilk, ancestor of the Rutherfords of Hundalee, got a charter under the great seal of the lands of Grubet.† In 1629, Andrew, Lord Jedburgh, was served heir to Andrew, master of Jedburgh, one of the senators of the college of justice, in the lands of Grubet, with the mills thereof.‡ In 1647, William

---

* Lib. de Mailros, p. 111. † Retours, No. 141.
‡ Douglas Peerage, 588.

Bennet was served heir to his father, Master William Bennet, rector of Ancrum, in the lands and barony of Grubet, with the mills of Grubet.* From the family of Bennet, the land passed into the family of Nisbett of Dirlton, and it now belongs to the Marquis of Tweeddale. The town of Grubet stood upon the right bank of the river Cayle, at a little distance from the mill. It now consists only of a shepherd's cot and byre. The banks on each side of the Cayle valley, particularly in the neighbourhood of Grubet mill, used to be covered with the broom; but this beautiful shrub, which might have vied with the broom of the Cowdenknowes, was rooted up several years ago. The "long yellow broom" might have been spared to adorn the steep braes of the lovely Cayle. Both broom and whin seem to be under the ban of the agriculturist.

WIDEOPEN, anciently written WYDEHOIPE, a name descriptive of its position on the peninsula where the Cayle enters the large valley extending from Cruickedshaws to Marlefield, formed a part of the barony of Grubet in the beginning of the 17th century. About 1700, it was the property of the maternal uncle of the poet Thomson, and where tradition says he was born, and in the neighbourhood of which he wrote his "Winter."† The

---

* Retours, No. 195.   † *Supra*, pp. 114, 115.

hill on which it is said the poem was written has two summits, and bears the name of Parnassus. Wide-open is again united to Grubet.

GATESHAW, which is situated on the left bank of the Cayle, was of old a possession of the abbey of Melrose, and was, at the end of the 15th century, *fermed* by Andrew Ker of Gateshaw, who, in 1498, appeared in the court of the abbot, and swore on the holy evangels, that he should not intromit with the herezeld of his tenants, but that the abbot should have them while they happened to be vacant, without prejudice or guile.* The lands of Gateshaw and Cliftoncote remained with the monks till the Reformation. In 1510, the same Andrew Ker of Gateshaw was accused at the Justiceaire at Jedworth, for the slaughter of John Murray of Falahill. Lancelot Ker, his son, and James Ker of Whiterig, were his sureties.† Lancelot succeeded his father; and, in 1530, along with the barons and lairds of the shires of Roxburgh and Berwick, submitted to the king's will for breaking their bonds.‡ In 1564, Richard Ker was owner of Gateshaw, and was a party to the contract between the Scotts and Kers. It would thus appear that the lineage, as given by Burke, of the family of Gateshaw, is not correct.

---

* Lib. de Mailros, p. 125.
† Pitcairn's Criminal Trials, vol. i. p. 69. ‡ Ib., p. 147.

William Ker, the present proprietor of the estate, is descended from the foresaid Lancelot. Gateshawbrae, on this estate, is hallowed as being the place where the covenanters worshipped, and where the first congregation of the Seceders in the south of Scotland formed a congregation in 1739, of whom Mr. Hunter was the first pastor. On the 17th October, 1839, about 3000 people assembled here to celebrate the centenary of the event, and the devotional exercises were sustained by dissenting ministers from the neighbouring towns and villages. "Nothing could be finer," says a writer who was present, "than when from the vast multitude there arose the song, the loud acclaim of praise, with a volume and majesty worthy of an occasion which had taken for itself that

> Temple not made with hands,
> The vaulted firmament.

It seemed to take the soul of that waste place with joy."

CORBET HOUSE, named after its early proprietor, Corbet, now belongs to Mr. Ker of Gateshaw.* It was repaired and renewed about the beginning of the century by Sir Charles Ker, the predecessor of the present owner of the estate. In 1522, it was

---

* Corbet is one of the oldest surnames in Scotland. *Supra*, p. 142.

burnt by the English, who ravaged the banks of Cayle and Beaumont, in retaliation of an inroad into Northumberland by Lancelot Ker. It was again destroyed by Hertford in 1545. It is named the "tower of Gateshaugh," in the list of places destroyed, and the present Gateshaw is called "New Gateshaugh." The tower seems to have been the principal mansion of the estate.

OTTERBURN, anciently Otirburn, appears in the beginning of the 15th century. Nicholas of Otirburn was a master of arts, a licentiate in degrees, a canon of the church of Glasgow, and vicar of St. Giles, Edinburgh. John of Otirburn appears about the same time. It was at the end of last century the property of Gilbert Elliot, and it is now the property of James Wilson.

The lands of TOFTS and COWBOG belonged to William Bennet, rector of Ancrum, in 1647, and then formed a part of the barony of Grubet. The small property of Heavyside has retained its name from the 12th century, without almost any corruption. It conferred a surname on William of Heuside in the 13th century. In the end of the last century it belonged to Andrew Henderson. It is now the property of Christopher Douglas.

LOCHSIDE and FOUMERDEAN were the property of Andrew Ker of Hoselaw, and now belongs to Robert

Oliver, whose beautiful mansion stands on the north margin of Primsideloch.

HUNUM,* HUNEDUNE,† HOWNAM,‡ HOUNAM,§ HOWNAM.—The name of this territory is said by Chalmers to be an abbreviation of *Howen-ham*, and derived from a person named *Howen* or *Owen*, who settled here.|| During the second century, *Howen*, the son of *Ruth*, witnessed a charter of Richard de Morville, the constable of Scotland, who died in 1189. But may the name not be derived from Roger de *Ow*, a follower of Earl Henry, the heir-apparent of David I., and who had large estates in Berwickshire? He may have first settled here, and conferred his name on the place. It is probable, however, that the true etymology may be found to be *Hodham*, signifying the *upper* village or town. The territory first appears in the possession of a person of the name of Orm,¶ before 1164, and who

---

* A.D. 1165, 1250; Regist. Glasg.; Lib. de Mailros.
† Ib. ‡ 1600; Lib. de Mailros.
§ 1650; Retours. || Caledonia, vol. ii. p. 165.
¶ The family of Orm is supposed to have come from Northumberland, in the days of David I. Orm, the son of Eilar, is a witness to a charter of Malcolm IV., before 1160, granting to the church of Glasgow the church of old Rokesburg and the chapel of the castle. He is said to have settled at Ormston, on the Teviot, from whom the place derived its name. Orm, the son of Hugh, acquired lands in the shires of Forfar and Fife during the reign of Malcolm IV., and from William

was succeeded by his son John.* In 1199, William, called De Laundeles, a son of John of Hunum, was in possession of the lands. About the same time, William built a chapel at Rasawe in honour of St. Mary, and gifted the lands of Rasawe, in pure and perpetual alms, to the monks of Melrose, on condition of their maintaining a chaplain to celebrate masses at the chapel.† This grant seems to have comprehended the territory from the Capehopeburn on the east, up to the ditch between Raweshawe and Cuthbertshope, and thence by the march between him and Richard de Umphravill,‡ to the Roman way on the west, and along that road to the boundary of the lands of Chatthou, and thence by the Chatthou march to the Capehopeburn. This district, attached

---

the Lion he obtained the manor of Abernethy, in Strathern, after which he assumed the surname of Abernethy. At the death of Alexander, Lord Abernethy, in the reign of Robert I., without male issue, his three daughters carried his estate and blood into the families of Stewart, Lindsay, and Lesley.

* This John is thought to have been the possessor of Over Crailling, now called Crailing Hall, on the Oxnam. He was one of the sheriffs of Roxburghshire. He is the second sheriff that can be traced at that period.

† Lib. de Mailros, p. 122.

‡ Gilbert de Umphraville granted to the monks of Kelso the tenth of his foals of his breeding mares in the forest of Cottonshope, which lay within the English border, opposite to the grant of William of Hunum; and these foals he allowed to follow their dams till they were two years old.—Lib. de Calchou.

to the chapel at Rasawe, appears to have included all the land lying between the Capehopeburn, Chatthou, and the English border. The grant was confirmed by William the Lion. After some time, William repented of his liberal gift to the monks, and endeavoured to regain forcible possession of the territory, but the commissioners of Pope Innocent decided that he should enjoy only a liferent of the lands, on the condition of their becoming the property of the monks at his death.* In 1225, William resigned the territory to the monks, and which was next year confirmed by Alexander II.† In 1237, the canons of Jedburgh agreed to find a chaplain to celebrate the masses for the souls of William, his wife, Donancia de Clerefei, and all the faithful dead, at Rasawe, as appointed by the bishop of Glasgow, instead of at the house of Melrose. John de Laundeles, who lived about 1245, confirmed the grant made by his father, or uncle, William, to the monks; and granted free passage to them between their grange at Hunedune and Rasawe. The monks of Melrose obtained a grant of lands on the east part of the territory of Hunum. Between 1164 and 1174, John, the son of Orm, granted to them certain lands which lay between his lands and the lands of Whitton, the lands of Grubet, the lands of Clifton, and the lands of Molle, as the boundaries were fixed

---

* Lib. de Calchou, pp. 124, 125.   † Ib., p. 246.

in presence of Bishop Ingleram and many good men, namely, "as far as the place where a small rivulet falls into Huneduneburn on the east side of Hulkilles, and thence upwards by this rivulet as far as its source, and thence westward to a little hill, and thence across the ridge between Brunecnol and Helle, and thence descending by the marches he made for them into Hawfurlungdene, and thence as the burn descends from Hawfurlungdene into Kalne."* This grant seems now to be represented by the farms called the Granges. The gift was confirmed by William the Lion and the granter's son William. Before 1227, the same William gave them the whole of that land called Brunocnollflat. John de Laundeles confirmed to the monks all the lands which they had in the territory of Hunum.† All these subjects remained with the monks till the Reformation. In 1471, James Rutherfurd of that Ilk got a charter, under the great seal, of the lands and barony of Hownam. In 1605, the Stewarts of Traquair were proprietors of half of the lands and barony of Hownam, comprehending the lands of Philogar and Cunzearton.‡ In 1650, the Earl of Roxburghe was retoured in the lands of Rasawe, which had formerly belonged to the monks of Melrose. The Duke of Roxburghe is proprietor of nearly a third of the

---

* Lib. de Melros, pp. 121, 122.   † Ib., pp. 244, 667.
‡ Retours, No. 30.

whole parish of Hownam. The church of Hownam is situated within a bend of the Cayle river, near to the place where Capehopeburn flows into it. It is said to have been originally in the form of a cross, but it is now a rectangular building, 50 feet in length, by 19 in breadth, 10 feet having been taken off its length in 1752.* It affords accommodation for 226 persons. The manse was built in 1776, and repaired and improved in 1832. The church belonged to William of Hunum before 1185. In 1220, it was in the possession of the monks of Jedburgh. At that time it was agreed between the monks and the bishop of Glasgow, that the whole tithes of corn within the parish should belong to the canons, the vicar receiving ten pounds annually, or the altarages, in his option, on his giving annually, at the feast of St. James, a stone of wax to the monastery of Jedburgh.† At this settlement, the convent reserved right to an acre of land, in some suitable place, on which to stack their corn.‡ In 1227, the monks of Melrose compounded with the canons of Jedburgh for the tithes of Rasawe, by a payment of 20s. annually to the church of Hunam. For the grange of Hunedun, the monks of Melrose paid forty pence in accordance with an agreement between them and William the parson, in 1185.

---

* New Statistical Account. † Regist. of Glasg., p. 96.
‡ "Ad reponendum bladum suum in loco competente."

But the monks of Melrose having disputed with the canons of Jedburgh as to their rights to the church of Hunum, and which they gave up on the canons agreeing to allow the lands of Hundune and Rasawe to go tithe free.* In 1567, the stipend of the reader of Hownam was £16, with the kirk lands. When parliament ratified the dissolution of Jedburgh and "Cannanbie" in favour of the Earl of Home, in 1621, it was enacted that the minister serving the cure of Hownam for the time should have for his sustentation three chalders victual, half bear and half oatmeal with the whole vicarage, manse, and glebe of the kirk.† In 1606, the patronage of the church of Hounam was in the hands of the Earl of Morton. In 1656, the advowson of the church was in the hands of the family of Rutherfurd. The patronage is now in the family of Warrender. The old town of Hounam stood a little way east from the Kirk Town, on the same bank of the river. The town of Hownam Kirk is situated near to the church between the Cayle and the Capehopeburn, consisting of a few modern houses, well built and cleanly kept. On the banks of the Capehope there are the ruins of a considerable number of houses, with the foundations of a mill. Here, it is said, the far-famed Rob the Ranter lived.‡ At Mainside, in the same locality,

---

* Lib. de Melros, p. 242.   † Acta Parl., vol. iv. p. 638.
 ‡ Vol. i., Addenda. The ancient name of this place was *Cuithenop.*—Lib. de Melros, p. 122.

there were of old nine cottages, but which were thrown down to make way for a farm-house and its offices. In 1544, the town was destroyed by Robert Collingwood, who also burned the towns of Sharplaw, Hownam, Heavyside, Hownam Grange, and other places. The town also suffered on the incursions of Eurie and Hertford. In 1545, Over Hownam, Nether Hownam, and Hownam Kirk, were burnt and cast down by Hertford. In 1684, John Ker of Hownam was executed at the Grassmarket, Edinburgh, for his share in the rebellion of Bothwell.* On a hill above the town there are traces of a camp or fortified place, called "the Rings." The steep sides of this hill, towards the north and west, are defended by several terraces or rings, and on the summit are the foundations of a number of circular huts. On the south the ground is level. It seems to have been intended as a defence against an attack from the north. This is the locality of the stones called "the Eleven Shearers." Tradition bears that these stones were eleven persons who had gone to that place on the Sabbath-day for the purpose of shearing corn, and while so engaged were turned into stone. No doubt the punishment of the eleven shearers was a pious invention of some good priest, to deter the rude inhabitants of that day from breaking the Sabbath. The clergy of that day were good and

---

* Crookshank's Hist., vol. ii. p. 208.

able, and knew well how to deal with the wild people amongst whom they laboured. But there must have been more persons engaged in shearing than eleven, for, on examining the locality carefully, I found that these stones, which are now broken, had only formed a part of a large circle, communicating with the summit of the hill. The view from this place is extensive and beautiful, and will repay a visit to it in July or August; and here, as well as "on every cairn-crowned" summit amidst the Cheviots, the violet abounds.

CHATTHOU, which derives its name from the mossy nature of the hill at which it is situated, seems to have been a separate estate at an early period, and to have conferred a surname upon several persons. Adam and John de Chatthou witnessed charters during the reign of William the Lion. Alexander de Chatthou was a witness to a charter in the reign of Alexander III. The same Alexander de Chatthou claimed, in 1226, portions of land lying within the boundaries of Rasawe, granted by William of Hunum to the monks of Kelso; but renounced the claim on being satisfied that it was unfounded. In 1296, Adam de Chatthou swore fealty to Edward I.* John de Chatthou got certain lands in Roxburghshire from King Robert Bruce, in

---

* Ragman's Roll, p. 127.

1322, which had been forfeited by the previous owner. The family of Chatthou seems to have possessed the property till the 15th century. In 1424, John Rutherford, second son of Richard Rutherford of that Ilk, progenitor of the family of Hunthill, got a grant of the lands of Chatthou, from Archibald, Earl of Douglas. Over Chatthou passed into the family of Ker about the end of the 16th century, and at the death of Christian Ker, Lady Chatthou, it became the property of the Synlaws family, who added the name of Ker to Scot. Nether Chatthou was at the beginning of this century the property of the Duke of Roxburghe. It now belongs to James Dickson.

PHILOGAR was at one time famed for its woods, but which were cut down many years ago. It was the property of the family of Rutherford, and is now enjoyed by Stavert of Hoscoat. Chatthou and Philogar were long famed for the produce of their dairies, which gave rise to the old proverbial distich:—

> "There's as good cheese at Chatto as e'er was chewed wi' chafts,
> There's as gude butter at Philogar as e'er was weigh'd wi' weights."

Owing to the farmers, generally, having given up the practice of milking the ewes, it is difficult to obtain cheese made from ewe milk.

BEIROPE, an ancient possession of Anselm of Whitton, afterwards of Molle. Anselm gave to the monks of Kelso a right of petary and pasturage for cattle, at certain seasons of the year, in Beirope. It seems to have conferred a surname on a family. In 1606, Robert Beirhope was accused of going to Littledene, belonging to Sir John Ker of Hirsel, and breaking up the byre doors, and stealing sixteen cows and oxen, with six horses and mares, and other goods. He was acquitted. The jury who tried him were John Mow of that Ilk, James Halyburton of Mertown, James Ker of Steelstockbraes, John Robson of Burvanes, and Patrick Dickson of Belchester, and others of little note.*

The BURVANES belonged to John Robson, and stood on the right bank of the river Cayle, a little below Heavyside mill.

BUCHTRIG, now belonging to James Wilson, seems to have been included in the district attached to the little chapel of St. Mary's. Near to the onstead is a hill called "the Moat," but I cannot ascertain the reason for its being called by that name. The hill does not appear to have been fortified. A road of sufficient breadth for a cart winds to the summit, with here and there stones placed so as to prevent a

---

* Pitcairn's Criminal Trials, vol. ii. p. 515.

vehicle going over the steep sides of the hill. My impression is that the top of the hill has been used as a quarry at some distant day. At the base of the hill, on the east, the foundations of houses can be distinctly traced. It may have been the locality of the little chapel of St. Mary. A high hill to the south of the Moat is called "Standard," evidently a corruption of *Stane*-ard, signifying "the Stone mountain."

OVER WHITTON, the ancient possession of Riddell, now belongs to John Ord, and *Chestres* to Christopher Douglas.

A yearly fair was formerly held at *Capehope*, and which was well attended, but it has long ceased to exist. A Border tryst is still held at *Penny Muir*, on the 31st July and 15th day of October, for the sale of lambs and draft ewes.

During the months of October and November, great numbers of salmon and sea trout ascend the Cayle for the purpose of spawning. The parr, which used to be very plentiful, is now extinct;[*] but the river contains a fine red delicious trout, some of large size, and in great numbers. A little to the westward of Hounam Kirk, the stream throws itself over a rock several feet high, forming a beautiful cascade called "the

---

[*] Is not this fact against the theory that the parr is the young of the salmon?

Salmon Leap." All the streams of this territory abound in trout.

The district was at one time richly wooded,* but only a few old trees are now to be seen at Capehope, and in the neighbourhood of the church. The extensive forests of hazel which once adorned the margins of the river may yet be traced on Chatto crags and other places; but the forests of oak, birch, and alder have been entirely cut up. The woods of Philogar have been cut within the last thirty years. It is gratifying, however, to notice that the present owners of the land are turning their attention to planting. On the estate of Chester House, there are 17 acres of plantations arrived at a considerable height. On the property of the Duke of Roxburghe about 21 acres have been planted, and Mr. Dickson has planted five acres of ornamental wood on his estate.

ECKEFORDE,† EKEFORD,‡ ECKFORD.—This territory derives its name from a ford on the river

---

* Cayle derived its name from the woody coverts through which it flowed, when the Gaelic language was spoken on the Borders.

† Circa 1165; Lib. de Melros, p. 80.

‡ During the 13th century; Regist. Glasg., p. 99; Lib. de Melros, p. 225. In the settlement between the bishop of Glasgow and the abbot of Jedburgh, the name is, by an error of the scribe, written *Heckford*.

Teviot, near to where the church is situated: *Oakford*. In the common dialect of the district, the *Oak* is still pronounced *Aik* or *Ec*. A road from Melrose, by *Eckford*, to the granges on the Cheviots, existed at a very early period. The oak must have flourished on the margins of the Teviot in ancient times, as trunks of oak trees of great size are occasionally, at the present day, exposed by a change of the channel of the river. The names of many places in the neighbourhood, evince that woods once covered the ground where not a trace of forest trees is now to be found.

The territory of Eckford seems anciently to have comprehended all the land lying between the Cayle and the Teviot, and the manors of Morebattle, Whitton and the two Craillings. It is doubtful whether any of the lands lying on the right bank of the Cayle were included in the old manor. The first family seen in connection with the manor is that of GEOFFREY. In 1250, Geoffrey of Ekkeford was possessed of land in the town and territory of Home. In 1296, Richard, the son of the said Geoffrey, took the oath of fealty to Edward I.* The family of Mowbray, who came to Scotland in the reign of William the Lion, appears as owner of the whole territory, but who lost Cessford about

---

* Ragman's Rolls, p. 142.

1316, and Eckford in 1322, in consequence of Roger de Mowbray being concerned with William de Sulis and Lady Strathearn in a conspiracy against Robert I. On the forfeiture of Mowbray, Robert I. granted the manor of Ecford to Walter, steward of Scotland, the husband of Marjory Bruce; the demesne lands of Cessworth were granted to Edmond Marshall, and to William de St. Clair he gave the remainder of the lands of Cesseworthe and the miln. Robert II., before 1390, conferred the barony of Eckford on Walter Scott of Kirkurd. In 1463, James III. granted to David Scott, son of Walter Scott of Kirkurd, a charter, erecting into a free barony the lands of Branxholm, Langtown, Lempitlaw, Elrig, Rankellburn, Ekfurd, and Whitchester, to be called the barony of Branxholm,* which charter was confirmed by James V. in 1528. In this charter were included the lands of Grahamslaw. The barony still belongs to the Duke of Buccleuch.

The principal messuage of the barony was *Moss House* or *Moss Tower*, so named from its situation in the midst of an extensive morass, and accessible only at one point by a causeway. In 1523, it was cast down by the English warden, Lord Dacre. In 1544, Sir Bryan Layton, Henry Eurie, Robert Collingwood, and others, attacked the tower, and, according to Eurie's report, won the "barnkyn and gate,

---

* Reg. Mag. Sig., lib. xxii. No. 205.

many naggs and nolt, and smoked very sore the towre, and took 30 prisoners, and so brought away 80 horses and naggs, 180 or 200 nolt, 400 sheep, and moche insight geare." The same party also ranged the woods of Woodin and the country around. In 1545, it was destroyed by Hertford. In 1570, it was burned by the Earl of Sussex. The ruins of the tower existed about the end of last century, but were taken down to afford access to materials for the erection of a new farm-house upon part of its site.

The town of Eckford seems to have been of some consequence during the Border wars. In all the English inroads, it shared the fate of other towns and villages which lay in the way of the destroying army.*

The church of Eckford stands on the right bank of the Teviot, in the midst of fine scenery, and commanding an extensive view of the vale of Teviot. It was built in 1662, completely repaired and new-seated in 1775. A few years ago, it again underwent a thorough repair, and is now capable of accommodating about 300 persons. At the east door of the church is still to be seen an iron collar, or *Jug*, suspended from the wall, and in which offenders were in former

---

* In the Statistical Account, it is stated that there formerly existed a tower at the village of Eckford, but there is no good reason for believing that there ever was any other tower than the Moss Tower, which was really the tower of the town.

days punished.* The church of Eckford was the property of the Jedburgh monks about the beginning of the 13th century, and with whom it remained till the Reformation. In 1621, parliament enacted that the minister serving the cure at Eckford should receive five chalders of victual, half beer, half oatmeal, with the hail vicarage, manse, and glebe of said kirk.† At the present time, the stipend amounts to fifteen chalders, half oatmeal and half barley, with £8, 6s. 8d. of communion expenses, forty-two pounds of cheese from the tenant of Cessford as vicarage tithes, with a servitude of turf on Woodinhill moor.‡ The manse was built in 1775, and has been repeatedly improved since that time. Eckford Brae, near to the manse, was in former times notable for tent-preaching. The writer of the New Statistical Account of the parish says that, "thither, at particular seasons, immense multitudes from the surrounding country were wont to resort. Here Boston and other eminent divines used to dispense to the people the bread of life."

The Moss Tower farm on this barony is celebrated as being the place where a superior kind of oats, called Church's oats, were first raised. It is said that the farmer, James Church, in the year

---

* It is said that the old bell of Eckford church was carried away in one of the English inroads, and placed in Carham belfry, where it remains to this day.

† Acta Parl., vol. iv. p. 638. ‡ New Statistical Account.

1776, got from a gentleman in Galloway about 60 grains of oats which were procured from abroad. These grains Mr. Church sowed by way of dropping in a common field of a blackish mossy soil. The return was fifty-fold. Next year, they were sown in a common field of a gravelly light soil. They were afterwards sown on different parts of the farm, and always produced a great crop. They were plump and short, but thick, weighed about 28 stones 6 lbs. per Teviotdale boll, and yielded a greater quantity of meal than other oats. They were ready about a fortnight before the Blainslee or Dutch oats. The name of the farmer was conferred on the oats. A descendant of Mr. Church still occupies the farm, and these oats are still grown on the fields where they were first planted.* The lands are now in a high state of cultivation.

GRAEMSLAW, part of the barony of Eckford, lies on the right bank of the Cayle river. The etymology of the name is doubtful. Some suppose that the name is derived from an early settler on the

---

* The black or small bearded grey oat was the only kind grown in the district till after the invasion of Cromwell, when it was displaced by the introduction of the white oat by an officer of the Commonwealth, named Blith.—Natural History of the Eastern Borders, p. 219. Of this oat there are now many varieties. "Unlike," says Mr. Stark (in his Essay on the Supposed Progress of Human Society from Savage to Civilized Life) "many other plants, with a circumscribed geogra-

banks of the Cayle of the name of *Gra*, who had a *ham* or dwelling at the *law*, while others think that the name is purely Saxon, and descriptive of the nature of the locality at the time the name was conferred; *Grame*, or *Graeme*, signifying " the savage or wild law." It may, however, have obtained the name from its situation at the deep cut or ditch through which the Cayle rushes. But it is thought the true etymology may be found in the Gaelic *Grim*, which means *war, battle*. *Grimslaw* would thus signify the *battle law;* and there are many reasons for believing that this place has been the theatre of deadly strife in ancient times. In this locality, tumuli abound everywhere. There are a number of caves in the red sandstone banks of the river, in one of which the Douglas league was signed, and where also the Covenanters found refuge. On the same bank of the Cayle, near to where it mixes its waters with the Teviot, stood a Spittal, or hospital for lepers. Graemslaw was spoiled by Surrey in 1523, and by Hertford in 1545.

---

phical range, wheats, barley, oats, and rye are found in almost every place where there are tribes of men. And it is, further, a curious and unaccountable circumstance, except in one view, that these grains are never found in a wild state available to any extent for the purposes of man. Their continuance depends upon their cultivation. Everywhere they are found to die out if left to the spontaneous care of nature."
—Trans. Royal Soc. Edinburgh, xv. 1, p. 204.

On the left bank of the Cayle, opposite to Graemslaw, is HAUGHEAD, anciently included in the territory of Eckford. In the 17th century, it belonged to Robert Hall, commonly called Hobbie Hall, a person remarkable for his piety and bodily strength. The mansion-house of the covenanting laird is still in existence, and an ash-tree near the house is pointed out as being the tree beneath whose shade tradition says his children were baptized. His son, Henry Hall, followed in the footsteps of his father, and afforded all the protection in his power to those who were persecuted for conscience sake. Like his father, he was of undaunted courage, and deeply imbued with religious zeal. He commanded the covenanting army at the skirmish of Drumclog and the battle of Bothwell Bridge, and was greatly distinguished for bravery and skill. His banner at both these places is still preserved, and described as being of blue silk, four and a half feet long by three and a half broad, with an inscription on it of three lines—the first, in the Hebrew character, "JEHOVAH-NISSI," Exodus xvii. 15; the second, "FOR CHRIST AND HIS TRUTHS;" the third, "NO QUARTER TO YE ACTIVE ENEMIES OF YE COVENANT."* After the battle of Bothwell Bridge he escaped to Holland, but ere long returned, and shortly afterwards was discovered, in company with Mr. Cargill, by the

---

* Transactions of the Antiquarian Society, Edinburgh, 1859.

governor of Blackness. Hall struggled with the governor till Mr. Cargill escaped, and he also would have got away, but for a blow on the head with the doghead of a carbine, causing a mortal wound. The townsmen turned out in a body and conveyed him out of the town, and being unable to walk, he was carried to the house of Robert Punton, whence he was taken by Dalziel and his guards. Although Hall was dying, Dalziel insisted upon taking him to Edinburgh, but he breathed his last before reaching that city. For three days his corpse lay in the Canongate Tolbooth, and it was with great difficulty that his friends obtained permission to bury him in the night. Four years afterwards, the said Henry Hall, *deceased*, John Menzies of Hanginshaw, Henry Boswell of Dunsytown, Robert Steel, portioner of Stain, John Mack, portioner of Hensilwood, were indicted in absence and found guilty, and forfeited, and were all, with the exception of Henry Hall, ordered to be executed when apprehended. This practice of hanging and trying afterwards, was not peculiar to this district, but was extensively followed in other parts of the country. It was usual in cases of high treason, where the party accused was dead, to place the corpse at the bar before an assize, lead evidence, obtain a verdict, and pronounce sentence, in the same way as if the person had been alive. The dead bodies of the Earl of Gowrie and Alexander Ruthven were produced at their trial, and sentence was pronounced against the corpses. In the case of Logan of Restalrig, his bones, which had been buried for many years, were dug up and produced at the bar, and trial had, and judgment pronounced, in the same manner as if he had been alive. During the time of the persecution, trials of this kind frequently occurred. A person of property refusing to swallow the abominable test, or resisting the servants of a tyrant, was shot on the hillside, his dead body was produced at the bar, and proof led of his guilt, a verdict returned, and sentence pronounced finding the person guilty, and forfeiting his estates, to enable the iniquitous government of the day to bestow them upon its willing tools. The Border land affords abundant examples of such proceedings.*

---

* They were proceedings of this nature that originated the reproachful phrase of "Jeddart justice," or "Hang a man first and try him after," which is known everywhere, and is alluded to by every one who imagines that the scales of Justice have not been held evenly. Historians, novelists, and essayists have all twitted the inhabitants of Jedburgh with the reproachful phrase, until it has become proverbial. The same reproach is directed against Cupar; and it appears, from a notice in the "Minstrelsy," that the same saying is applied to a place called Lydford, in England. Some imagine, mistakenly, that the severity of George, the fourth Earl of Home, the father of one of the abbots of Jedburgh, gave it birth, and this view is adopted by Morton in his "Monastic Annals;" but it is evident that it was not from a rigorous enforcement of the law, but the peculiar manner in which it was administered in a class of cases. Such a form of trial took place in

A few hundred yards above Haughead, between the steep red scaur banks of the Cayle, is the place where the Covenanters met for preaching, and where one of the two great conventicles was held. The locality was well suited for such meetings, being lonely and retired, and in the neighbourhood of a number of places of concealment in the banks of the river and the mountain fastnesses. Here the zealous Richard Cameron was licensed, and sent first to Annandale to preach the gospel.*

---

all cases of treason, where the party accused was slain or had died. Without a trial, the goods and estate of the traitor could not be forfeited. The Justice aires, for nearly sixty miles of Border land, were held at Jedburgh, where many members of rebellious clans were tried and condemned to death, and where, also, the corpse of the rebel who had been slain, or died previous to trial, was placed at the bar, and sentence pronounced, forfeiting his goods and estate. The first trial of this kind was that of Robert Lesly, in 1540. After the action with the Covenanters at Pentland Hills, in November, 1666, the authorities in Scotland had recourse to a new process: that of trying in absence parties accused of being present in the action at Pentland; and in August, 1667, a number of landed men were tried in absence, convicted, their lands declared forfeited, and adjudged to be executed when taken. After this trial it was not deemed necessary to produce the corpse or bones at the bar. On this change of practice, Lord Hailes remarks, "The bones of a traitor can neither plead defences, nor cross-question witnesses, and upon this matter there is no difference whether the accused person be absent in body or present in bones." No doubt, from these trials arose the phrase which has passed into a proverb.

* On the appointment being intimated to Cameron by Mr.

In the immediate neighbourhood of Haughead is a place called PRIEST'S CROWN, a corruption of Priest's *crum*, signifying the priest's meadow, and thought to have derived its name from its being the meadow of the vicar or priest. Originally both Haughead and Priest's Crown were church lands, and at the Reformation belonged to the vicar. In this locality small hills of sand abound, which many persons imagine to be artificial, but they are not so. Among these gravelly knolls there are many sand cones, and where the ridge is highest, there are

---

Welsh, "he said, How can I go there? I know what sort of people they are. But Mr. Welsh said, 'Go your way, Ritchie, and set the fire of hell to their tails!' He went, and the first day he preached upon that text, 'How shall I put thee among the children,' &c. In the application, he said, Put you among the children! the offspring of thieves and robbers! We have all heard of Annandale thieves! Some of them got a merciful cast that day, and told afterwards, that it was the first field meeting they ever attended, and that they went out of mere curiosity to see a minister preach in a tent, and people sit on the ground."—*Life of Cameron.* In a note to the "Border Minstrelsy," it is stated that he was chaplain in the family of Sir Walter Scott of Harden, who attended the meetings of the indulged Presbyterians; but Cameron, considering this conduct as a compromise with the foul-fiend Episcopacy, was dismissed from the family.—This good man was slain at Air's Moss, in the parish of Auchinleck, in 1680, where he behaved with the greatest bravery. He and Mr. Hackston commanded the horse. It seems that his labours in the family of Sir Walter Scott of Harden had borne fruit, for, in 1684, Sir Walter was fined £2944, 8s. 10d., and his son, £3500.

several of these little hills. One of these, situated in a field to the east of the turnpike, existed till the autumn of 1857, at the side of a meadow; and the farmer of the land, desirous to fill up a morass at the corner of the field, thought the best way to do so was to cart the little *law* into it. To work the labourers went, when they found the knoll to be pure sand, and in the centre of it, a few feet from the top, they came upon a stone kist, lying east and west. It was formed of rough sandstone slabs, taken from the banks of the Cayle—at least they are of the same kind as the stones in the channel of the river, and one or two of them, I observed, were water-worn. The kist was about three feet ten inches in length, and two feet four in breadth. Within it lay the bones of one of the ancient people. The head lay to the west, and it appeared to me that the body had been doubled up and laid on its side, as was usual in early times. Along with the bones were found a few beads of shaly coal, and part of a fibula of the same material. Nothing was found in the grave to mark the period at which the interment took place, or the sex. From the smallness of the skull and other bones, and the absence of all weapons, I am inclined to think that the inmate of the stone coffin belonged to the female sex. The kist is now protected by a wall, erected at the expense of the Duke of Buccleuch, the owner of the lands.

From the apex of this knoll, a fair panorama is

presented to the vision. Bonnie Teviotdale lies on the west, with the waters of Teviot sparkling as they wind through the lovely vale, like an inland lake; on the east, the scene is fair of its kind, and both united form such a picture as is rarely to be met with in

> " Lands that afar do lie
> 'Neath a sunnier day and bluer sky."

CESSFORD barony lay to the south-east of Eckford manor, and seems to have included all the lands between it and Whitton. It was formerly written *Cessworth, Cessworthe,* and *Cessforth,* &c. The origin of the name may be sought for in its situation on the lake, *i. e.*, the town on the lake or moss. It is thought that this lake was formed by the waters of the Cayle, in the valley above Marlefield. About the 15th century it came to be called Cessford, probably from a passage in the lake at this place. In addition to a ford, there also seems to have been a boat upon the lake. In 1684, James Muir, at *Cessford-boat,* was, with John Kerr of Hownam, indicted before the Justiciary at Edinburgh for treason, for not owning the King's authority as then established, nor Sharp's death, murder; nor account Bothwell, rebellion; and condemned to be hanged at the Grassmarket. Roger de Mowbray appears to have been one of the earliest proprietors of the manor. On his forfeiture, King Robert I., in 1316, gave to Edmund Marshall the whole demesne lands of Cessworth, and William St. Clair of Hirdmenston got all the other lands and miln. About this time the Douglas was over-lord of all Teviotdale, which he had won by his gallantry. According to the author of the "Memorie of the Somervills," a family of Oliphant possessed the barony during the beginning of the 13th century, and to Lady Elizabeth Oliphant Sir John Somerville was married.* The same author states that one of the barons of Linton was served heir to his father in the barony of Linton in April, 1381, before Sir Robert Kerr of Cessford, in the town of Jedburgh.† Although this author may not be correct as to the dates, it is probable that the Kers were in possession of this barony at a much earlier period than is generally supposed. It is not clear, however, to whom the Kers succeeded. It is said that in 1446 the Earl of Douglas confirmed a charter to Andrew Ker of the barony of Cessford. In 1474, James, Lord Hamilton, granted a charter of the lands of Cessford to the same Andrew Ker. James IV. gave to Walter Ker, in 1494, the barony of Cessford, which belonged to William Cockburn of Skraling. The barony is still possessed by his descendant, the Duke of Roxburghe.

The CASTLE of Cessford stands upon a ridge in-

---

* Memorie of the Somervilles, vol. i. p. 50.   † Ib. p. 136.

clining towards Cayle valley, having the deep glen through which Cessford burn flows on the west, and on the south-east the ground slopes to a rivulet which joins the burn a little to the north of the castle. The castle is now a ruin, but enough of it remains to shew that it must have been, when entire, of great strength. The principal building is 67 feet long, 60 feet broad, and 65 feet high. The walls are of an average thickness of 12 feet. The castle has been surrounded by an inner and outer wall; no part of the former is to be seen, but portions of the latter, especially on the north-east, as well as a part of the offices, still remain. The whole course of the outer wall, which is about 300 yards, may be traced by its foundations, which are perfectly distinct. It was surrounded by a moat, furnished with water, it is said, from a spring above the farm-house. At the end of last century the remains of the moat were to be seen, but the plough has now destroyed every vestige of it. In the month of May, 1523, the castle was besieged by Surrey, in the absence of its owner, with a numerous army, well provided with powerful ordnance, with which he battered the donjon with little effect. While the guns were playing against the castle, the Lord Leonard, Sir Arthur Darcy, Sir William Parr, and others, by means of scaling ladders, entered the barnkin, where they suffered severely from the iron guns of the castle and stones cast down upon them. They then attempted to scale the donjon, while the archers and ordnance kept the besieged engaged, but notwithstanding all the efforts of the besiegers, they could not prevail against the castle, which was gallantly defended. At last, when Surrey was despairing of success, the warden came within a mile of the castle, and not knowing how matters stood within the castle, but fearing the worst, offered to give up the place on his men being allowed to leave with their bag and baggage, to which Surrey was but too glad to accede, as he could not have taken the castle by force of arms. In a letter to Henry VIII., written by Surrey after returning to Alnwick, he says, "I was very glad of the said appointment (capitulation), for in maner I sawe not howe it wolde have been won if they within wold have contynued their deffending."* On the castle being delivered up, it was thrown down by the ordnance, and, while the destruction of its walls was going on, another party went to Whitton fort and cast it down. In 1545, Cessforthe, Cessforthe burn, and Cessfort maynes, are in the list of places destroyed by the army of the Earl of Hertford. In 1666, Henry Hall of Haughead and a number of Covenanters were imprisoned in the castle.† It is said that the castle ceased to be the dwelling-place of the Kers after 1650.

---

* Cotton MS.   † Wodrow, vol. ii. p. 134.

A number of ash-trees of considerable size, some measuring eight feet in circumference, are at present growing in the courts of the castle, and within the ruined walls of the office-houses. About fifty yards west from the castle stands a solitary ash-tree, and a place on the south where a number of trees grow is pointed out as the site of the ancient gardens.*

MARLEFIELD lies between the modern baronies of Eckford and Cessford. It anciently formed a part of the territory of Eckford. About the beginning of the 17th century, it was called Mowmaynis, and the property of Mr. William Bennett, rector of Ancrum. In 1677, William Bennet was served heir to his father in the lands and barony of Grubet, comprehending among others the lands of Mowmaynis.† He was succeeded by his son, Sir William Bennet, who suffered many hardships for conscience sake. In 1677, he was fined 400 merks for

---

* In the Old Statistical Account, the minister of Eckford parish gives an account of a remarkable ash that stood at the castle. It was called the Crow-tree, and measured at the base 27 feet 8 inches in girth; at six feet from the ground, 15 feet; and at the cleft where the branches diverged and spread, 14 feet 6 inches. The tree expanded its branches on every side. It was computed to contain 300 feet of wood. Although very old, it was in a healthy state in 1793, and was much admired. It does not now exist.

† Retours, No. 195.

VOL. III.   Z

attending conventicles, and for hearing and conversing with Mr. Welsh, and ordered to remain in the Bass till the fine was paid. His son, Sir William, was born at Marlefield, where he lived during the greater part of his life. He took an active hand in raising the county of Roxburgh against the rebel forces in 1715. He was the intimate friend of Ramsay and Thomson, who often visited at Marlefield House. In 1721, Ramsay is said to have written a poetical address to Eolus, on the night of a high wind, at the house of his patron. There are good grounds for believing that this Sir William is the *Patie* of the " Gentle Shepherd," and that the scene of that beautiful pastoral is laid on the banks of the Cayle, in the immediate neighbourhood of Marlefield House. The description in the poem answers exactly to the scenery in this locality. The rocky, caverned banks of the Cayle correspond with the opening scene, where *Patie* and *Roger* are introduced—

> " Beneath the south side of a craggy bield,
> Where crystal springs their halesome waters yield,
> Twa youthfu' shepherds in the gowans lay,
> Tenting their flocks ae bonny morn of May;—
> Poor Roger granes till hollow echoes ring,
> But blyther Patie likes to laugh and sing."

Habbie's Howe is also to be found within a short distance of the mansion, through which a burn wimples between two verdant banks to the Cayle. It is of consequence to notice that a remarkable personage lived in the immediate neighbourhood, of the name of Habbie or Hobbie Hall, a friend and fellow-sufferer with Sir William in the cause of religious liberty. Their estates lay together, and were bounded by the burn, which

"Kisses wi' easy whirls the bord'ring grass."

There existed also a cottage on the estate, called Symon's House, and a field adjoining known as Symon's Field. Mowses Burn and Mowses Knowe are also on the estate. In every respect, the scenery at this place corresponds with the scenes of the drama. And further, the poem is an historical description of Sir William Bennet and his son. Sir William was imprisoned, and afterwards forced to leave his native land, leaving his son behind him under charge of a faithful tenant, to be brought up as his own. When a better sun shone on Scotia's hills and dales, the exile returned to his native vale, and found his son as described by his guardian. *Patie's* love of learning, as described by *Symon*, is a true representation of the character of Sir William Bennet, who was a man of taste and great literary attainments. Other localities may point to scenes answering the description of the poet; but here are to be found, not only scenery exactly fitting the drama, but a pictorial representation of the owner of the lands and his son. Everything considered, I cannot entertain a doubt that the scene of the

"Gentle Shepherd" is laid on the margins of the Cayle. Sir William Bennet died in 1724, and was interred in the family aisle adjoining the church of Eckford. Over the entrance to the aisle is the following inscription:—"*Hoc monumentum sibi et suis bene merentibus, ponendam curavit Dominus Gulielmus Bennet eques auratus anno salutis, 1724.*"

The mansion of Marlefield stands at the west end of the Cayle valley, commanding a fine view of the vale and the distant Cheviots. In the grounds are a number of magnificent lime-trees, and on the banks of the river, near to the cottages, are a few fine oaks and beeches. The estate now belongs to the Marquis of Tweeddale.

CAVERTON.—The name of this ancient territory is derived from the Cambro-British *cae ver*, signifying little fields or enclosures, and the Saxon *ton* added describes the town at the fields or enclosures. This place is thought to be the *Keveronum* of the Inquisitio of Earl David in 1116, and belonging at that early period to the church of Glasgow. The name of this place is a proof that farms existed during the British period. The territory is situated on the right bank of the Cayle, opposite to Cessford and Marlefield, lying between the river and the baronies of Linton, Lempitlaw, Sprouston, Heaton, and Eckford. It belonged to the family of *Suli*, and who obtained the name of Sules from two bailiewicks of that name in Northamptonshire. Ranulph de Sules followed David I. to Scotland, and got from him Liddisdale, Nisbet, and Caverton, in Teviotdale. He was butler to William the Lion. At his death, in 1170, he was succeeded by his nephew Ranulph, the son of his brother William. Ranulph was assassinated at Castleton in 1207.* Nicholas, the son of Fulco, succeeded, and was a man remarkable for his great wisdom and eloquence. He married a daughter of the Earl of Buchan, by whom he had two sons, William and John. He died at Rouen, in Normandy, in 1264. William became justiciary of Lothian under Alexander III., and he was one of the *Magnatus Scotæ* who pledged themselves to support the succession of Margaret to her father, Alexander III. He was present at the Parliament at Brigham in 1290. Nicholas de Soulis claimed the crown of Scotland, in right of his grandmother Margery, who was a daughter of Alexander II., but withdrew his pretensions, as her legitimacy could not be established. The barony of Caverton was forfeited while in possession of William de Soulis,† in

---

* Chron. Mailros, p. 106: "Ranulfus de Sules occisus est in domo a domesticis suas."

† This is the person whom tradition says was rolled up in a sheet of lead for a funeral pall, and melted in a cauldron on the Ninestane Rig. But unfortunately for the tradition, and the minstrel who sung of the event, Sulis was seized at Berwick, confessed his guilt before Parliament, and his life

consequence of his having entered into a conspiracy against Robert I., with the view of elevating himself to the throne. The plot was discovered by the Countess of Strathern. In 1216, it was granted by Robert I. to Robert Stewart, the son of Walter Stewart.* It was out of the forfeited lands in Teviotdale belonging to Soulis and Moubray that the £2000 granted by Robert I. to the monks of Melrose, to enable them to restore their house, which had been destroyed during the war of Independence, was raised. On Edward, the English king, obtaining possession of Teviotdale, the barony of Cavertoun was conferred on the family of De Coucy. In 1335, Edward III. granted a charter of confirmation of the barony of Cavertoun.† Three years after, the barony was given by the same king to James de Loyrens; but as it was so destroyed by the war, he added an annual pension of twenty pounds sterling.‡ The barony was valued during peace at £58 yearly, but, owing to the war, did not yield £8 sterling. About the middle of the 15th century, Walter Ker, designed as of Caverton, but probably of Cessford, was in possession of lands in Caverton.

---

was spared by the king, but his estates forfeited, and himself confined in Dumbarton Castle, where he died. Chalmers says there never was a *Lord* Sulis, whatever the minstrel may sing.

 * Robertson's Index, p. 10, No. 13.
 † Rotuli Scotiæ, vol. i. p. 352   ‡ Ib., p. 825.

In 1478, he was summoned before the Lords Auditors, at the instance of Dougal M'Dougall of Makerstoune.* About the same time, Rutherfurd of Hundole had a third part of the lands of Caverton.† In the beginning of the 17th century, families of the names of Pott and Pringle appear to have been in possession of lands in Caverton. In 1623, William Pott was served heir to his father, John, called *Laird Pott*, in three-pound lands called Langislands, in the territory of Caverton.‡ In the same year, George Pringill, in Schairpitlaw, was served heir to his father in two husbandlands in the barony of Hounam.§ In 1628, John Pott was retoured heir to his father, William Pott, of the lands commonly called Langislandis, in the barony of Caverton.|| In 1675, Robert, Earl of Roxburghe, was served heir to his father, William, Earl of Roxburghe, Lord Ker of Cessford and Caverton, amongst others in a husbandland in Caverton, called Huntlilands.¶ The territory of Caverton, with the exception of the lands of Mainhouse, belong to the dukedom of Roxburghe. The town of Caverton was of importance in early times, but now consists of only a few farm cottages. On the east side of the town stood a little chapel, which served the inhabitants of that terri-

---

* Act. Dom. Aud., p. 69.   † Reg. Mag. Sig., lib. xii. No. 320.
‡ Retours, No. 120.   § Ib., No. 117.
|| Ib., No. 168.   ¶ Ib. No. 267.

tory, but every vestige of it had disappeared before the end of last century. As said before, this chapel is believed to have existed at a very early period, and to be the *Keveronum* in the inquisition made by Earl David in 1116, as to the property of the church of Glasgow in Teviotdale.* Very few notices are to be met with of this chapel. In the end of the 15th century, Walter Ker of Cessford burdened the lands of Caverton with a yearly payment of ten pounds to the officiating chaplain. He also granted to the chapel two cottages which lay near to the orchard, two acres of land with *crums*, meadow, and four *soums* in Caverton, with a manse and yard. In 1500, James IV. confirmed this grant. The small graveyard of the chapel was used by several families of the parish, and by others, because their forefathers were interred there up to 1793. Since that time, it has scarcely been used for burial. In a field north of the churchyard, a fountain was called the Holy Well, and occasionally the Priest's Well, from its connection with the chapel, but the name is beginning to be lost among the now ever-changing inhabitants of the country hamlets.

To the west of Caverton hill-head cottages are the scarcely perceptible remains of a tumulus which was of considerable extent, and called the *Black Dyke*. When examined by Mr. Paton, the minister of the

---

* Reg. Glas., pp. 5, 7.

parish, in 1793, it measured 342 feet in length, over 27 feet at the east end; it measured 42 feet at the western extremity; it was 33 feet from side to side. It lay in a direct line east and west. It was composed of fine loose mould, intermixed with large stones covered over with heath. No human bones or remains of any kind have been found in it. Tradition has it that the bodies of those dying of the plague were buried here in 1349; but the shape of the mound and the absence of remains seem to indicate that the people who raised the dyke had a very different object in view than burial.

MAINHOUSE, which was included in the territory of Caverton, belonged to a family of Chatto, in the end of the 16th century. Thomas Chatto was baillie of Kelso in 1717. In 1817, the lands were acquired by James Syme, a merchant in Glasgow. In 1847, the estate was purchased by Thomas Nisbet, who was, at his death, succeeded by his brother, Ralph Compton Nisbet, with whom it now remains. Since the estate came into the hands of Mr. Nisbet, it has been greatly improved, and the lands are in a high state of cultivation. The house occupies a fine situation, overlooking the vale of Cayle, with the Cheviot mountains in the distance. Mainhouse was destroyed by Hertford in 1545.

The territory of Caverton suffered severely during the wars between England and Scotland, owing to its position between the Tweed and Cayle, the ground over which the invading army chiefly passed. The greater portion of the land must have been a moor, especially on the east. Caverton Edge, on which Kelso races were formerly run, is now planted, and the remainder is let into farms capable of producing crops of every kind, and is highly cultivated.

ORMISTON.—This ancient barony derives its name from *Orm*, the son of Eilar, who settled on the bend of the Teviot in the beginning of the 12th century. The dwelling of *Orm* was at the place now called Old Ormiston, and a lovelier situation is rarely met with in the Border land. It commands a fine view of the valley down which Cayle flows, and the green mountains which form the boundary line between the two kingdoms, appear in the distance. The river Teviot bends around the barony, and hastens over its rocky bed to meet with the Tweed. The scenery around Old Ormiston far excels that in the vicinity of the new mansion higher up the river. *Ormeston* became, in the end of the 13th century, a surname of the family. John de Ormeston swore fealty to Edward I. in 1296.[*] After that time, a family of Dalmahoy appear to have been in possession of part of the lands of

---

[*] Ragman's Rolls, p. 126.

Ormeston. John Copeland, Edward's sheriff of Roxburgh, occupied for a time the lands which belonged to Dalmahoy, and on their being restored, he got a pension of twenty pounds yearly, as compensation for their loss.* In 1347, Andrew of Ormeston, James de Sandilands, and Patrick le Clerk, got a safe-conduct from Edward III. to visit William Douglas, chevalier, a prisoner of war in England, and convey to him certain things which he required.† In 1358, a safe-conduct was granted to the same Andrew and four kinsmen to visit England. Andrew is styled "familiaris David de Bruys, prisonerie."‡ In 1476, Andrew Ormeston possessed the lands.§ Ormeston seems to have been a follower of Scott of Branxholm, and at feud with the Kers; for, in the contract between the Scotts and Kers in 1564, the laird of Branxholm took burden upon him for James Ormeston of that Ilk.|| The same James Ormeston, and his uncle *Hob* Ormeston, were concerned in the murder of Henry Darnley in 1566, and for which he was executed at Edinburgh in 1573. While lying in the castle of Edinburgh, under sentence of death, he confessed to John Brand, minister, his share in the murder, and that he was urged to the deed by Bothwell; but declared that the Queen never spake to him on the subject.

---

* Rotuli Scotiæ, vol. i. p. 558.   † Ib., 706.   ‡ Ib., 806.
§ Acta Dom. Aud., 56. || Pitcairn, vol. iii. p. 391.

Having made his confession as to the murder of Darnley, he asked the minister to pray for him, for he had been a great sinner otherwise : " for of all men in all the earth, I have been ane of the proudest and heich-myndit, and maist filthie of my body, abusing myself dyvers ways. Bot specially I have shed innocent blood of ane Michael Hunter, with my awin hands. Allace, therefore! Because the said Michael hevand me lying upon my back, haveing ane fork in his hand, might have slain me gif he pleasit, and did it not; quhilk of all things grieves me maist in conscience : Alswa in a rage I hangit a poor man for ane horse, with mony other wickit deids; for the quhilk I ask my God mercy: For it is not mervel that I have been wickit, for the wickit companie that ever I have been in, bot specialie within thir seaven years byepast, quhilk I never saw twa guid men, or ane guid deid, bot all kind of wickedness. And that my God wald not suffer me to be lost, and hes drawn me from them as out of hell, and has given me layer and space with guid companie to repent; for the quhilk I thank him, and is assurit that I am ane of his elect."* It is said that he died, to the appearance of men, one of the most penitent sinners, and a great example of God's mercy. On the death of Ormeston, the barony passed into the hands of Captain Robert Anstruther,

---

* Pitcairn, vol. i. p. 513.

by whom they were afterwards resigned into the hands of the king, who granted to William Ker of Cessford, warden of the middle marches, the said lands and barony, together with the tower, fortalice, mills, and fishings, of the same, and also the twenty-merk lands of Maxton, called Govanis lands. This grant was ratified by Parliament in 1581.* In 1585, his Majesty and the Parliament held at Linlithgow revoked and rescinded all deeds granted by the said James Ormeston previous to his execution, in favour of his children and friends; and in 1592, the Parliament of new ratified the grant in favour of William Ker, of said lands and barony in liferent, and to Mark Ker, his second son, and his heirs male, whom failing, to return to the said William and his house of Cessford.† Under that grant, Mark Ker entered into possession of the barony of Ormeston, and in 1606, Robert, Earl of Roxburghe, was served heir to his brother, the said Mark, in the lands and barony, with the twenty-merk lands of Maxton, called Govanis lands.‡ In the end of last century it was the property of William Elliot of Wells, from whom it passed into the hands of William Mein, whose ancestors seem to have been long connected with the district, and to have intermarried with the Kers. He greatly improved the lands, built a new mansion,

---

* Acta Parl., vol. iii. p. 269.   † Ib., p. 612.
‡ Retours, No. 35.

and erected, at his own expense, for the accommodation of the public, an elegant suspension bridge for carriages over the Teviot at Cayle-mouth. Previous to that time there was not a bridge over the river between Ancrum Bridge and Kelso.

In 1523, Ormiston was cast down by Lord Dacre. The barnkyn of Ormeston was taken and burnt by Lord Eurie in 1544. In 1545, the town of Ormeston was burnt and the tower destroyed by Hertford.

HETON, HETAINE, HETOYUN, HEITOUNE.—This ancient manor derives its name from its position on the summit of a ridge which slopes down to the banks of the Teviot. From this place fine views are obtained of Teviotdale and the Merse. The first person who appears as owner of the manor is Alan de Perci the younger, who followed Earl David to Scotland, and fought by his side with all the spirit of a Percy, at the battle of the Standard, in 1138. After this battle, he obtained from David I. the manors of Heton and Oxnam. Alan granted a carrucate of land in Heton to the monks of Whitby for the salvation of his own soul, for the salvation of the souls of David the king, and of his son Earl Henry, and for the souls of his father, Alan de Perci, and of his mother. This grant was witnessed by his four brothers, William, Walter, Geoffrey, Henry, and it was confirmed by David the king, by Malcolm

IV., and by his two brothers, Geoffrey and Henry. Alan, dying without issue, was succeeded by his brother Geoffrey, who also died without issue. His nephew Walter, the son of Henry, next possessed the manor, and imitated his uncle in liberality to the religious houses. To the house of Kelso he gave a ploughgate, containing 104 acres, in Heton, next to the land belonging to the hospital of Roxburghe.* He also granted the monks of Dryburgh two oxgangs of land in Heton, with all the pasture and easements of the same town belonging to so much land, for the safety of his own soul, and the souls of all his ancestors.† This grant was confirmed by William the Lion, by Pope Lucius, by Philip Colville, by Pope Gregory, and by Alexander II., before 1230.‡ The next owner of the manor was Philip de Colville, an Anglo-Norman, who settled in Scotland during the reign of Malcolm IV. It was the first possession the family acquired in North Britain. He was succeeded by his son Thomas, who witnessed many charters of William the Lion, between 1189 and 1199. In 1210, he was suspected of a conspiracy against the life of his king, and imprisoned in Edinburgh Castle; but having made his innocence appear, he was liberated, after a confinement of six

---

* Lib. de Calchou.
† Regist. de Dryburgh, p. 163.
‡ Ib. pp. 180, 195, 163, 164, 181, 199.

months, and restored to favour.* He is a witness to several charters of Alexander II. He acquired the lands of Whitsome in Berwickshire, and died in 1219.† William de Colville, his son, acquired the manors of Kinaird in Stirlingshire, and of Ochiltree in Ayrshire. The laird of Heton, like the other lairds in the district, swore fealty to Edward I. in 1296.‡ Robert de Colville possessed Heton and Oxnam during the reign of Robert I. About 1330, he quit-claimed to Roger of Auldton, "an annual revenue of five shillings, in which he was bound to him for two oxgangs of land which he held of him in the town and territory of Heton,"§ and liberty was granted to Roger to convert the said oxgangs to pious uses or perpetual alms. Under that leave, Roger granted the two oxgangs of land for the maintenance of a chantry and officiating priest, in the church of St. James, Roxburgh. The two oxgangs lay on the south side of the town of Heton, between the land of Robert de Colville and the land

---

* Chron. Mail., p. 109: "Et Thomas de Couilla captus est et apud Edenburc custodie mancipatur propter sedicionem quam contra regem suum et dominum Machinatus est, ut infamia narrando clamat qui ad festum Sancti Martini si redemit."

† Chron. Mail., p. 135.

‡ Ragman's Rolls, p. 128.

§ These two oxgangs are thought to have amounted at that period to 38 acres: not twopence per acre for land which now lets at more than £2 per acre.

of Thomes, called *Walker*,* on the west side.† In the Register of Glasgow, the name of Heton is mistakenly written *Reton*. In 1336, Edward III. appointed Alan of Heton warden of the town and territory of Heton.‡ The barony of Heton was granted by Robert II. to Duncan Wallace, and his wife, Elenor de Bruges, Countess of Carrick. In 1456, John Heytone sat in the Parliament of Scotland as commissioner for the burgh of Haddington. In 1502, Sir William Colville was in possession of the barony of Heton. At the Jedworthe Justiciare, in November, 1502, Robert and Henry Douglas were permitted to compound for the theft of three oxen from Sir William Colville of Synlaws.§ Sir William was slain in the same year, leaving two daughters. In

---

* The origin of the name of Walker is said to have been derived from Rolla, a Danish chieftain, who was, from his height and weight, unable to use a horse, and therefore compelled to walk a-foot, and from whence he obtained the sobriquet of the *Ganger a-Walker*. Giants must have lived in those days if we are to believe the accounts of the Danish period.—Beauties of England, vol. i. p. 215, 234, 265; View of Derbyshire, vol. ii. p. 426; Glover's Derbyshire, vol. ii. p. 457.

† Regist. Glasg., p. 244: "Et duas bovatus terre in Villa de Reton quarum toftum jacet in parte australi ejusdem ville inter terram Roberti de Colville domini de Reton ex parte orientali et terram Thome dicte Walker ex parte occidentali."

‡ Rotuli Scotiæ, vol. i. p. 903. § Pitcairn, vol. i. p. 33.

1510, at the Justiciare at Jedworthe, George Halyburton was accused of art and part of the murder of Sir William Colville, and not appearing, Mark Ker of Dolphinstone, his surety, was fined in 100 merks, the said George denounced, and his goods escheated to the king. In 1509, half of the barony belonged to Andrew Ker of Primsideloch, and the other half to Ralph Ker of Ferniehirst. The lands are now possessed by Sir George Douglas and William Scott Ker of Chatto.

The town consists of a row of houses on each side of the turnpike road leading from Berwick to the western districts of the country. The houses are generally of an inferior kind, but the proprietor, Sir George Douglas, has begun the erection of very elegant cottages at the east end of the town. Heyton-on-the-Hill is in the list of places destroyed by Earl Hertford in 1545.

Between 1190 and 1456, a number of persons bore the surname of Heton.

APPENDIX.

ADDITIONS AND CORRECTIONS.

KELSO.

Page 41.—The following is a translation of the confirmation charter of Malcolm IV., preserved in the archives of the Duke of Roxburgh, a fac-simile of which is in volume i. of the Lib. de Calchou:—

"Malcolm by the grace of God King of Scots to all his friends French English and Scots and to all the sons of God's holy church wisheth perpetual health. Know all men now and hereafter that David King of Scots my grandfather of pious memory whilst he was earl founded an abbey at SELESCHIRCHE in honour of the holy Virgin Mary mother of God and Saint John the evangelist; for the health of his own soul and the souls of his father and mother his brothers and sisters and all his ancestors and successors. But when by Divine mercy after the death of his brother Alexander he succeeded him in the kingdom by the council and advice of John of revered memory bishop of Glasgow and his nobles men who feared God he removed the aforesaid abbey because the former place was not a convenient situation for a monastery to Roxburg to the church of the blessed Virgin Mary which is situated on the bank of the river Tuede in the place which is called KELCHO. Which church Robert bishop of St. Andrews in whose diocese it was from love to God and of his own free will granted that it should be free from all episcopal authority insomuch that the abbot and monks might receive their consecrated ointment and oil and the ordination of the abbot himself and the monks from whatsoever bishop they pleased in Scotland or Cumbria.* This privilege with the other privileges and possessions which they enjoy through the liberality of my grandfather King David my father Earl Henry or my own I concede to them as far as my right extends for ever and by my royal power confirm to them for perpetual alms: viz. the town of KELCHO with its due bounds in land and water discharged quit and free from every burden; also the land which Gerold gave me near the confines of the said town which land comes down to the road that goes to NEITH-ANSTHYRN.† And when ever I hear the service of God in that church on holidays or other days I confirm to the same all my offerings and the offerings of all those who shall be with me. Also from the milne of EDENHAM twelve chalders of malt every year; and liberty to dig peats in the muir of Edenham from the ditch that comes down the other muir crossing that muir in a straight direction to the three large stones on the other side. Also forty shillings a year from the revenue of the burgh of ROKESBURGH and a toft beside the church of St. James and another in the new town and the land which was Walter Cementar's. Also in the churches of the same burgh with their land as freely and fully as ever Ascelline the archdeacon possessed them. Also the half toft which was Acculf's; and twenty chalders half meal half wheat at the milns; and the seventh part of a fishing. Also in SPROSTON a ploughgate of land and ten acres with the buildings belonging to the ploughgate; and three acres of meadow; and the church of the same village; with the land belonging to the church; and two oxgangs of land

---

* The Cumbria of King David extended from the Solway, the Esk, and the Kersope on the south, to the upper Forth and Lochlomond on the north, and from the Frith of Clyde and the Irish Sea on the west. It extended eastward to the boundaries of the Lothians and the Merse.

† Nenthorn.

beside PRESTERBRIDGE which I gave them in exchange for
two oxgangs with which the monks accommodated me of
the land of the church of St. Laurence at BEREWIC. Also
the village of RAVENDENE* in land and water; and the
pastures of Sproston and the muirs for digging turfs common
as well to the inhabitants of Ravendene as to those of Sproston. Also in Berewich a ploughgate of land and a dwelling
belonging to the same beside the church of St. Laurence; and
another dwelling in the burgh and forty shillings out of the
revenue of the same burgh yearly and the half of a fishing
which is called Berewicstrem. Also the seventh part of the
milns and the land of Dodin in the same town and the land
of Waltheof the son of Ernobold. Also the village of MIDDLEHAM and BOTHELDENE† with their due bounds in lands and
waters in woods and cleared grounds. Also thirty acres of
land in the domains of LILLESCLIVE‡ between the ALNA and
the brook that divides the grounds of Middleham and
Lillesclive and the tithes of the miln of the same village viz.
Lillesclive. Also WHITELAU and WHITEMERE with their due
bounds; and the lands of SELESCHIRCHE with its due bounds
in lands and its waters in woods and cleared ground and my
waters about Seleschirche as free to them to fish in with their
fishermen as to me with mine and my pastures as free to
their people as to mine; and my woods for building their
houses and for fuel as free to them as to me. Also the church
of the other Seleschirche with half a ploughgate of land; and
the church and the land of LESMAHAGU with its due bounds;
and TRAVERLIN§ with its due bounds as Vineth fully and
freely possessed and enjoyed it with all the easments of

---

* Redden. † Bowden. ‡ Lilliesleaf.

‡ Morton, in the Monastic Annals, page 116, mistakenly
states that this place is Crailing, on the Oxnam water; but the
name of Crailing was in use before Malcolm IV. wrote this
charter. Besides, Crailing was granted to the abbot of Jedburgh. It is clear that Traverlin and Crailing cannot be the
same.

the adjoining strother which is called Cameri; and the crag of the same village (as the Lord Alfwin abbot of Halyrude and Ernald abbot of Kelso came to a mutual agreement concerning a dispute which was between them about that same crag—before these witnesses Ralph abbot of Newbottle; William abbot of Strevelin; Osbert prior of Jeddeword; Richard the clerk; Machbet.) For my grandfather gave this Traverlin to the foresaid church of Kelcho in exchange for the ten-pound lands which they had in Hardiggasthorn near Northamtun. Also in RINFRIV a toft and one net exempted quit and free from all customs; and in EDINBURG a toft; and in PEEBLES a toft; and in LANNARCH a toft; and the church of KETH; and half of the fat of the craspies* that shall have been stranded in the Forth. Also the tenth of the beasts and swine and kain cheese of that part of Galwey which my grandfather had during the lifetime of King Alexander; and the tenth of the cheeses of TUEDALE in like manner annually; and the half of the hides of all the beasts slaughtered for my kitchen so that whenever I or any of my successors have one hide the monks may have another. And they shall have a like share of the suet and tallow of the hides; and all the skins of the rams and lambs; and the tenth of the skins of the deer taken by my huntsmen. These products of my kitchen and of my slain beasts the monks shall have over all that territory only which my grandfather possessed when king Alexander was alive. Also a salt work in KARSACH. Likewise as far as it depends upon me I grant and confirm to the said church by the gift of Earl Gospatrick the church of HOM with two ploughgates of land and a meadow in the precincts of the same village; also the church of FOGHO with a ploughgate of land; the church of MACCHUSWEL† by the gift of Herbert de Macchuswell; the church of SIMPRIG by the gift of Hye and his son Peter; the church of ST. LAURENCE of Berewic by the gift of Robert the son of William the church of MALCARVASTON‡ with a ploughgate of

---

* Whales.   † Maxwell.   ‡ Makerston.

land by the gift of Walter Corbeth the church of MOLLA* with the adjacent land by the gift of Uctred of Molla; the church of WITHAS-TOWN by the gift of Witha; the church of CAMBUSNEITHAN by the gift of William Finemund; and the church of LINTONRUTHERC† by the gift of Richard Cumin. All the above named lands and possessions therefore I grant to the church of the Blessed Virgin Mary of KELCHO; and to the monks serving God there; to be freely and peaceably enjoyed by perpetual right; and by this my charter I confirm the same to them as perpetual alms; so that none of my successors shall presume to demand anything of the foresaid church or any of its possessions but only prayers for the good of their souls. And this charter is confirmed in the year one thousand one hundred and fifty-nine after the incarnation of the Lord; the following persons being witnesses: Herbert bishop of Glasgow; William bishop of Moray; Gregory bishop of Dunkeld; William and David my brothers and Ada my mother; Gaufrid abbot of Dumfermline; Osbert abbot of Jeddeword; Amfred abbot of Newbottle; Alured abbot of Strevelin; Walter the chancellor; Robert prior of St. Andrews; Matthew archdeacon of St. Andrews; Tor archdeacon of Lothian; Herbert the chamberlain; Nicholas the clerk; Richard the chaplain; Master Andrew; Master Arthur; Walter clerk to the chancellor; John the nephew of bishop Robert; Serle the clerk; Solomon chaplain to Bishop Herbert; and Helias clerk to the same bishop; Godfrey king of the isles; Earl Gospatric; Earl Ferteth; Gilliebride carl of Anagus; Uctred the son of Fergus; Gillebert de Umframvill; William de Summervill; Richard de Morvill; Ranulph de Sulas; David Olifard; Richard Cumin; Robert Avenil; William de Morvill; William Finnemond; Walter Corbet; Asketer de Ridale; Henry de Percy; Liulph the son of Maccus; Orm the son of Hailaph, and many other clerks and laymen.

At Rokesburg."

---

* Mow.   † Linton in Peebleshire, see page 206.

SMALHAM.

P. 135.—In 1451, the barony of Smalham was given in free regality to William, Earl of Douglas.*

MAKERSTON.

P. 144.—The first Macdoual who appears in connection with lands in Roxburghshire, is Fergus Macdoual, the son of Duncan Macdoual of Galloway and Margaret Fraser his wife. Margaret Fraser inherited in her own right the baronies of Mackerston, Yetholm, and Clifton. In 1374, she resigned these baronies into the king's hands in favour of her son Fergus, and on the third day of May of that year, Robert II. granted him charters of said baronies.† The Macdouals were one of the most powerful families of the British race in Wigtonshire, and are thought to be descended from Roland Macdoual, Lord of Galloway. Fergus Macdoual and Dougal Macdoual of Wigtonshire took the oath of allegiance to Edward I. at Berwick, in 1296.‡ During the Succession War, Dougal Macdoual took part against Bruce, and for which their lands were forfeited. In 1306, he defeated Thomas and Alexander Bruce and Sir Reginald Crawford, took all the three prisoners, and carried them to Carlisle Castle, and were immediately ordered for execution by Edward I. Next year, Robert Bruce marched into Galloway to revenge the death of his brothers, and carried fire and sword through the territories of his enemies. Macdoual raised the men of Galloway, and Edward II. ordered a large force to oppose Bruce, which caused him to retire into the northern fastnesses. In 1308, the gallant Edward Bruce invaded Galloway, defeated Macdoual and the other chiefs who had joined him, and took Dougal Macdoual prisoner. His son, Duncan M'Dougal succeeded, and, like his father, adhered to the English king.

---

* Reg. Mag. Sig., lib. iv., No. 148.   ‡ Ib., Rot. ii. 32, 33.
‡ Prynne, iii., p. 654-663.

On Galloway being subdued, Robert I. conferred on his brother Edward the lordship, and all the estates in that territory, forfeited by the heirs of the lords of Galloway. The grant was made in 1308. When Edward III., in 1332, set up Edward Baliol to claim the crown of Scotland, during the minority of David II., every part of Galloway became involved in the miseries of civil war. Those proprietors who had been settled on the forfeited lands by Robert I. shed their blood for his son; but many of the old owners of the land, who had been allowed, by the leniency of the king, to possess their estates, went over to the English king. During the first seven years of the war, Duncan Macdoual, who was the chief of the Clan Macdoual, remained true to the young king, but in August, 1339, when the star of Edward III. was in the ascendant, he took the oath of fealty to that king, and was pardoned for his past offences.* At the death of the Regent Randolph, David II. granted in 1341 the whole of Wigtonshire in free earldom to his faithful follower Sir Malcolm Fleming. On obtaining this grant, Sir Malcolm resolved upon punishing Duncan Macdoual for his revolt in 1339, and notwithstanding all the aid of the English king, he was subdued and forced to submit to the king of Scotland. Duncan Macdoual, and his son Duncan, fought with David II. at the battle of Durham in 1347, and were taken by the English army, and imprisoned in the castle of Rochester, from whence they were removed to York. Duncan, the father, was liberated, on promising to act against the Scots. His wife, brother, and two of his sons were hostages for him. In 1353, Duncan Macdoual renounced the authority of Edward III., and swore fealty to David II. in the church of Cumnock, and ever afterwards remained faithful to his sovereign.† On this fact becoming known to Edward, he ordered John de Boulton, his chancellor of Berwick, to seize all the lands, goods, and chattels of Duncan Macdoual, and the lands of his wife,

---

* Rotuli Scotiæ, vol. i. p. 571. † Fordun, l. xiv., c. 15.

their family and adherents.* The like command was issued to John Coupland, Edward's sheriff of Roxburghshire. Margaret Fraser was the wife of Duncan, and the mother of the said Fergus Macdoual, who was the first of the name that inherited the lands of Mackerston, &c., in the south of Scotland. Chalmers supposes that she was the second wife of Duncan Macdoual, as Fergus only inherited his mother's estates in Roxburghshire, and not those of his father in Galloway.† The principal seat of the Galloway family, from whom Fergus Macdoual sprung, was Garthland. The old Tower of Garthland was forty-five feet high, with the date of 1274 on its battlements.‡ *Macdougal* was the original name of which *Macdoual* is an abbreviation.

STOCKSTROTHER.

P. 170.—In noticing Ringley Hall, and the tumulus in front of Mackerston House, I omitted to call attention to Stockstrother, which is situated a little to the south of Ringley Hall. Its name has been imposed by the Anglo-Saxon dwellers on the Tweed, *stock* in that language signifying a *place* or *mansion;* and *strother, meadow,* or *marsh, i. e.,* Stockstrother, the place at the meadow. It is possible, however, that the name may have been conferred upon the place from its being the residence of one of Edward's sheriffs of the county of Roxburgh, of the name of *Strothers:* Stockstrothers, the place of Strother. It must have been a place of importance in early times, and strongly fortified. Part of the old building is still to be seen in the walls of several of the cottages at the onstead. The walls are of great thickness, and the stones with which they have been built, of immense size, many of

---

* Rotuli Scotiæ, vol. i. p. 761. The order is dated from Woodstock, August 18, 1353.

† Caledonia, vol. iii. p. 378.

‡ Old Statistical Account of Stoney Kirk Parish, vol. ii. p. 56.

them measuring about five feet in length, and of proportionate deepness. Stockstrother had its full share of visits from the armies of England.

LINTON.

P. 217, *Foot Note.*—In May, 1729, an ox, six feet four inches high, was sold in the Canongate market, Edinburgh.*

YETHAM.

P. 229.—I have mistakenly included *Zedon* as one of the names of this place in 1388. It is so given in Froissart's Chronicles, vol. iv. p. 3, and by other writers, but they have mistaken Yetham for *Suden* or Southdean, as explained in p. 264.

Pp. 235, 236.—In 1669, an addition was built at the west end of the church. It is probable that the old part to which the addition was made, was the original church of Yetham. It was covered with reeds.

---

* Courant, No. 644. Caledonia, vol. ii. p. 734.

END OF VOL. III.

Fifth Edition, handsomely bound, price 6s.,

Quiet Hours.

BY

THE REV. JOHN PULSFORD.

"This is a remarkable book. It is unique in appearance; and there is a ring in its substance which reminds us of the pith and weight by which not a little of our old English authorship has been characterized. The thought and feeling are truly and deeply Scriptural and Christian. But there is a strength in both which is not a little refreshing in these days of so much formal and conventional authorship. Give it as a present, reader, where you wish to induce a Christian thoughtfulness, a reverence of sacred truth, and all things sacred. You feel that it is a strong hand that comes upon you as you read these pages."—*British Quarterly Review.*

"From the unmeaning nonentities of the teeming modern press this book starts out with a dignified character of its own, stamped thereon by genuine godliness, vigorous intellect, rich and elegant imagination, and rare faculty of speech. The 'Aids to Thought' remind us of the 'Fragments' of Novalis, and the chapters that alternate with the former are priceless jewels. Amongst these sparkles most brightly that which is inscribed 'Jesus Revealing the Heart of God,' which we are glad to find is circulating separately."—*The Homilist.*

ALSO,

Quiet Hours.

SECOND SERIES.

Handsomely bound, price 7s. 6d.

EDINBURGH: THOMAS C. JACK.

www.ingramcontent.com/pod-product-compliance
Lightning Source LLC
Chambersburg PA
CBHW032032220426
43664CB00006B/443